IMAGES
of America

BRADDOCK, ALLEGHENY COUNTY

On the cover: **COAL DOGS AND JOE BOATS.** When coal mining was a significant industry in the early 1800s, the "Sixth Street ravine" served as a pathway for miners and dog teams transporting coal to the Pennsylvania Railroad or to "joe boats." As the population grew and more business came, the ravine became a true roadway. The Braddock Avenue and Sixth Street intersection has evolved over time, with each evolution succinctly reflecting the changing conditions and economic circumstances of the generation traversing its path. Its relevancy and context are gracefully recorded in this late 1940s image. (Courtesy of Braddock Carnegie Library.)

IMAGES
of America

BRADDOCK, ALLEGHENY COUNTY

Robert M. Grom

ARCADIA
PUBLISHING

ISBN 978-0-7385-6302-2

Published by Arcadia Publishing
Charleston, South Carolina

Printed in the United States of America

Library of Congress Catalog Card Number: 2008924491

For all general information contact Arcadia Publishing at:
Telephone 843-853-2070
Fax 843-853-0044
E-mail sales@arcadiapublishing.com
For customer service and orders:
Toll-Free 1-888-313-2665

Visit us on the Internet at www.arcadiapublishing.com

To Carol, Adam, Jessica, and all things Braddock.

Contents

ACKNOWLEDGMENTS

When assembling materials for this work, I found it difficult to periodically not run afoul of family obligations. To my family, Carol, Adam and Jessica, I hope that you understand my passion for this work and that you will forgive any transgression that it may have caused. Without your support and deference, I could not have completed even my very first sentence. To my friends and colleagues, I hope that once this book is in hand, you too will understand my enthusiasm for all things Braddock. For those who have provided me with the stories and visual records of their lives and of local history, I am forever in your debt. In particular, I wish to recognize Jeffery Au and Victoria Vargo of the Braddock's Field Historical Society and Carnegie Library of Braddock. Please know that your support, materials, and many considerations have meant much to the project. May both of your organizations continue to receive the level of resources and attention needed to continue serving as the "center of light and learning" that Andrew Carnegie so appropriately envisioned many decades ago.

Images included in this work (and many others that have been given but could not fit within its context and physical constraints) are gratefully acknowledged. Braddock Carnegie Library, Carnegie Library of Pittsburgh, Library of Congress, U.S. Steel Corporation, Rankin Christian Center, Senator John Heinz History Center, UPMC Braddock Medical Center, Rivers of Steel National Heritage Area, and the American Society of Composers, Authors and Publishers have all substantially added to this effort. People, their stories, and friendships have helped cast the human dimension. Your family albums, odd collections of photographs, and news clippings have all brought life to this work. My heartfelt thanks are offered to Tony Buba, Susan and John Cosgrove, Richard Farrell, Kenneth Goldsmith, Victoria Hruska, John Katz, Joe Kirsch, Chuck Klausing, Robert Messner, Joanne (Szwarc) Naugle, Mimi (Szwarc) and Joe O'Donnell, Joanne Schleifer, Lisa Silberman, Yvonne Spencer, James Spindler, Anna (Trasky) Sullivan, John L. Sullivan, Anna (Gilarski) Szwarc, Gaye Velar, and Ron Zdrojkowski for supporting me in my quest for pictures and just the right words.

INTRODUCTION

In many ways the story of Braddock, Allegheny County, is the story of America. It is the place where our country's tenderest young roots first took hold and where the fabric of our national character first took shape. Emerging from an area of uncharted waterways and raw forests teeming with abundant wildlife, to our nation's first major battlefield of international consequence, its history is rich, varied, and unique. What has occurred in little more than 250 years, on and around Braddock, and the mere 328 acres of ground that comprise Braddock's Field, is captivating and worthy of wider recognition and broader understanding.

The area now described as Braddock, Allegheny County, emerged slowly over time. Huge areas of land once defined as Cumberland County stretched across Virginia and into what we now know as western Pennsylvania and extended well into the "Ohio" country. In 1771, Bedford County was carved out of Cumberland County; two years later, Westmoreland County was established in much the same manner. Once begun, the carving of territory reflected what by then were becoming established patterns of exploration, settlement, trade, continued population growth, and politics. In 1781, the County of Washington was created and shortly thereafter, again subdivided to create Fayette and Greene Counties. The cascade of settlement and development continued like the waves of water over sand; each year's waves reaching further, but infrequently staying long on a defined course. Tracts of land ranging in size from 200 to 350 acres were sold throughout western Pennsylvania for sums ranging in price from three pence to eight shillings per acre. Unsold properties were later distributed via warrants.

It was not until 1788 that Allegheny County would finally manifest itself from parts of Washington and Westmoreland Counties. The final redaction resulting in most of the boundaries that we now recognize occurred not long afterward, when Allegheny County was subdivided to create Armstrong, Beaver, Butler, Crawford, Erie, Mercer, Venango, and Warren Counties. Between 1788 and 1813 the entire Allegheny County area was either sold or warranted. The Borough of Braddock was incorporated much later, in 1867, being carved out of a part of Wilkins Township. Rankin Borough came next in 1891, with North Braddock following in 1896 and Braddock Hills in 1946.

As I began assembling materials for this work I could not help but stop periodically to marvel at the rich and unique history of such a small area of ground that comprises Braddock, Allegheny County. Braddock's history is packed with historical relevance—so much so, that many more volumes could and should be written.

Having a lifelong interest in history is a curious addiction. Once begun, the search for that elusive image or illustration needed to depict an important event frequently is the cause of great anxiety. Worse perhaps, is locating that singular, remarkable image, that truly is worthy of a thousand words—but finding its provenance or descriptive detail elusive. The reality is that not all such scenarios are successfully rewarded; but yet, both the search and the obsession continue.

The desire to know something more about the stories extolling the historic significance of a building, a person or an event often evoke a flood of questions. What do you mean? Where did you hear that? Can you tell me more? Where did you find that? All of these questions and more help create this wonderful treasure hunt for knowledge.

I confess! I have often been seduced by history, but never before had I succumbed so dramatically as with this work. I am now afflicted with a desire—or rather, the compulsion—to know more about the ground that I walk on every day. Is this where George Washington stood? Did Gen. Edward Braddock's blood feed the earth beneath our footsteps? On what corner near the mill did Capt. William Jones buy his cigars? Which country did the family who lived in this home come from, and what became of them? How could the son of a second-hand furniture dealer write such beautiful music during a time when smoke from the mills declared that there was no sun in the sky? What forces could compel a young man to leave his hometown to travel across country and create a national fervor for conservation resulting in the creation of an entire travel and tourism industry in the Grand Canyon? I hope that like me, you too will succumb to the richness of the questions and the value of learning more about the fascinating history of Braddock, Allegheny County, Pennsylvania.

In April 1917, Swissvale, Pennsylvania, writer Hugh P. Meese stated, "A history is not evolved from some historian's inner consciousness. It is, on the contrary, the result of a vast amount of digging and refining, the value of the history depending upon the patience with which the historian has delved and the clarity and judgment of his presentation." To you, dear reader, I hope and trust that in your judgment, you will find this presentation of much value.

One

Exploration, Settlers, and Early Trade

Native Americans and fur traders were the first to come to this area just nine miles east of Pittsburgh's point. Nestled favorably along the Monongahela River and adjacent to the Turtle Creek, the region's earliest known English settler was John Frazier (this spelling is the most often encountered in historical accounts, however, he himself spelled his name Fraser). Frazier first came to the area in 1742, after being threatened by the French and forced to vacate his trading post in Venango County. During the spring of 1753, he permanently established his new cabin and trading post here.

King George II had granted one-half-million acres of the upper Ohio region to gentlemen from Virginia and Maryland in 1748, formally constituting the Ohio Land Company. Wishing to capitalize on this opportunity to expand trade and grow profits, plans were quickly developed to explore the region's full potential and better understand the substance of reported French incursions. In late 1753 and early 1754, young George Washington and his guide Christopher Gist visited Frazier as they surveyed the region, assessed its resources, and further determined its strategic advantage. What they found of the natural advantages was impressive, but their visit also confirmed the presence of the French and an unappealing potential for British loss.

The area along the river that held this nascent setting was ultimately named after the British general that met his demise here and ignited one of the most pivotal wars in America's history. The river that transported the earliest traders and settlers was named Monongahela after its Native American name, meaning that it was "the river with high banks which fall in." Decade upon decade brought change to the land around the water's edges, but the rivers advantageous position and natural bounty continued to draw countless waves of people after Braddock's defeat. As the 20th century emerged, writers were still boasting of the region's attributes, with one author acclaiming, "No other city in the Monongahela Valley combines in its natural location a greater wealth of endowments than Braddock."

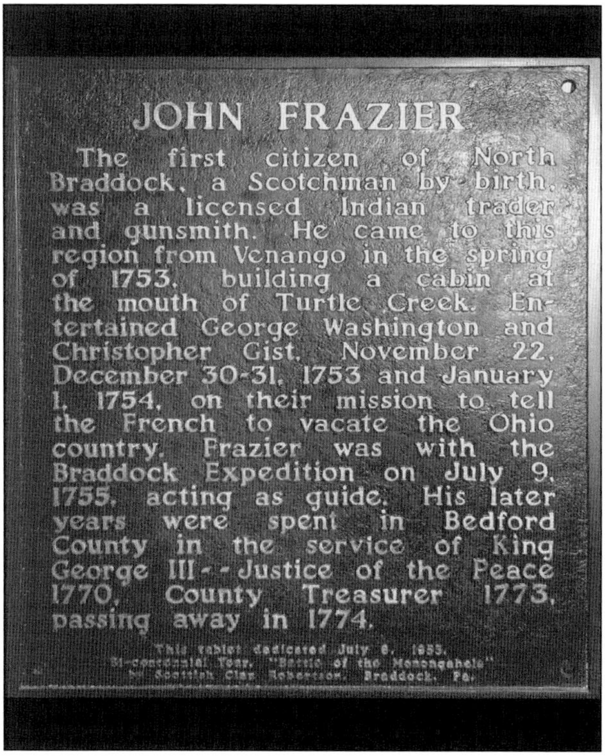

JOHN FRAZIER HISTORICAL MARKER. John Frazier, a Scotsman, came to the area along the Monongahela River at the mouth of Turtle Creek in 1742 and settled on land granted by Native American queen Aliquippa in 1753. Virginia's governor Robert Dinwiddie, in a February 1754 communication, refers to Frazier's cabin in mentioning a report he had received from George Washington. Guide Christopher Gist noted in his journal that he and Washington stayed at Frazier's on three occasions during 1753 and 1754. Frazier's cabin was located on ground upon which Andrew Carnegie's Edgar Thomson Steel Works was later built. For years the marker noted the property's historical significance until it was displaced during construction. The marker is currently displayed in the museum and gallery at Braddock Carnegie Library. (Author's collection.)

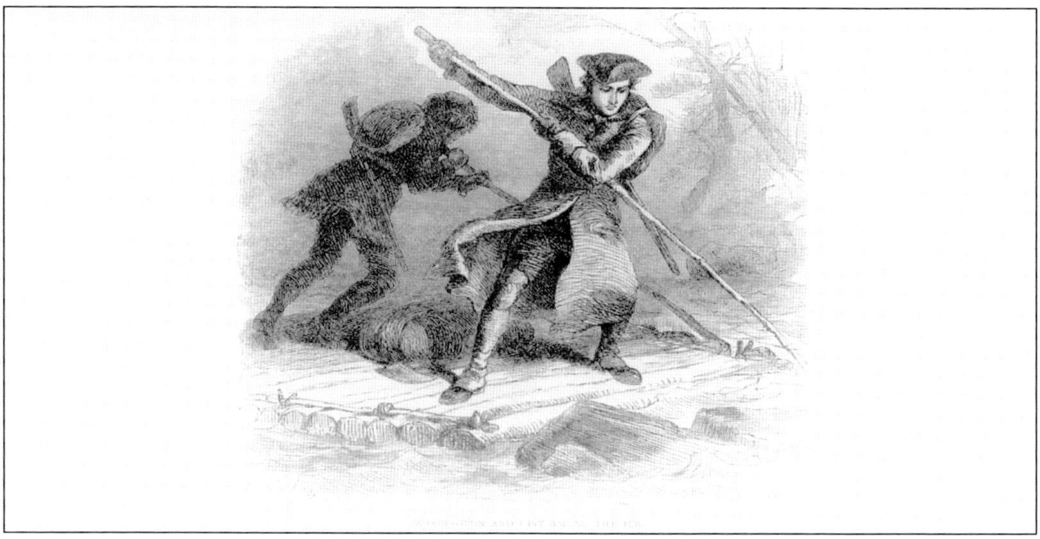

CHRISTOPHER GIST AND GEORGE WASHINGTON. Sent to explore the region by Governor Dinwiddie, George Washington and his guide Christopher Gist found the area of strategic advantage and of considerable value as it contained seemingly endless natural resources. Unfortunately, the presence of the French and confirmation of their intentions to control the region created much anxiety when reported. In December 1753, Washington almost lost his life when he fell into the Allegheny River's icy waters using a raft like the one pictured. At the time of the Battle of the Monongahela, Gist was 49 years old. He served as a captain and as Gen. Edward Braddock's main guide. (Courtesy of the Library of Congress.)

Two

Braddock's Defeat and Washington's Rise

Greed, pride, and competition grew between the French and English. As the urgency for control of this territory grew, the risk of asserting ownership was underestimated. Like movements of players on a chessboard, the resulting actions and counteractions caused a cascade of political and military events that became the genesis of Braddock's Field. Maps were drawn and redrawn as information became available, new outposts were established, minor military skirmishes began to occur routinely, and small ramparts and larger forts were developed in succession to protect the various rival interests.

All of these intrigues resulted in one of England's earliest and most humiliating military defeats on American soil. The loss of more than 1,200 of Edward Braddock's elite British troops and Colonial soldiers at the hands of 250 French and Canadian troops and 600 Native American allies, who sustained only nominal losses, was a disaster. While the immediate result of the carnage was significant, its greater impact was felt not long afterward as it became evident that the futures of England, France, and America were to be forever changed as a result. Prompting a series of tactical responses, England learned some valuable lessons; most notably that far larger forces would be required to dislodge the French and Native Americans and that those they sent to claim the territory would need to learn the ways of native combat. Americans on the other hand, learned that the highly touted British army was not invincible.

Had a motion picture of the Battle of Braddock's Field been created, the marquee announcing its stars and supporting cast would be extraordinary by modern standards. Braddock was the star of course, with other key actors including George Washington, Daniel Boone, Benjamin Franklin, Horatio Gates, Thomas Gage, Hugh Mercer, Daniel Morgan, George Croghan, Christopher Gist, Charles Lee, and many others. Not long afterward, many of the cast appeared again, albeit this time in leading roles during America's war for independence.

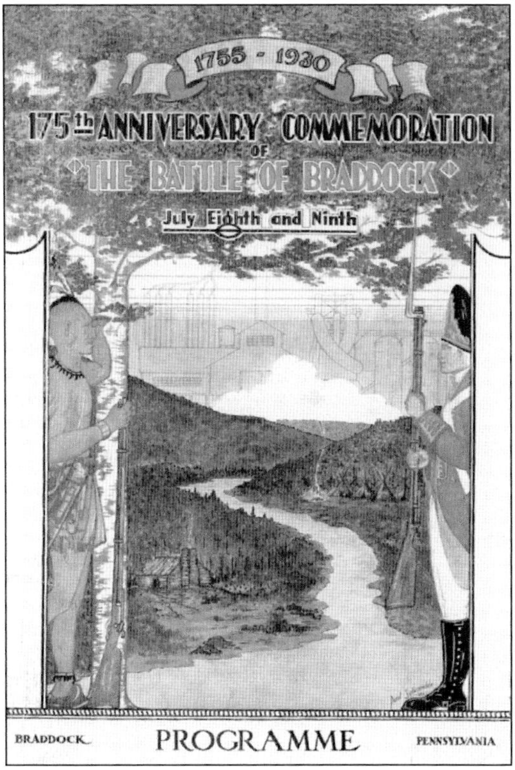

Artist Rendering of Frazier's Cabin. Paul Sylvander created this rendering of Frazier's cabin and nearby Native American camps in 1930 for the cover of the 175th anniversary commemoration of the Battle of Braddock. The drawing depicts the traditional story of how John Frazier came to the area in 1742 as a trapper and trader befriended by Queen Aliquippa. She allowed Frazier to build a cabin at the junction of Turtle Creek and the Monongahela River, granting him land for the purpose. Frazier's cabin and Queen Aliquippa's "royal wigwam" are gracefully depicted in Sylvander's rendering. (Courtesy of Braddock Carnegie Library.)

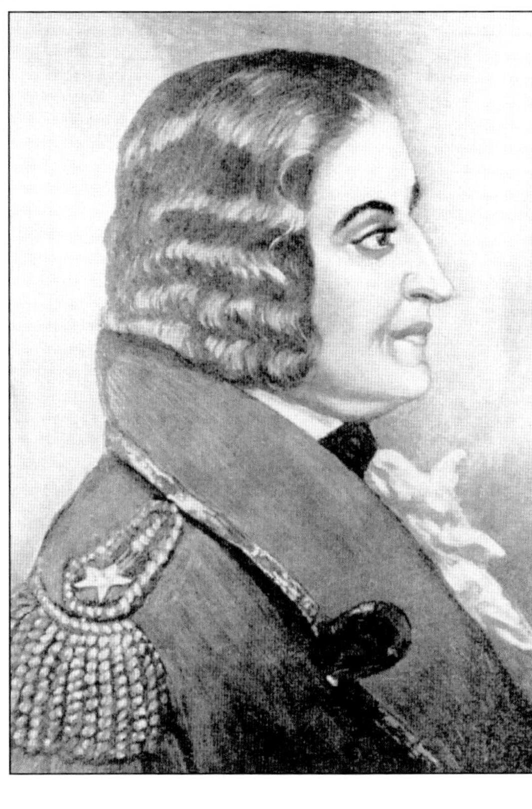

Gen. Edward Braddock. Fearing the loss of the "Ohio Country" to the French, Virginia's governor Robert Dinwiddie decided to mount an expedition against them at Fort Duquesne. Edward Braddock, general-in-chief of his majesty's forces in America, was to lead the expedition. The failure to heed Benjamin Franklin and George Washington's warnings about the fighting style of the natives was a costly error for Braddock; as a result, he lost his life and much of his army. (Courtesy of Braddock Carnegie Library.)

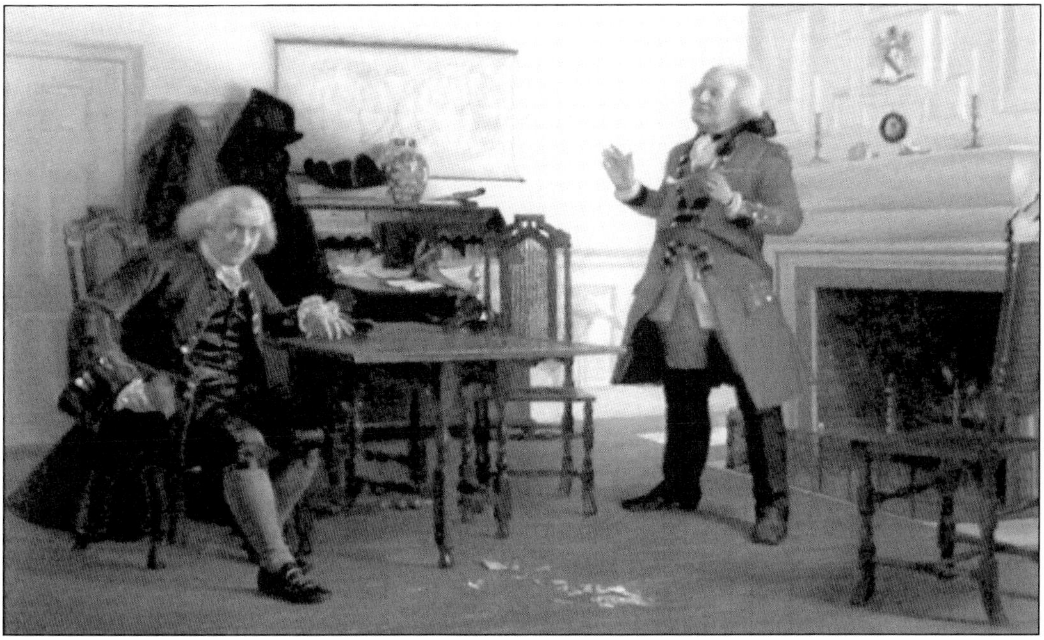

BENJAMIN FRANKLIN AND GENERAL BRADDOCK. Prior to leading his army against the French, Braddock sought the counsel of Pennsylvania's leadership, including that of Benjamin Franklin. When it was suggested that Braddock take precautions against the Native Americans, Franklin quotes Braddock as stating "These Savages may indeed be a formidable Enemy to your raw American Militia; but upon the King's regular and disciplined troops, Sir, it is impossible they should make any impression." His brash misunderstanding cost him his life. This painting was created by artist Frederick James. (Courtesy of Braddock Carnegie Library.)

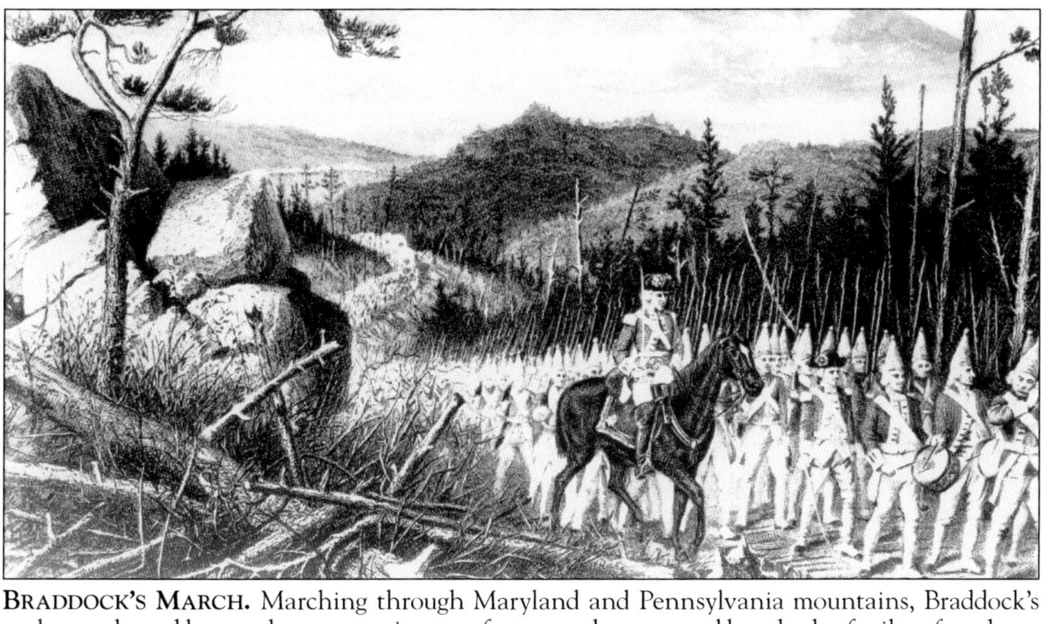

BRADDOCK'S MARCH. Marching through Maryland and Pennsylvania mountains, Braddock's path was cleared by an advance contingent of axmen who prepared hundreds of miles of roadway. The passage of Braddock's army over such a long distance was considered by many to be one of his most significant accomplishments. (Courtesy of Carnegie Library of Pittsburgh.)

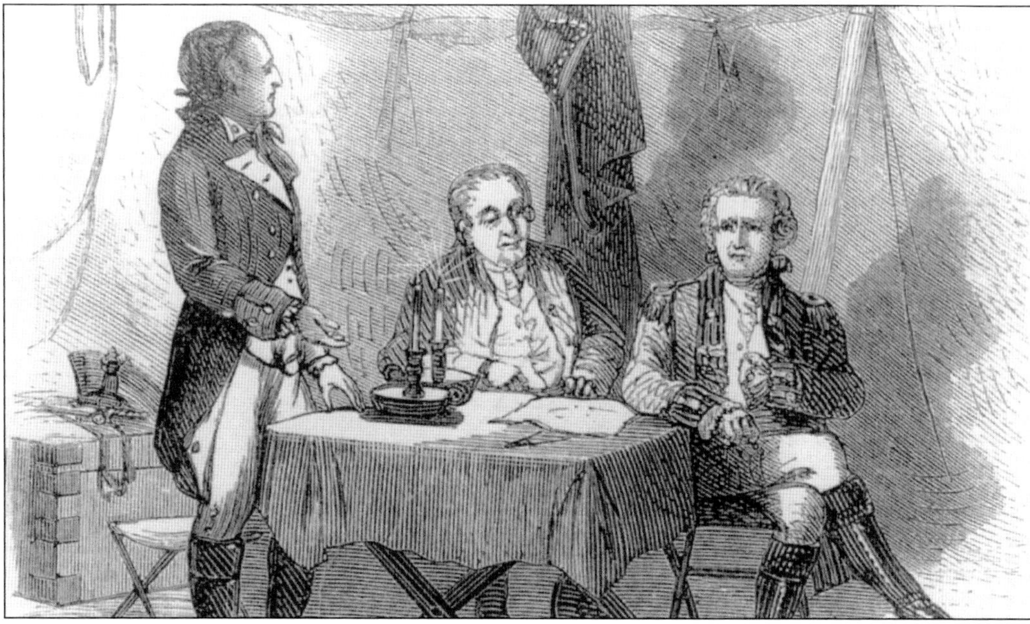

WASHINGTON WARNING BRADDOCK. Auguste Levasseur, secretary to Marquis de Lafayette, stated in his journal published in 1829: "If General Braddock had not disdained the advice of his young aide-de-camp Washington, he would not have engaged his troops so imprudently on a terrain that was to the advantage of his enemies, and he would not have lost his army, his glory and his life there." (Courtesy of the Library of Congress.)

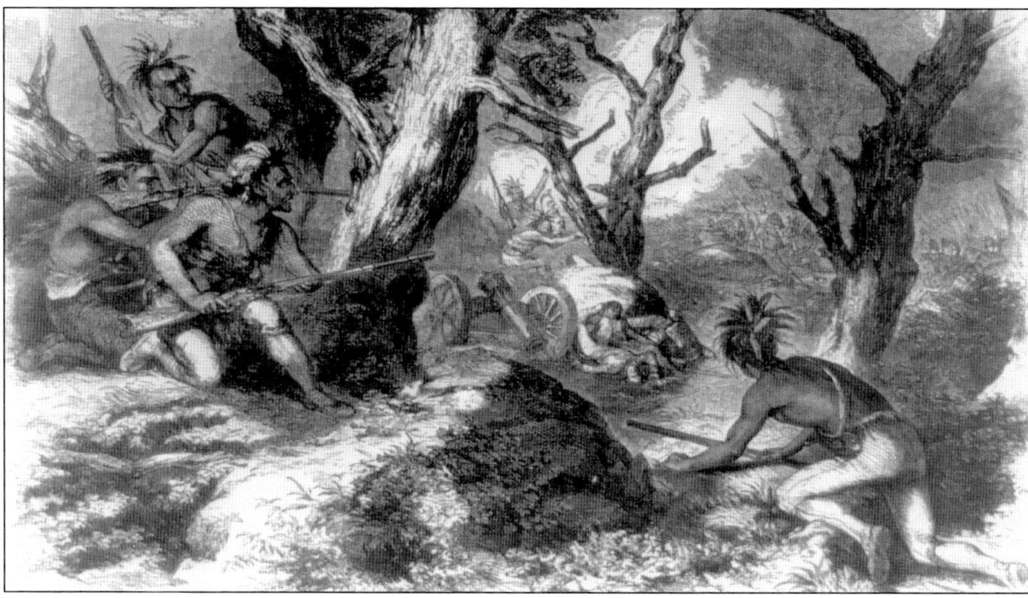

THE INVISIBLE FOE. Using tactical advantage of heavily forested terrain, the French and Native Americans attacked Gen. Edward Braddock's forward columns. Lacking the backwoods fighting acumen of their provincial counterparts and unwilling to adopt untested Native American fighting style, Braddock ordered a traditional British military response with disastrous consequence. Amid panic and confusion, the rigidity of the traditional military regimen only exacerbates the number of fatalities. (Courtesy of the Library of Congress.)

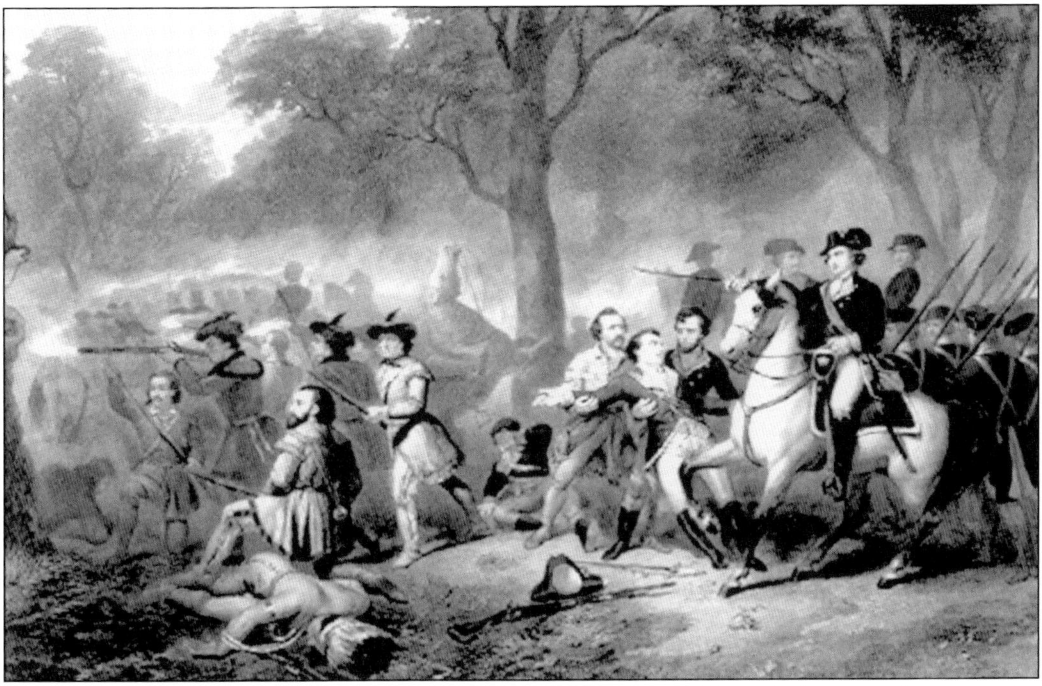

WOUNDING OF BRADDOCK. It was reported that Braddock acted bravely, but naively during the height of the three-hour battle. Attempting to marshal distraught troops caught in ambush, he had several horses shot from under him. He fought with courage until a bullet struck his arm and side, taking him out of the battle and requiring his troops to evacuate him from the main battle site. (Courtesy of the Library of Congress.)

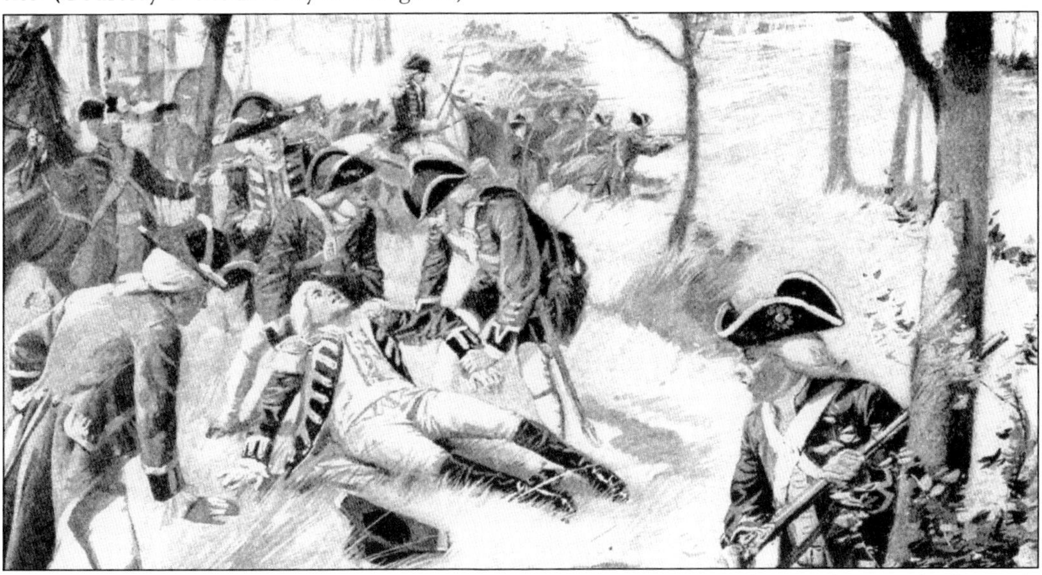

GENERAL BRADDOCK AIDED BY TROOPS. The battle raged for three hours, during which nearly half of Braddock's army was lost; among them many of his best soldiers and officers. Confused and in disarray, soldiers fired at unseen enemies and during the most chaotic action it was reported that many members of Braddock's army were consumed by friendly fire. (Courtesy of the Library of Congress.)

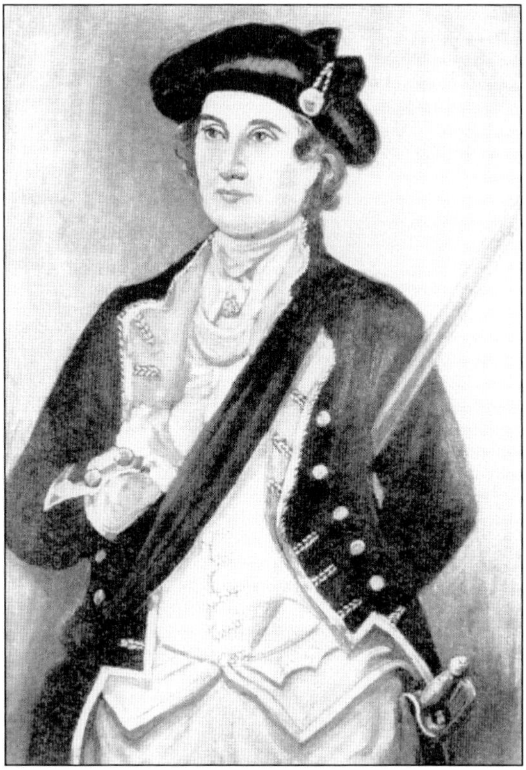

GREAT SPIRIT PROTECTS WASHINGTON. Many years after the Battle of Braddock, George Washington and his physician and friend, Dr. James Craik, traveled to the area. While visiting with a group of local Native Americans, one old chief reported that he himself had taken part in the great battle. He noted that he and his warriors had especially targeted Washington, repeatedly firing at him to no avail. He stated that the purpose of his visit was to offer his respect to the valiant soldier protected by the Great Spirit. (Courtesy of Braddock Carnegie Library.)

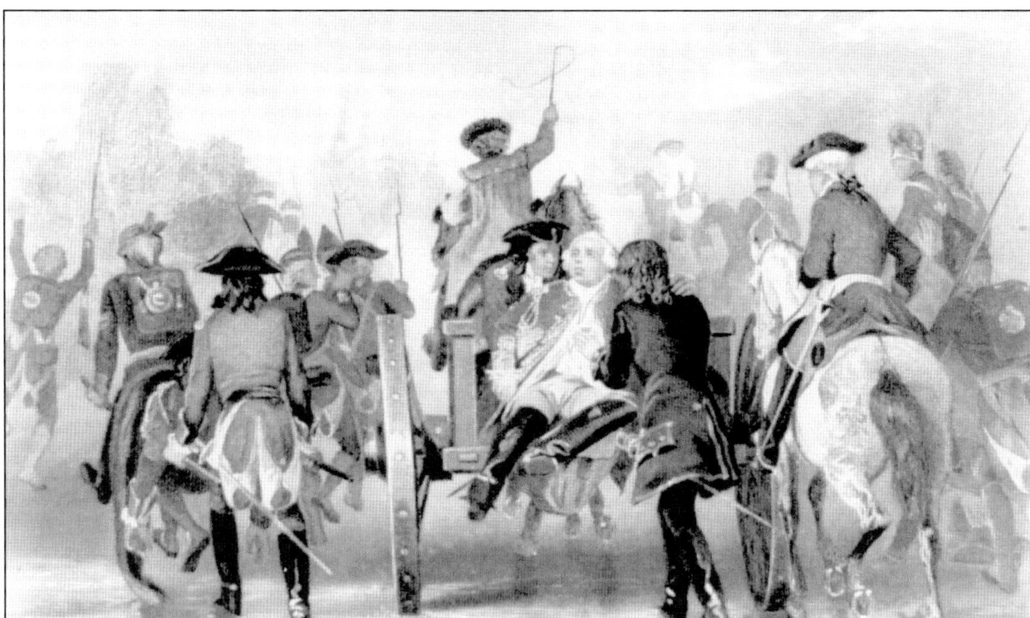

GENERAL BRADDOCK EVACUATED FROM BATTLE. The battle was lost when the general was severely wounded. He is seen here being transported from the battle site in a military cart. He was later transferred to horseback, and finally carried by his soldiers as they retreated. (Courtesy of the Library of Congress.)

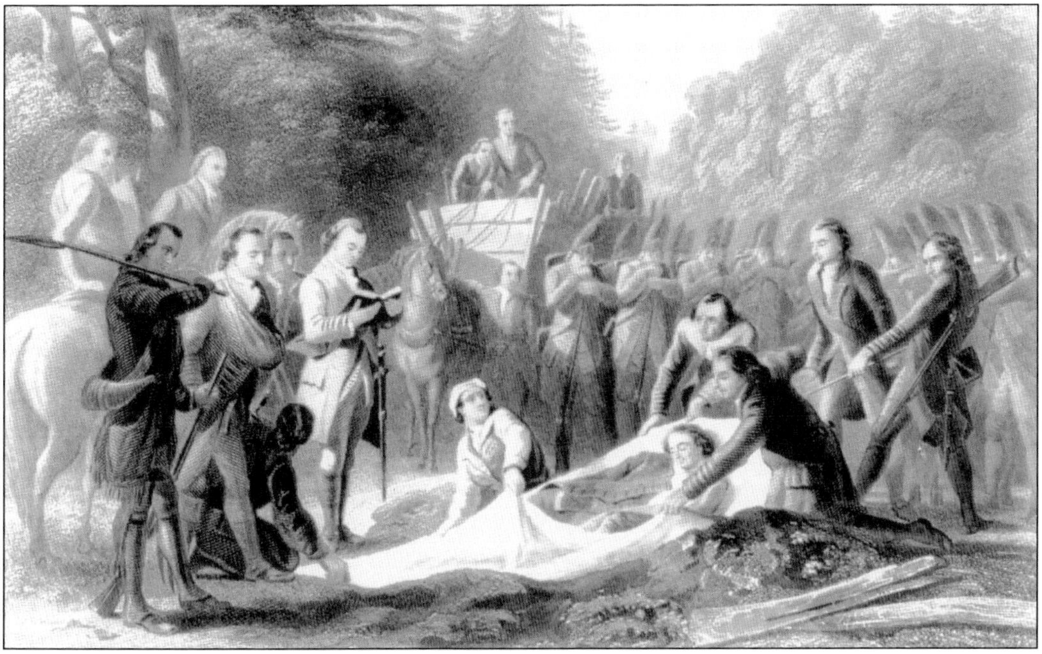

BRADDOCK'S BURIAL. Gen. Edward Braddock succumbed to his wounds four days after the battle. As the remnants of the retreating army approached Fort Necessity, he was buried in the road to protect his grave from Native American or French degradation. The army's chaplain was incapacitated, so Colonel Washington offered the eulogy. (Courtesy of the Library of Congress.)

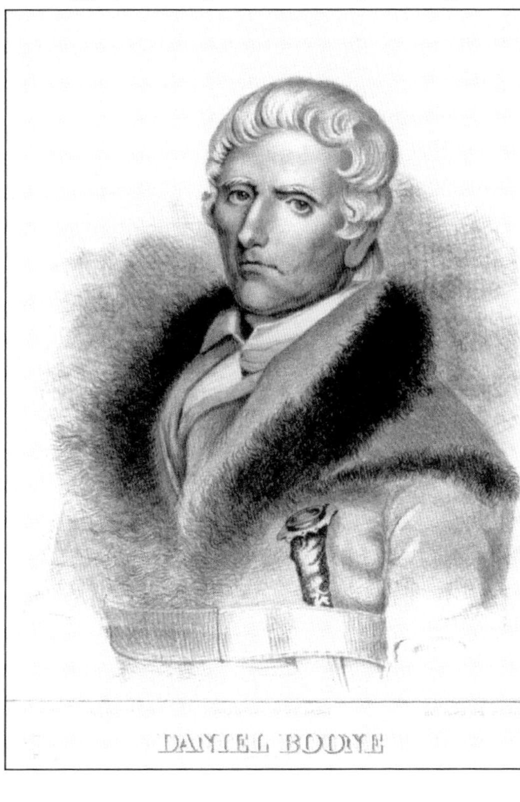

DANIEL BOONE. At the time of the battle, 21-year-old Daniel Boone was engaged in Braddock's forces as a teamster and blacksmith with the North Carolina contingent. Much remembered as an early-American pioneer, Native American–fighter and backwoodsman, he gained valuable experience on Braddock's march and at the Battle of the Monongahela. (Courtesy of the Library of Congress.)

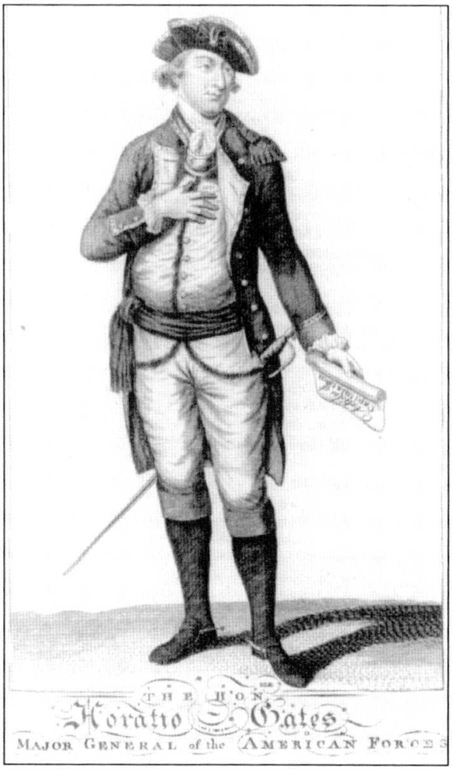

HORATIO GATES. A professional British soldier, Horatio Gates was 27 years old when Edward Braddock's army moved across the Monongahela River on their way toward Fort Duquesne. Like many other soldiers, he too was wounded in battle. Gates would later serve as a continental army general, winning one of his most impressive battles at Saratoga where he defeated Gen. John Burgoyne in 1778. (Courtesy of the Library of Congress.)

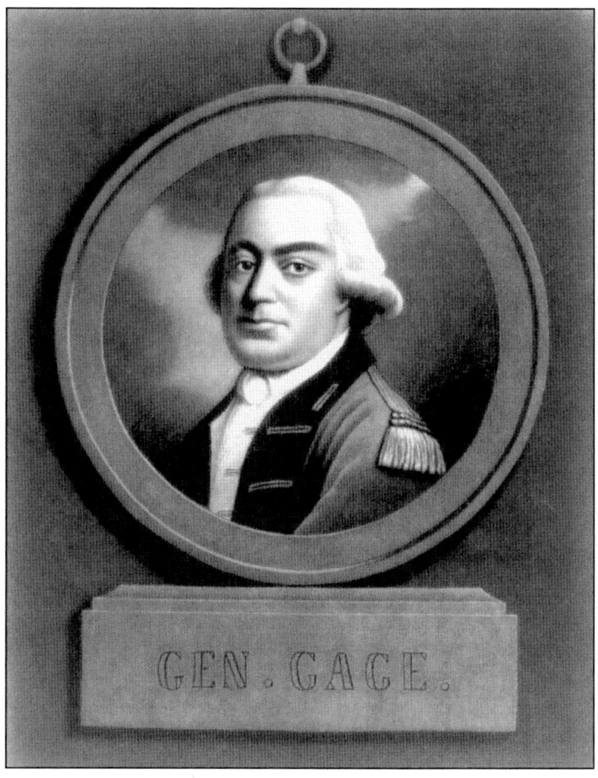

THOMAS GAGE. Thomas Gage was a very lucky soldier during the Battle of the Monongahela. He was a 34-year-old lieutenant colonel who led Gen. Edward Braddock's advance guard. He was wounded in the battle but survived. Gage later became commander of the British royal forces in North America and it is he who is credited with starting the American Revolution by sending troops to destroy military stores in Concord and Lexington. (Courtesy of the Library of Congress.)

CHARLES LEE. Charles Lee was 24 years old at the time of the Battle of the Monongahela. He later became George Washington's chief rival for appointment as commander in chief of the continental army. He was consistently in opposition and in competition with Washington. His actions frequently became bitter and spiteful. Lee was eventually discredited and court-martialed for treason. (Courtesy of the Library of Congress.)

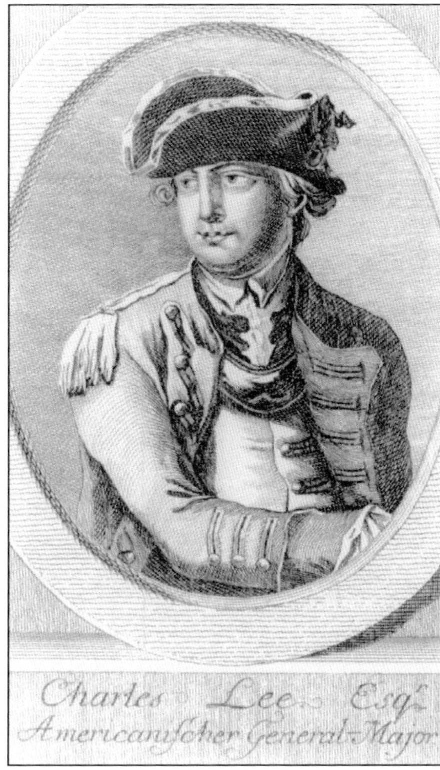

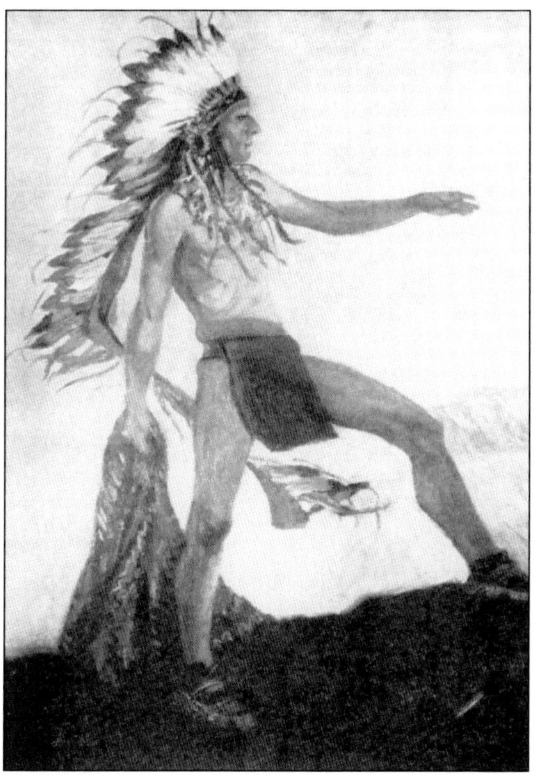

KING SHINGISS. Chief Shingiss of the Delaware Indians reportedly aided the French in defeating Braddock's army in the Battle of the Monongahela. Following Braddock's defeat, he and his warriors joined the French and raided towns and villages throughout western Pennsylvania and Virginia. (Courtesy of Braddock Carnegie Library.)

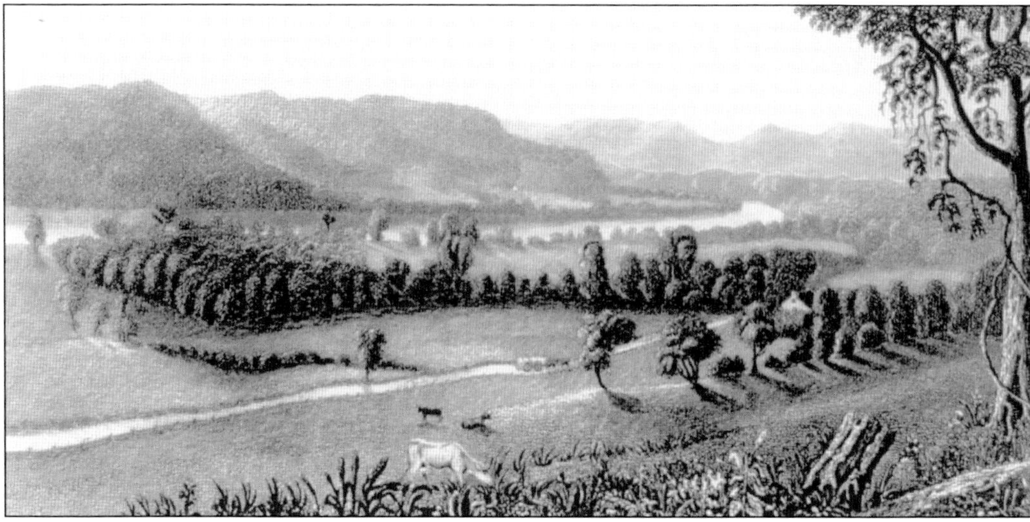

BRADDOCK'S FIELD. This engraving offers a calm and peaceful view of Braddock's Field as it looked many years after the famous battle. Lush pastures are evident in the foreground and the Monongahela River is seen in the background. This engraving was made by W. C. Jackman from a painting by William C. Wall. (Courtesy of the Library of Congress.)

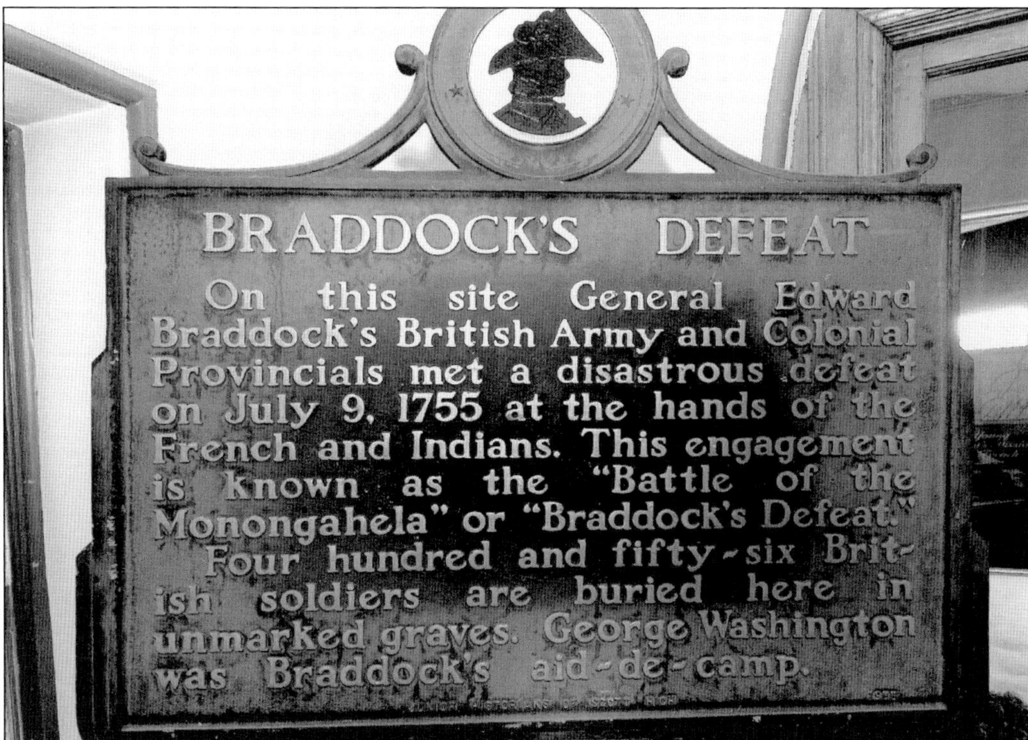

BRADDOCK'S DEFEAT MARKER. The Scott High School Junior Historians had this marker created to commemorate the Battle of the Monongahela. It was displayed on the high school property in North Braddock. The school was built on land considered by most historians as having had the significant elements of the battle. When the school building was torn down, the plaque was removed to Braddock Carnegie Library. (Author's collection.)

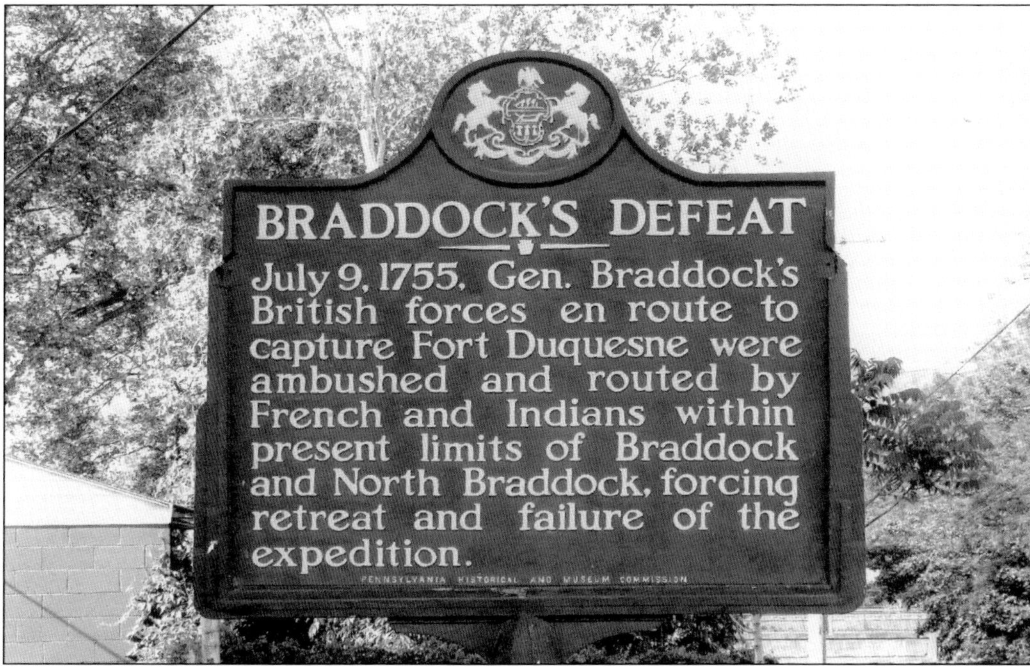

BRADDOCK'S DEFEAT BATTLEFIELD MARKER. This Pennsylvania Historical and Museum Commission marker commemorates the place of Gen. Edward Braddock's defeat. The marker is located on a publicly accessible site on Library Street in North Braddock, a short distance from Braddock Carnegie Library. (Author's collection.)

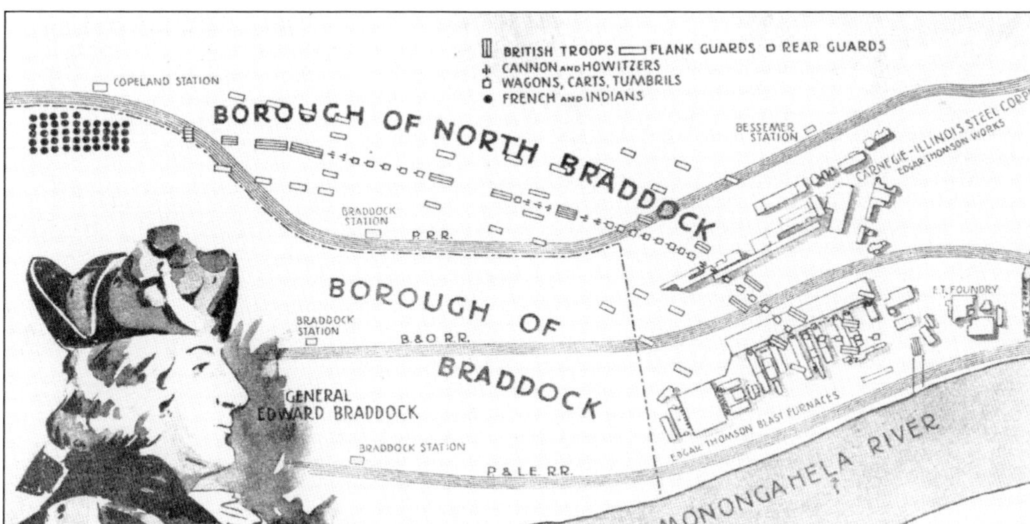

BRADDOCK'S FIELD BICENTENNIAL MAP. In celebrating the bicentennial of the Battle of the Monongahela in 1955, Braddock borough officials prepared this diagram showing the various positions of the battle's participants. The map shows these positions relative to the Monongahela River, Edgar Thomson Steel Works, and the area's various railroad stations. (Courtesy of Braddock Carnegie Library.)

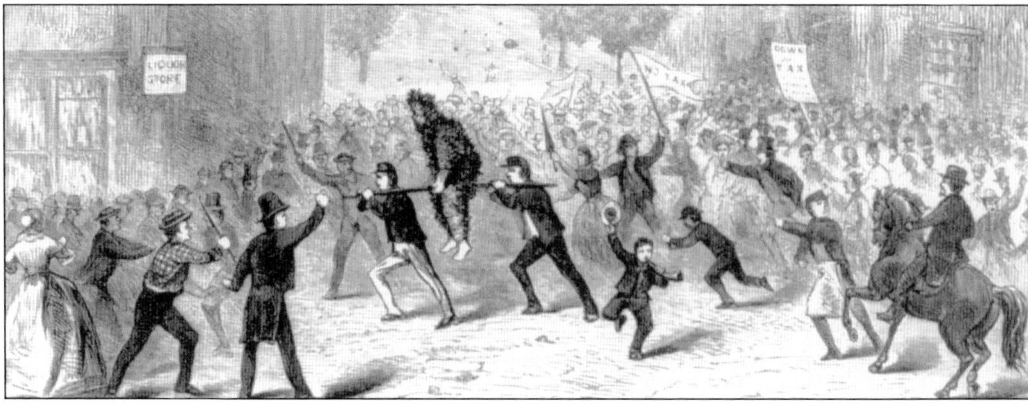

WHISKEY REBELLION. In 1794, western Pennsylvania farmers protested what they believed was an unfair federal tax on whiskey. Seeking to assemble for a march on the city of Pittsburgh, the rebels met on Braddock's Field. The site was then one of Pennsylvania's most recognized landmarks. On August 1, 1794, several thousand men assembled and were ready to march until it was announced that Pres. George Washington had issued orders deploying federal troops. The mob quickly disbanded and little more resistance occurred. (Courtesy of the Library of Congress.)

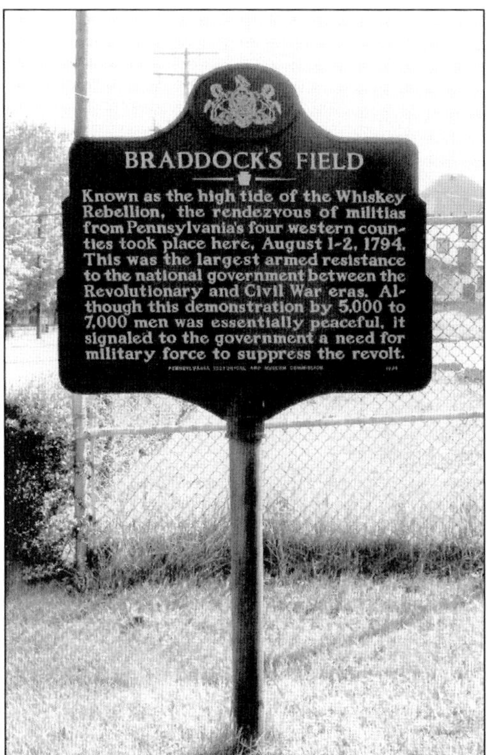

BRADDOCK'S FIELD MARKER. This Pennsylvania Historical and Museum Commission marker notes the gathering point where farmers-turned whiskey tax protestors met during the height of the Whiskey Rebellion in 1794. This marker is located a few short blocks from Braddock Carnegie Library. (Author's collection.)

Three

Andrew Carnegie and Industrialization

History was again about to be made on Braddock's Field, when another Scotsman came to town. This time, however, it was not a result of military glory, but rather, of industrial and entrepreneurial destiny. It was also not a British general or a Virginia planter turned president that would make the world turn on end. On this occasion it was a young Scottish emigrant named Andrew Carnegie who acquired the honor. In this case, it was hot metal and not military mettle that was about to set the stage for an extraordinary change of fortune for the area.

For many years after Gen. Edward Braddock's defeat, the ground around Braddock was considered prime farmland, and the area around John Frazier's old homestead held many orchards. From the beginning of the 19th century through the Civil War, the area continued to evolve with large tracts of land being subdivided and new homesteads begun. The last reported Native Americans left the area around 1820. When business and industry began to crowd the confines of Pittsburgh, new development followed rivers and rail. Braddock's advantageous position along the Monongahela River was easily discernable and began to draw the attention of business leaders and investors. One of the first businesses so attracted to the area was a barrel factory that first opened in 1850, right around the time that the Pennsylvania Railroad laid its first track through Braddock. Eleven years later, the McVay-Walker foundry was built and Braddock's steel-making future determined. In 1873, Braddock's relevance was again thrust upon the world when Carnegie-McCandless and Company began operating and became the mighty Edgar Thomson Steel Works. Much as the history of the world had changed with the conclusion of the Battle of the Monongahela little more than a century earlier, it was now about to hear the roar of Carnegie's blast furnaces; a fitting tribute to yet another impetuous Scotsman.

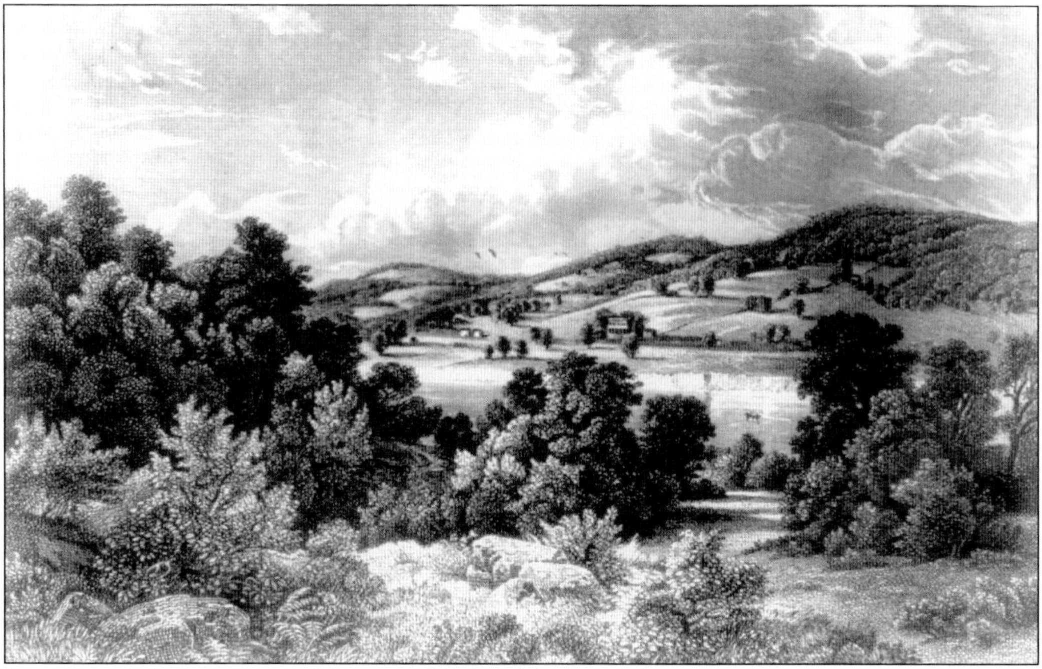

BRADDOCK'S BATTLEFIELD. The main battlefield was well known and respected for many years following the battle. After the battle, Braddock's Road continued to serve as a major artery for soldiers, traders, and settlers. In 1854, painter Paul Weber prepared this depiction of how Braddock's Field looked almost a century later. The riverbank and the rolling hills remained much the same as at the time of battle, but forested areas had been removed as the land was converted for farming. (Courtesy of the Library of Congress.)

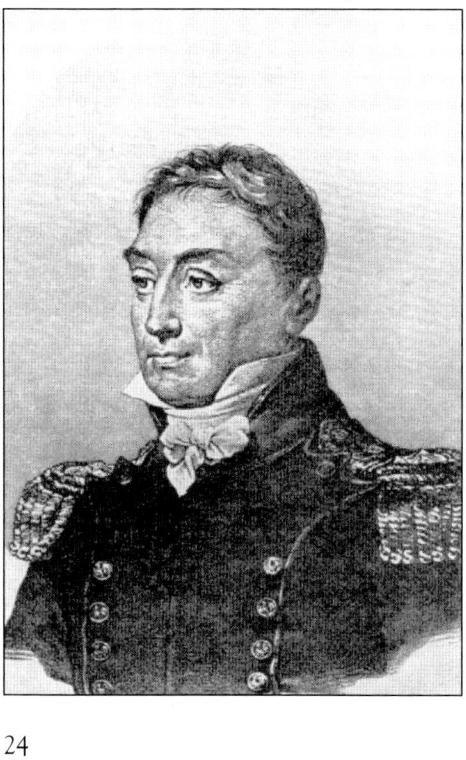

MARQUIS DE LAFAYETTE. On May 28, 1825, George Washington's friend the Marquis de Lafayette came to Braddock while making his way from former U.S. senator and secretary of the treasury Albert Gallatin's home at New Geneva, Pennsylvania (near Uniontown), to Pittsburgh as part of his "guest of the nation" farewell tour. In Braddock, he stayed at the home of George Wallace, whose mansion was located on one of the primary areas of Braddock's battle. (Courtesy of Braddock Carnegie Library.)

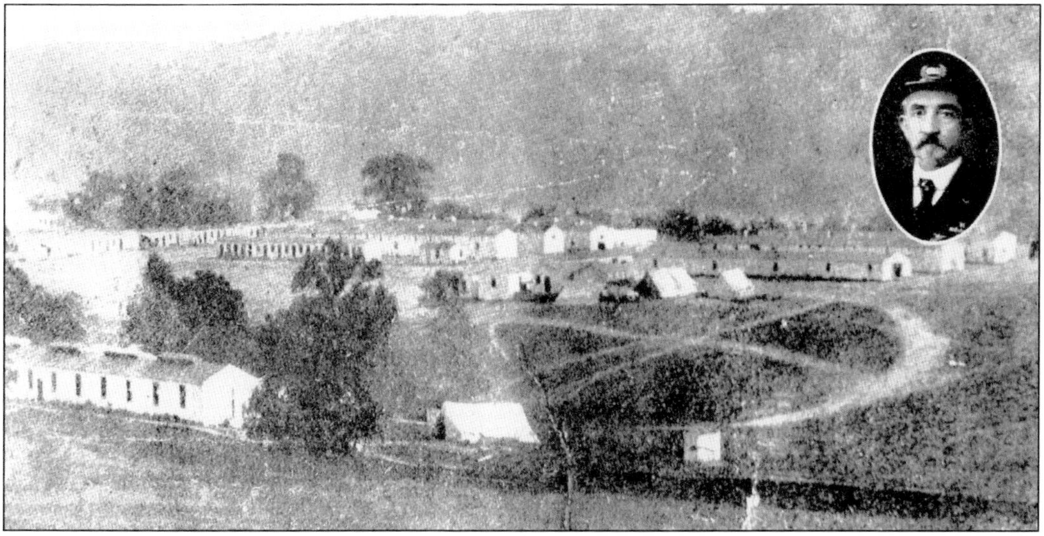

CAMP COPELAND. A Civil War military camp was opened in Braddock during August 1863. The camp was named after Brig. Gen. Joseph T. Copeland of Maine. It was located on the portion of Isaac Mills's farm property that was situated adjacent to the Pennsylvania Railroad tracks that were located near the uppermost portion of Fourth Street. Over a two-year period, thousands of troops were posted there and numerous buildings, including a hospital, were constructed. This image is reproduced from editor George H. Lamb's *The Unwritten History of Braddock's Field*, published in 1917.

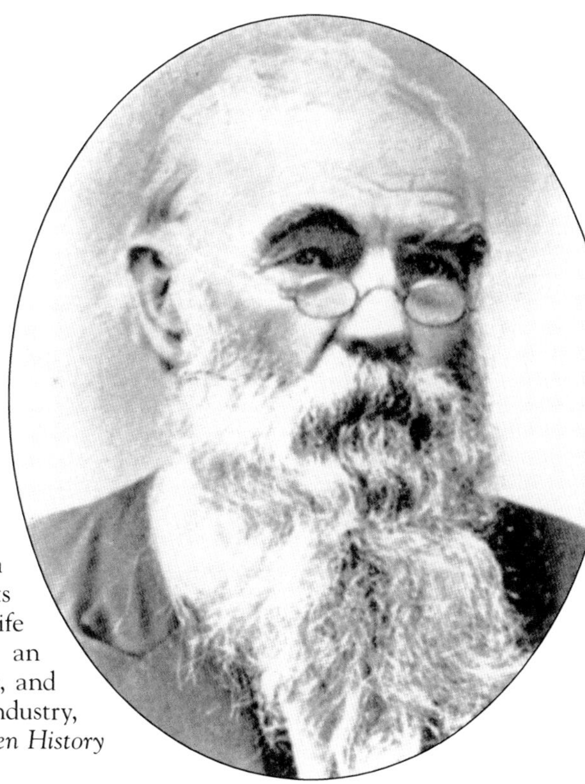

ISAAC MILLS SR. Isaac Mills Sr. came to Braddock's Field in 1804. As the eldest son, he arrived with his family in a Conestoga wagon from Morristown, New Jersey. They lived in a cabin until 1847 when they moved to a more substantial home built on a hill between Fourth and Fifth Streets above Braddock Avenue. Isaac, his wife Elizabeth, and their children took an active role in Braddock's development, and they were active in civic activities, industry, and church. (Courtesy of *The Unwritten History of Braddock's Field.*)

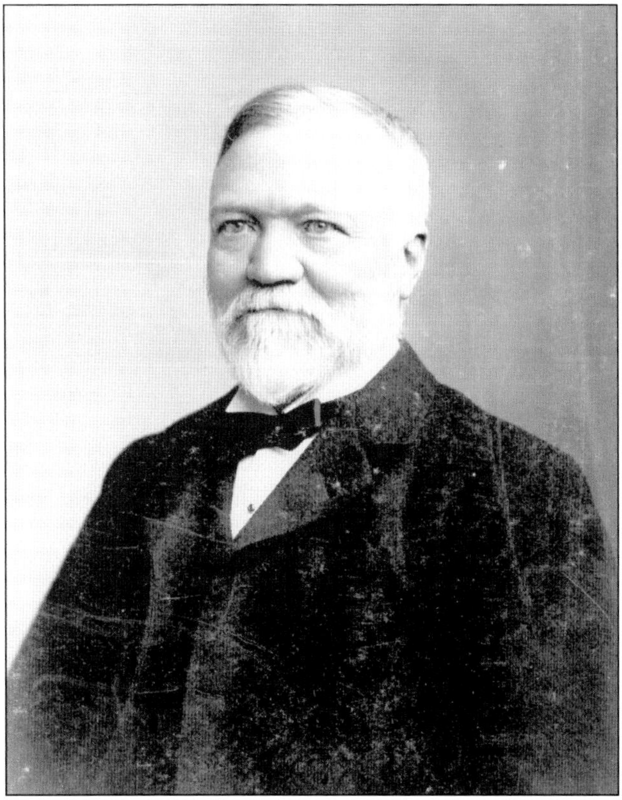

ANDREW CARNEGIE, 1835–1919. A young man of enormous potential, Andrew Carnegie came to America in 1848. Starting with little money and an attraction for hard work and reading, he soon learned the ways of business. His working career began as a bobbin boy in a cotton factory. Due largely to self-education and his tireless work ethic, he soon found work as a secretary and telegraph operator for the Pennsylvania Railroad Company. From that point onward, he seized opportunity as it was presented. (Courtesy of the Library of Congress.)

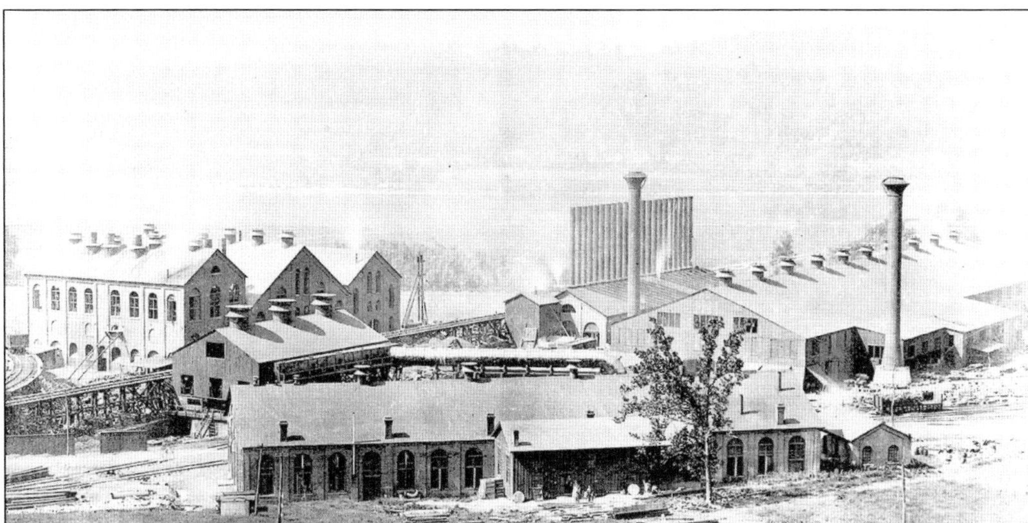

EDGAR THOMSON WORKS IN 1875. Shortly after Carnegie's initial investment in the Iron City Forge Company, he and his brother Thomas and partner William Coleman purchased the option for more than 100 acres of land in Braddock. They felt that the location was attractive for construction of a new steel-making plant. In 1872, the deal to purchase the Braddock property was finalized. Beginning construction in 1873, it took two years to complete the mill. When it opened in August 1875, it was considered the country's most modern steel-manufacturing facility. (Courtesy of the U.S. Steel Corporation.)

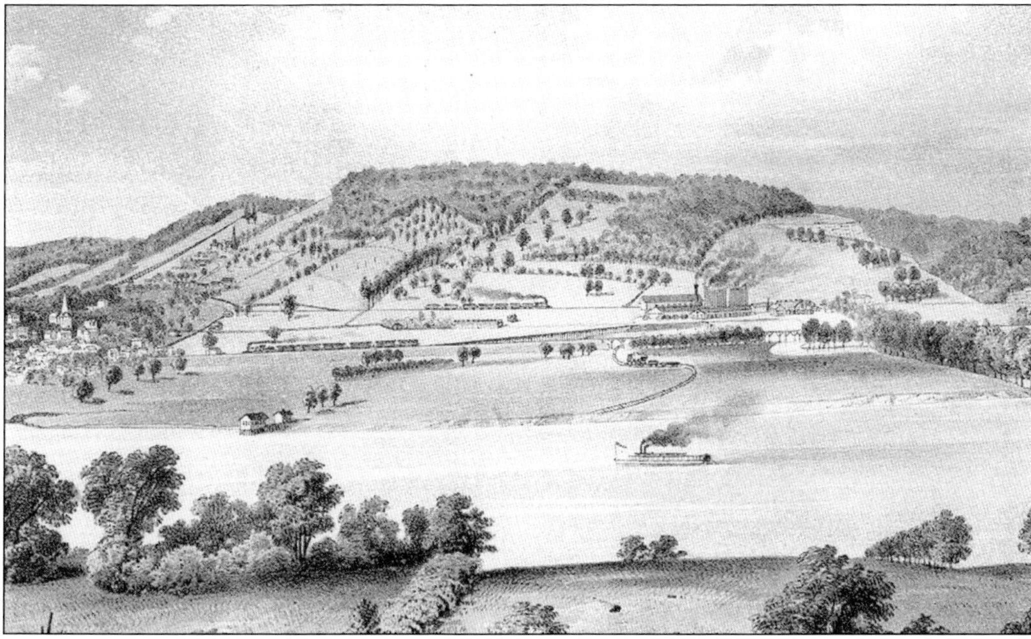

BRADDOCK, 1876. At a distance it was easy to grasp the rationale for Carnegie's placement of the Edgar Thomson mill's various structures. Some buildings were constructed between Braddock's main road and the Baltimore and Ohio Railroad tracks, others between the road and the Pennsylvania Railroad tracks. As the mill grew, more land was required. In 1893, Turtle Creek was diverted upstream and new mill buildings were erected on its old bed. (Courtesy of *The Unwritten History of Braddock's Field.*)

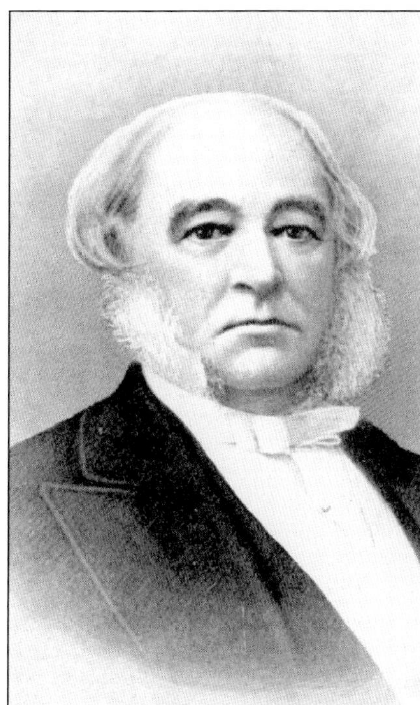

J. EDGAR THOMSON. As president of the Pennsylvania Railroad, J. Edgar Thomson was in many ways responsible for Carnegie's initial business success. At the time when Carnegie was developing his business plan and investing in construction of the Braddock mill, it was Thomson's business that he most desired. As one might imagine, it was not by happenstance that Carnegie named his first steel mill after his potentially largest client. (Courtesy of *The Unwritten History of Braddock's Field.*)

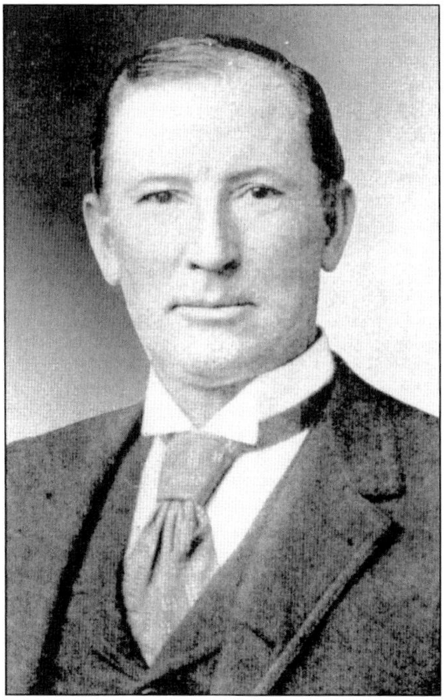

Capt. William Jones. Capt. William Jones was the first superintendent of the Edgar Thomson Steel Works. He was born in Luzerne County in 1839. During his early years, he was trained and worked as a machinist. In 1859, he worked for the Cambria Iron Works in Johnstown and later that same year he went to Chattanooga, Tennessee, where he assisted in the construction of a blast furnace. In 1873, he accepted the position at Andrew Carnegie's new Edgar Thomson mill. His leadership, management, and mechanical skills were legendary. (Courtesy of *The Unwritten History of Braddock's Field*.)

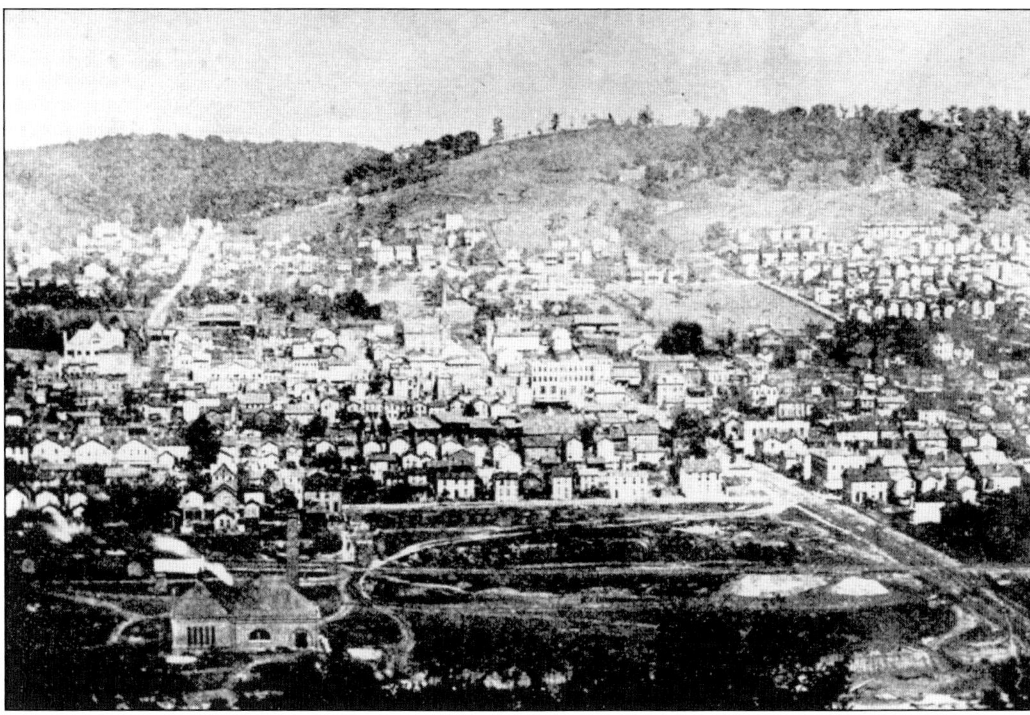

Braddock and North Braddock, c. 1887. Business was good and the town was booming by 1887, but the best was yet to come. Braddock's Ninth Street is seen at the far right extending from the Monongahela River up the hill to North Braddock. No longer a small village, the areas around the mills and factories were now rapidly spreading up the hillsides to North Braddock and beyond. (Courtesy of Braddock Carnegie Library.)

Four

Immigration and Economic Vitality

Opportunity draws people like moths toward flame. Initially it was trapping and trade that drew the area's first settlers. Soon their endeavors gave way to farming as the British occupation of Pittsburgh assured relative safety. The fertility of the land and the proximity of waterways allowed easy access to tools, foodstuffs, and markets. It was the Scotch and Irish who came first. Initially many of these earliest residents were exposed to the area by direct or indirect connection to British military forces.

As early industries were developed and rich veins of coal discerned, those of Welsh heritage were drawn to the area. Success compounded success as new industries and markets emerged—all requiring human capital to complement natural resources and a growing entrepreneurial spirit. In order to make the machines necessary for the manufacture of new products, additional talent was required. Soon it was the resident mechanical inclination of German and Nordic peoples that were needed. As the increased demand for labor ran headfirst into industry's desire to reduce costs, the need for unskilled or less costly labor rose dramatically. This tension created both a need and an opportunity for more people to come to the area and mix into the ever-enlarging pool of nationalities drawn to the growing flames of industry.

Soon the floodgates opened wide as a sea of mankind was drawn from Italy, Eastern Europe, and Russia, all seeking to improve their prospects by making their mark among the industrial behemoths emerging along the area's riverbanks. By 1890, more than 8,500 people called Braddock home; by 1920 there were almost 21,000 residents representing a wide variety of nationalities, traditions, and languages.

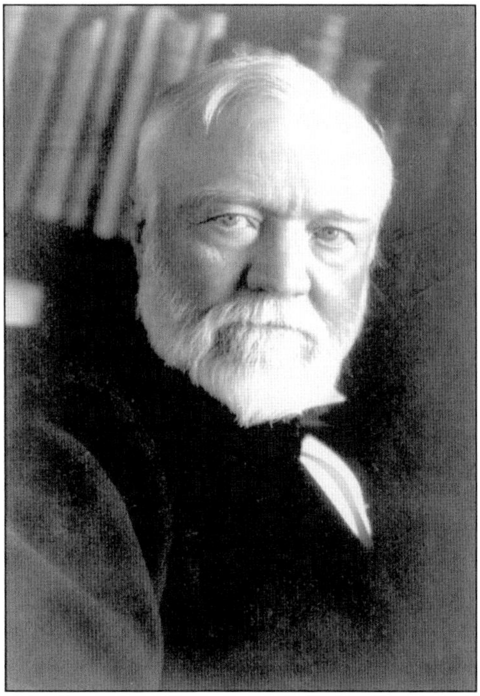

ANDREW CARNEGIE'S LIBRARIES. Andrew Carnegie conceived, developed and funded the construction of Braddock Carnegie Library. Its prime purpose was to support and benefit Edgar Thomson employees and their families. The Carnegie library of Braddock was to be his very first in America and served as a singular act of beneficence that subsequently led to the development of many hundreds of similar libraries around the country over a 30-year period. (Courtesy of the Library of Congress.)

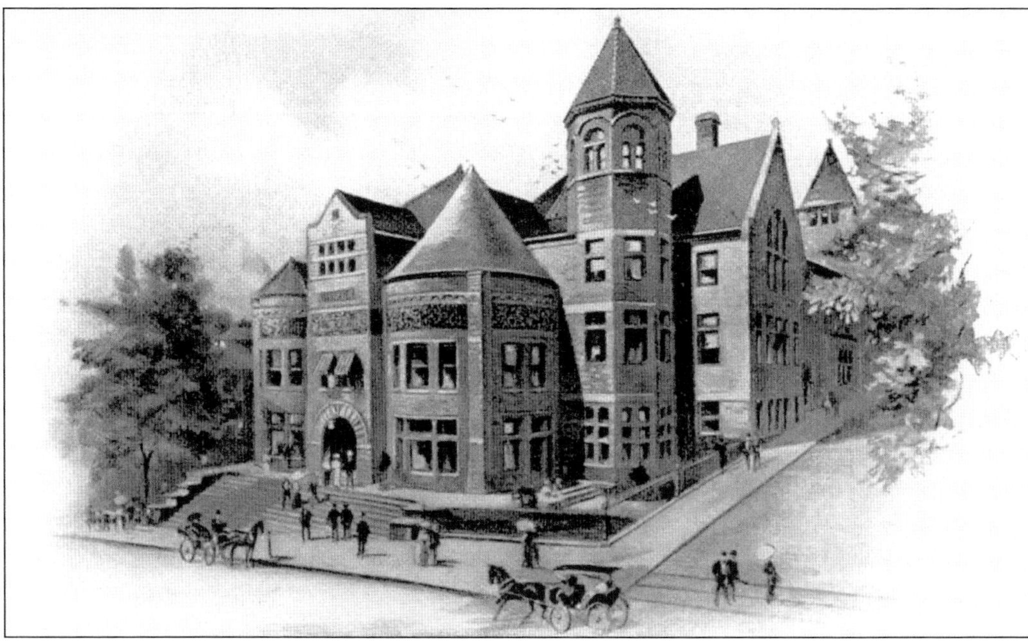

CARNEGIE LIBRARY OF BRADDOCK. America's first Carnegie library was dedicated on March 30, 1889. Construction took slightly more than a year to complete. Among Carnegie's dedicatory remarks, he stated, "I venture to predict that when generation after generation shall have passed away, this Library will remain and be recognized as a center of light and learning; a never ending spring of all good influences; and perhaps it may serve to remind those generations that are to come, that the duties of capital towards labor, even in this age, are not altogether forgotten." (Courtesy of Braddock Carnegie Library.)

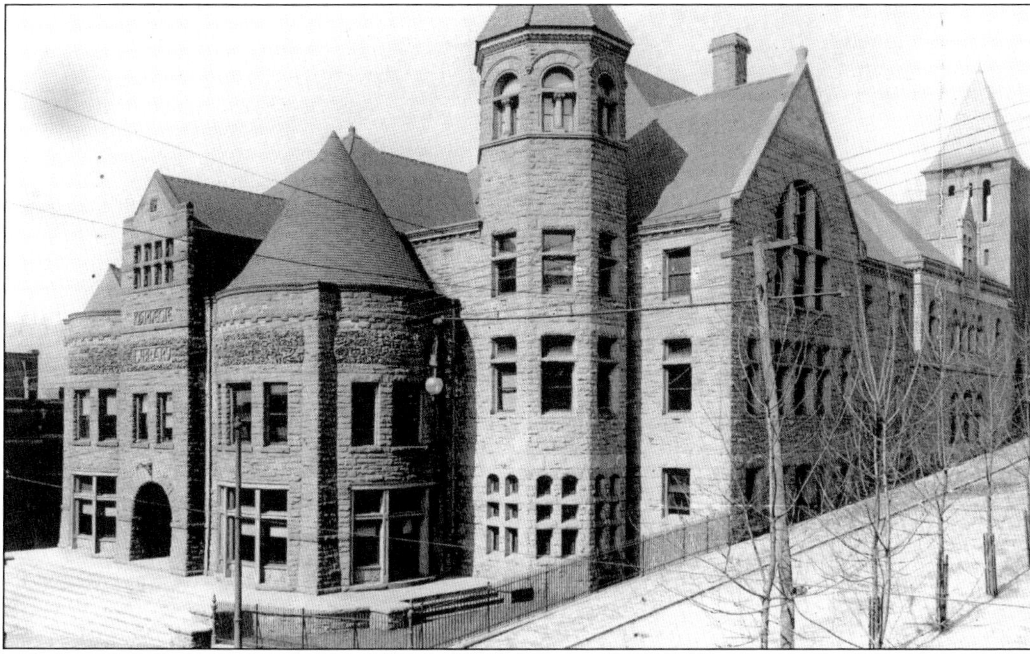

Carnegie Library Addition. An addition designed by the architectural firm of Longfellow, Alden and Harlow was added to the library in 1893. The addition significantly increased its space and included a gymnasium, duckpin bowling alley, music hall, and swimming pool. (Courtesy of the Library of Congress.)

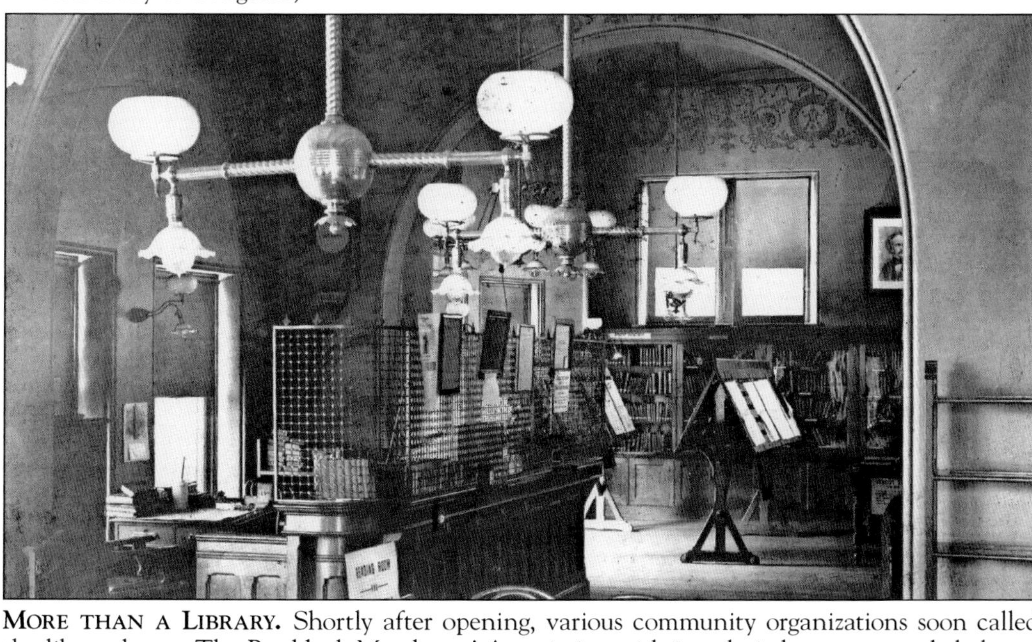

More than a Library. Shortly after opening, various community organizations soon called the library home. The Braddock Merchants' Association with its salaried secretary and clerk was headquartered there. Other organizations operating at the library included: Braddock Medical Society, Carnegie Round Table, Braddock Druggists' Association, Jewelers' Organization, and Aquatic Club. The music hall was used for all sorts of public assemblies, with particular uses including amateur theatricals, lectures, and concerts. (Courtesy of Braddock Carnegie Library.)

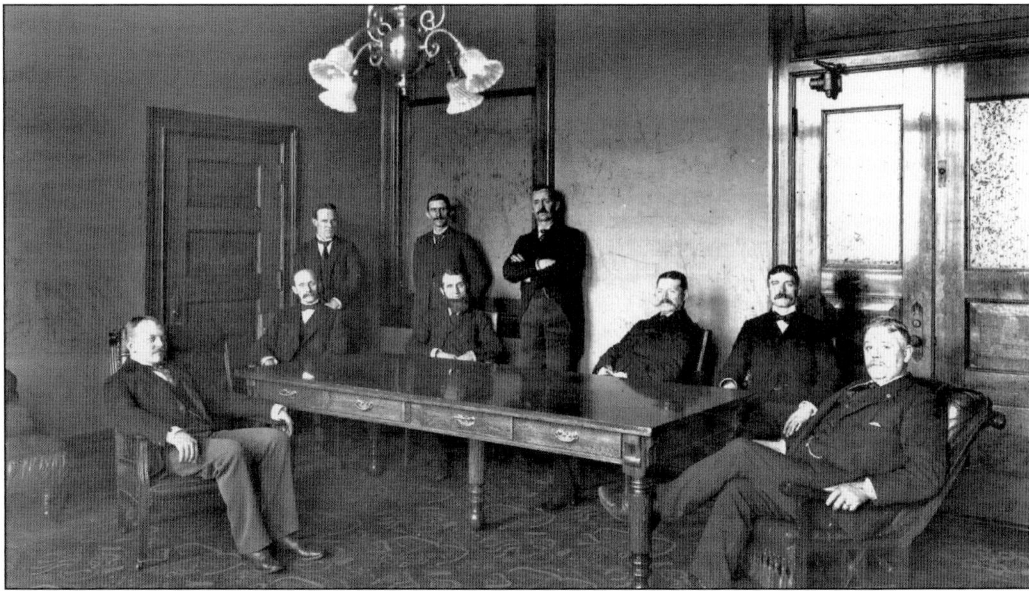

Carnegie Club Board of Directors. The Carnegie Club was organized in 1893 upon completion of the new addition. While receiving direction from the same directors as the library, the club was opened as a separate operating entity. Around 1898, the management functions were merged. The purpose of the club was to complement the library's work by providing health, exercise, recreation, and amusement activities to improve the soundness of their bodies. (Courtesy of Braddock Carnegie Library.)

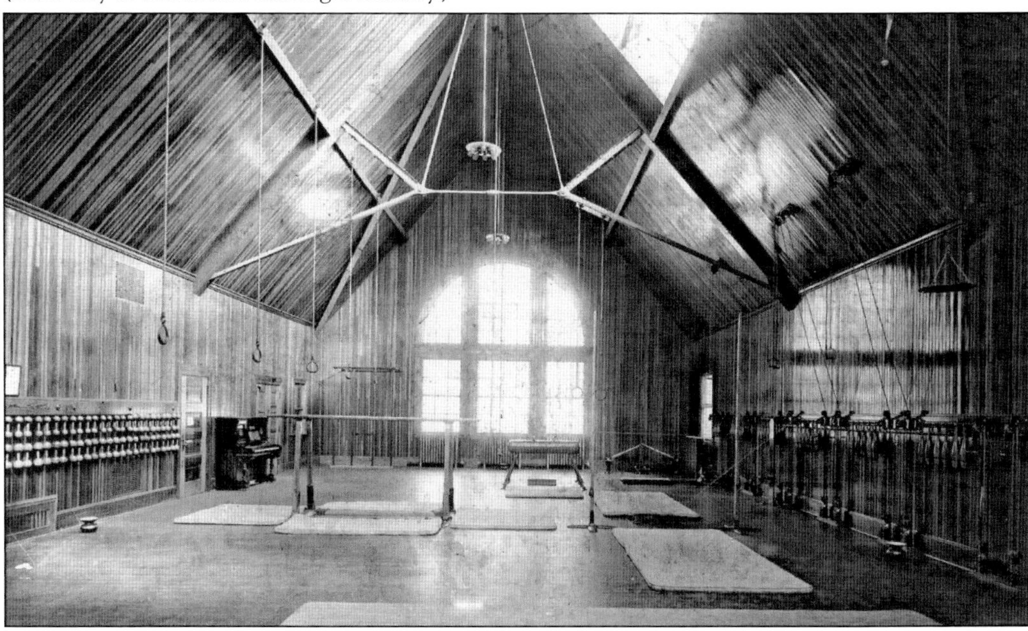

Carnegie Club Gym. At the dedication of the library in 1889, Andrew Carnegie stated, "I trust you will not forget the importance of amusements. I hope the upstairs is to be provided with all the means possible for playing of a game of billiards and so forth, and for gymnastic exercises. Life must not be taken so seriously." Seen here, the gymnasium is well equipped for exercise and sport. (Courtesy of Braddock Carnegie Library.)

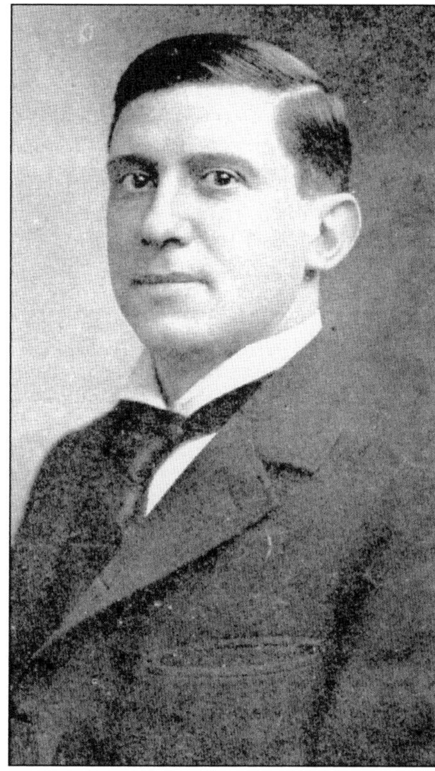

CHARLES M. SCHWAB. Charles M. Schwab served as the first president of the U.S. Steel Corporation upon its formation in 1901. He began his spectacular rise in the industrial world from very humble beginnings in Braddock. Upon graduation from college, he took a job in Braddock as a grocery clerk. Within months he went to work in the engineering department of the Carnegie Steel Company as a stake driver. Schwab was a quick learner, and he soon became the company's chief engineer. (Courtesy of *The Unwritten History of Braddock's Field.*)

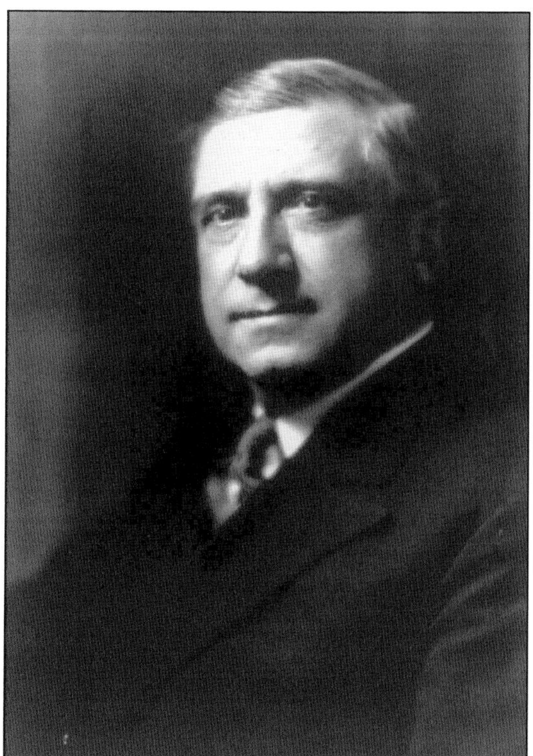

SCHWAB SAVES BETHLEHEM STEEL. In 1887, Schwab was named superintendent of Andrew Carnegie's Homestead Works. In 1889, he returned to Braddock to take over operations of the Edgar Thomson mill. After the Homestead steel strike in 1892, he was given charge of both plants. In 1897, he became president of the Carnegie Company. He resigned his position as president of U.S. Steel Corporation in 1903. In 1907, he took on the job of rebuilding the Bethlehem Steel Corporation. (Courtesy of the Library of Congress.)

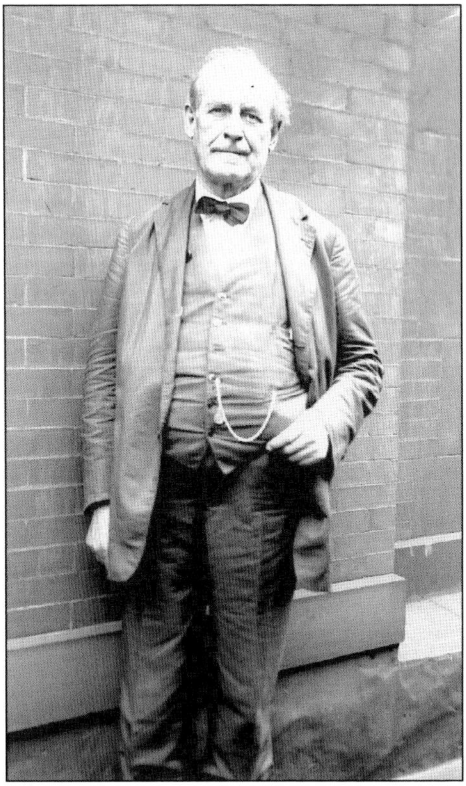

WILLIAM JENNINGS BRYAN. Braddock has always drawn a diverse range of people, including political, military, industrial, and religious leaders. On March 3, 1903, it attracted William Jennings Bryan. That afternoon Bryan delivered one of his famous speeches at Carnegie Hall. He was an active and forceful member of the Democratic Party and well known for his passionate and eloquent speeches. One of the most famous was his "Cross of Gold" speech, given at the 1896 Democratic national convention. (Courtesy of the Library of Congress.)

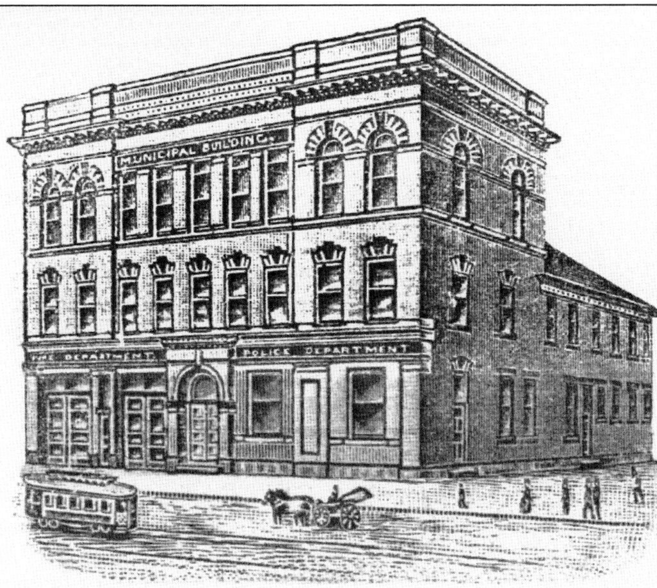

BRADDOCK MUNICIPAL BUILDING.

BRADDOCK MUNICIPAL BUILDING, 1903. Located at 723–729 Braddock Avenue, the Braddock Municipal Building served as the meeting place for the Braddock Council. The building also held offices for burgess, board of health, police department, fire department, and public works department, solicitor, treasurer, and other offices. (Courtesy of Braddock Carnegie Library.)

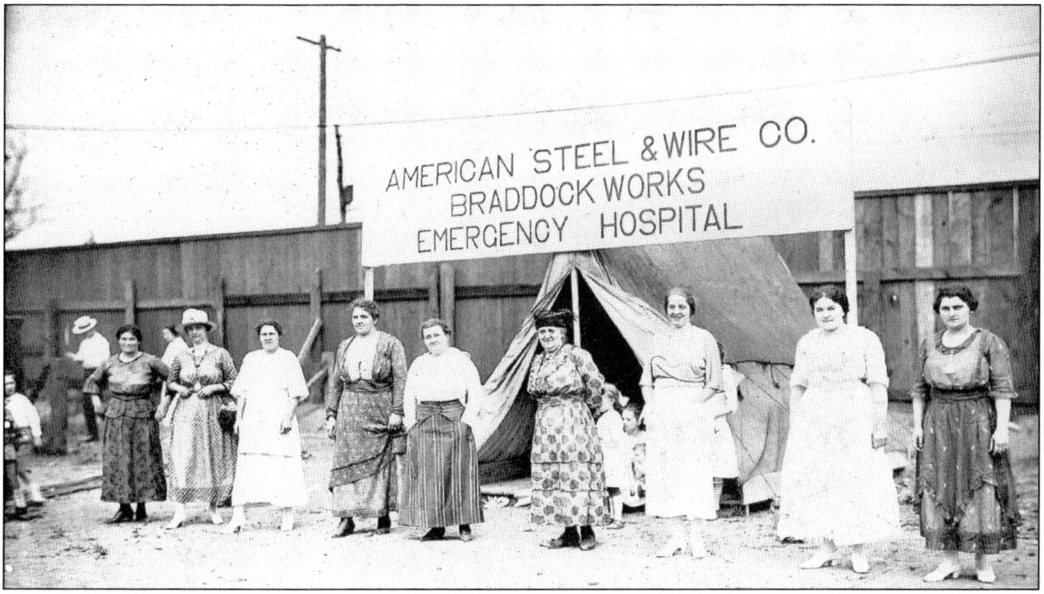

AMERICAN STEEL AND WIRE COMPANY EMERGENCY HOSPITAL. During the last decade of the 19th century, industry and railroads caused an alarming increase in the number of industrial accidents. In 1890, Fred Oakley, a reporter for the *Braddock Daily News* made what was considered the first efforts—in words—to engage local citizens in the process of opening a hospital. Until a permanent hospital could be established, however, temporary hospitals like this were common. (Courtesy of UPMC Braddock Medical Center.)

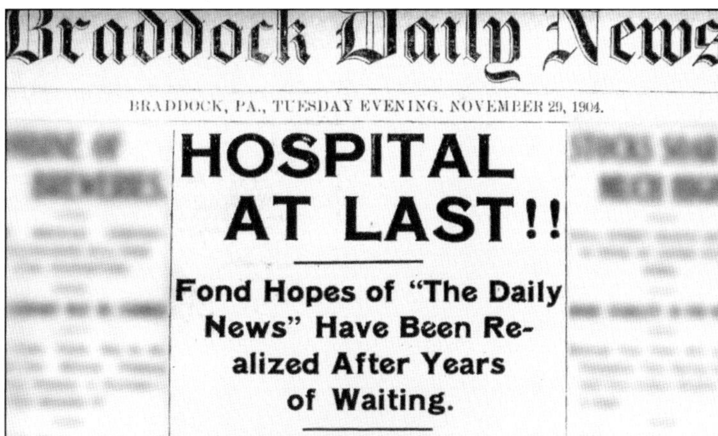

Braddock Daily News

BRADDOCK, PA., TUESDAY EVENING, NOVEMBER 29, 1904.

HOSPITAL AT LAST!!

Fond Hopes of "The Daily News" Have Been Realized After Years of Waiting.

PROPERTY PURCHASED

The Elizabeth Clay Mansion and a Plot of Ground 200 Feet Square Has Been Secured by the Hospital Association for Hospital Purposes

AT A COST OF $30,000.

BRADDOCK GENERAL HOSPITAL ANNOUNCEMENT. During October 1894, it was reported that an anonymous donor had committed $200 toward the establishment of a hospital. Initially referred to as a "Hebrew merchant of Braddock," it soon became known that the donor was Jacob Katz, a local tailor. Other business owners offered additional subscriptions shortly thereafter. It was not until February 1905, however, that sufficient funds had been gathered to allow for the successful chartering of Braddock General Hospital. (Courtesy of Senator John Heinz History Center.)

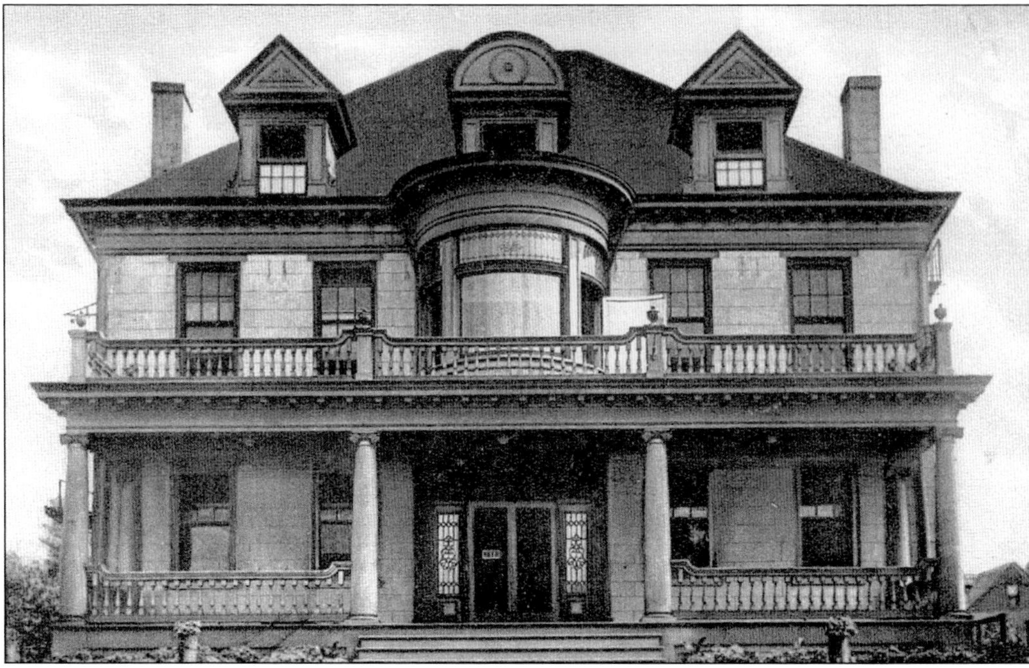

THE MILLS MANSION. On April 14, 1905, the Braddock Hospital Association reached an agreement to purchase the Mills homestead, including the family's mansion, which was slated to serve as the initial hospital building. The property was considered among the most beautiful in the area as it was situated on a knoll just above Braddock Avenue on the corner of Fifth Street and Holland Avenue. (Author's collection.)

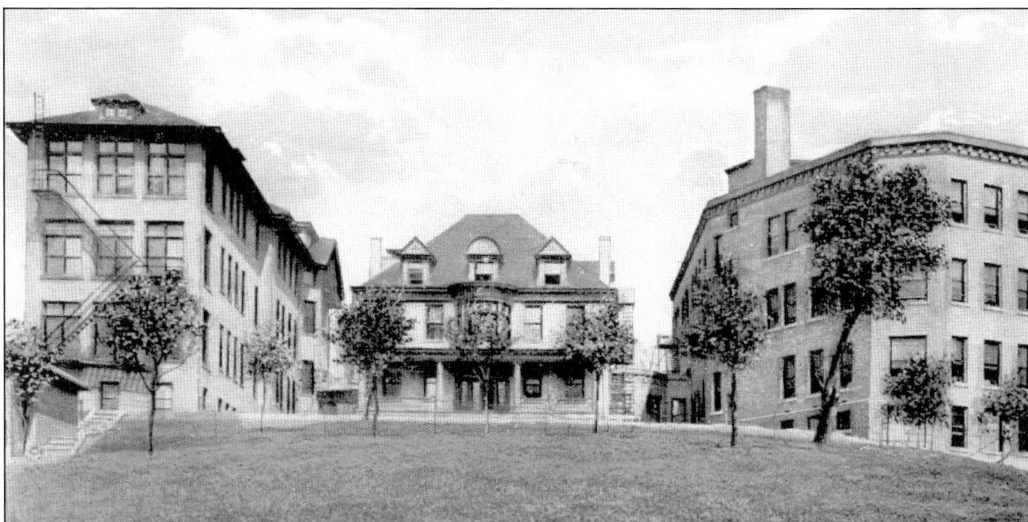

BRADDOCK GENERAL HOSPITAL'S EARLY GROWTH. Braddock General Hospital opened its doors on June 27, 1906. However, the hospital's board of managers soon found that its facility of 30 beds was too small. Before the first mortgage could be settled, additional funds were being solicited for the construction of a new 70-bed wing. In 1911, the west wing was completed and the Mills mansion was converted to accommodate student nurses and hospital administration. (Author's collection.)

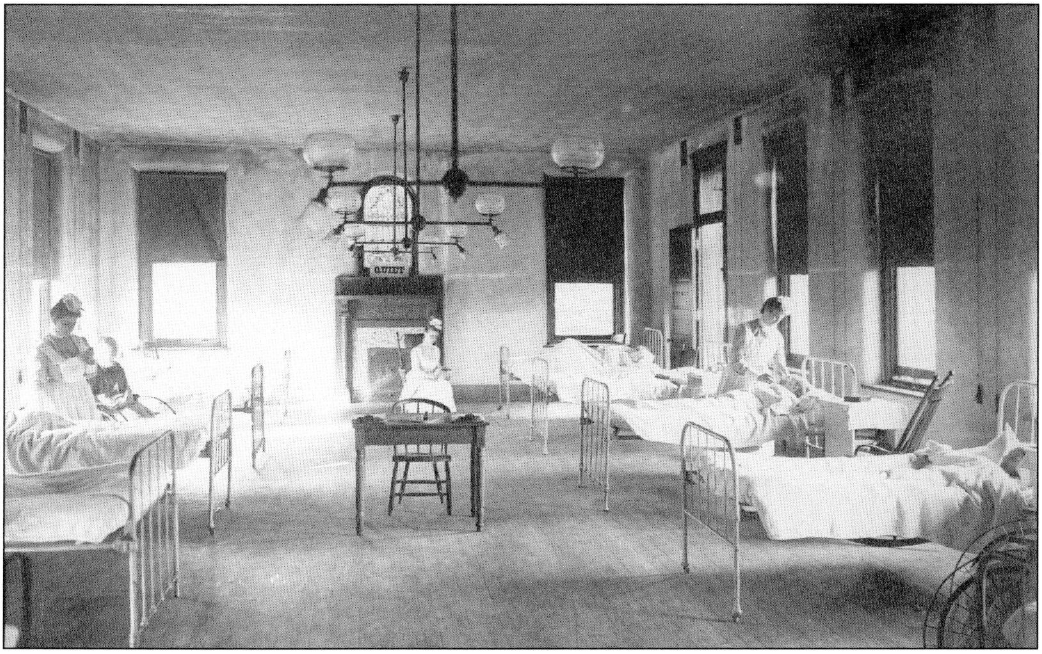

SCHOOL FOR NURSES OPENS. Upon completion of the new wing, the original building was used to house a dormitory for student nurses and hospital administration. The Braddock General Hospital Training School for Nurses graduated its first class in April 1910. (Courtesy of UPMC Braddock Medical Center.)

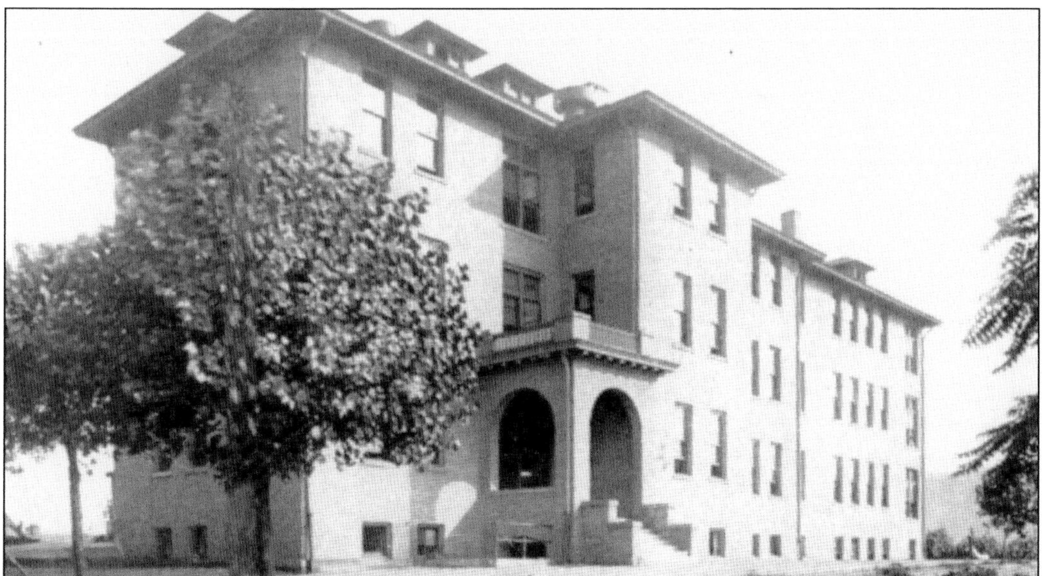

BRADDOCK GENERAL HOSPITAL WEST WING. History repeated itself in 1913 when the hospital's managers found that they were again out of space and routinely falling 20 beds short of demand. Funds for yet another hospital expansion were solicited by the board of managers and an army of volunteers was led by C. E. Dinkey, superintendent of the Edgar Thomson Steel Works. On April 19, 1917, a new 60-bed "east wing" was opened. (Courtesy of *The Unwritten History of Braddock's Field.*)

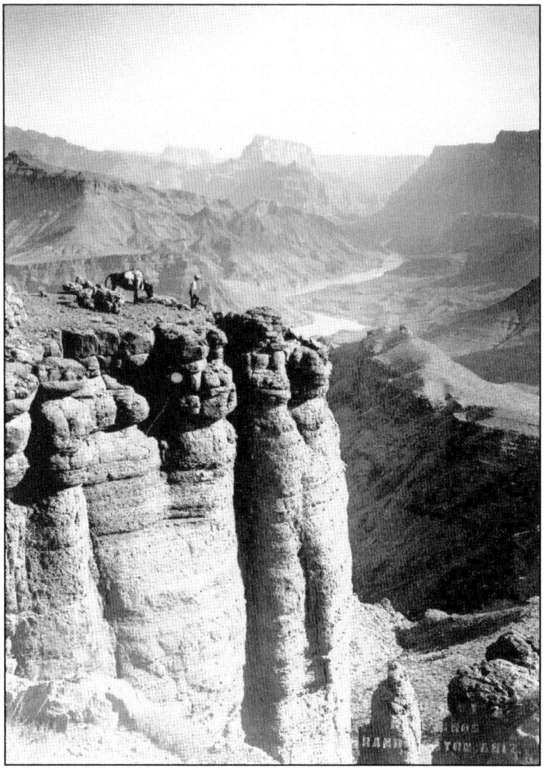

EMERY AND ELLSWORTH KOLB. Arriving from Vienna with little more than 25¢ in his pocket in 1847, John Kolb Sr. became a well-respected and affluent resident. His sons Emery and Ellsworth left the area to become famous in the early motion picture and travel business with their exploits in the Grand Canyon. Their work is regarded as critical to the nation's interest and preservation of the Grand Canyon. This Kolb brothers photograph shows a man and donkey on Tanner Ledge Grand Canyon around 1913. (Courtesy of the Library of Congress.)

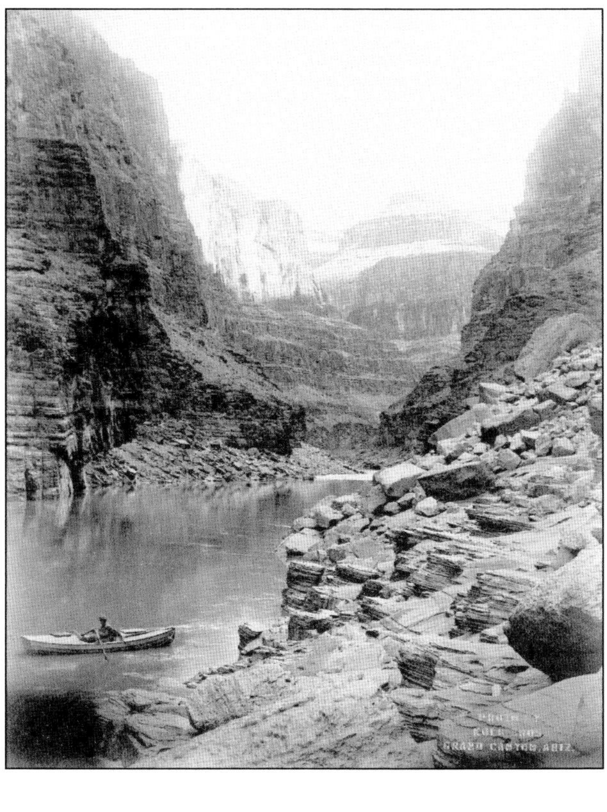

THE KOLB BROTHERS MOVE WEST. Leaving his job in the mill, Ellsworth Kolb left Braddock in 1900 to see the west, arriving at the South Rim of the Grand Canyon in 1901. His brother Emery, a photographer, joined him in late 1902. In 1911, they ran the Colorado River from Wyoming to Mexico and recorded their voyage on motion picture film, reportedly the very first motion pictures of the canyon that the world had ever seen. In 1914, a story of their adventures was published by the National Geographic Society. Shown here is a Kolb brothers photograph of the Grand Canyon sometime around 1913. (Courtesy of the Library of Congress.)

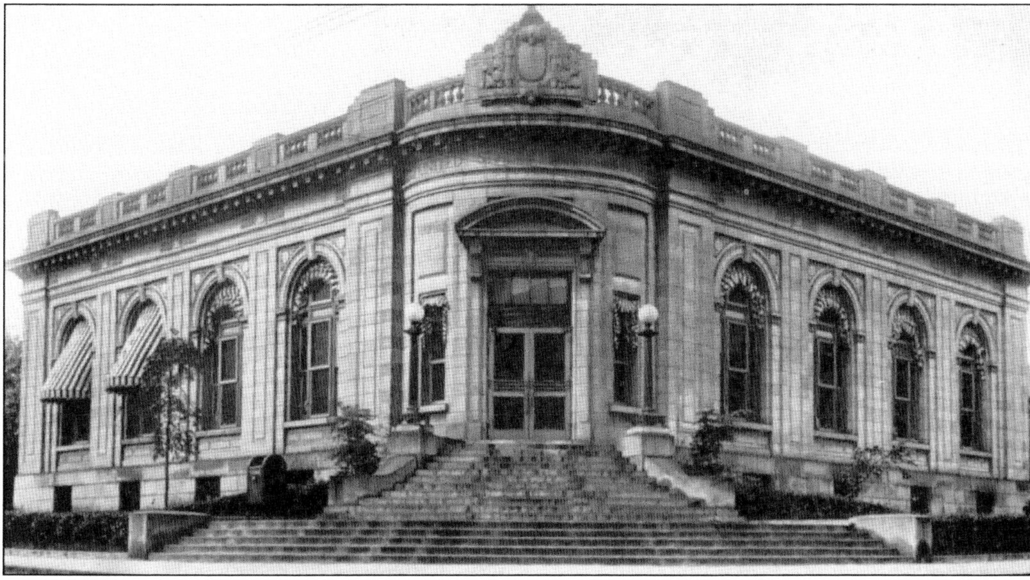

NEW POST OFFICE AND GOVERNMENT BUILDING. Between 1900 and 1910, the population of Braddock grew by almost 5,000 people and post office business was booming. Business was so good in fact that Congress authorized $125,000 for the construction of a new post office. In searching for an appropriate site, it was determined that property along Braddock's main street was cost prohibitive at almost $1,100 per foot. Lower cost property on Parker Avenue was subsequently acquired and the new post office opened on June 10, 1913. (Courtesy of *The Unwritten History of Braddock's Field.*)

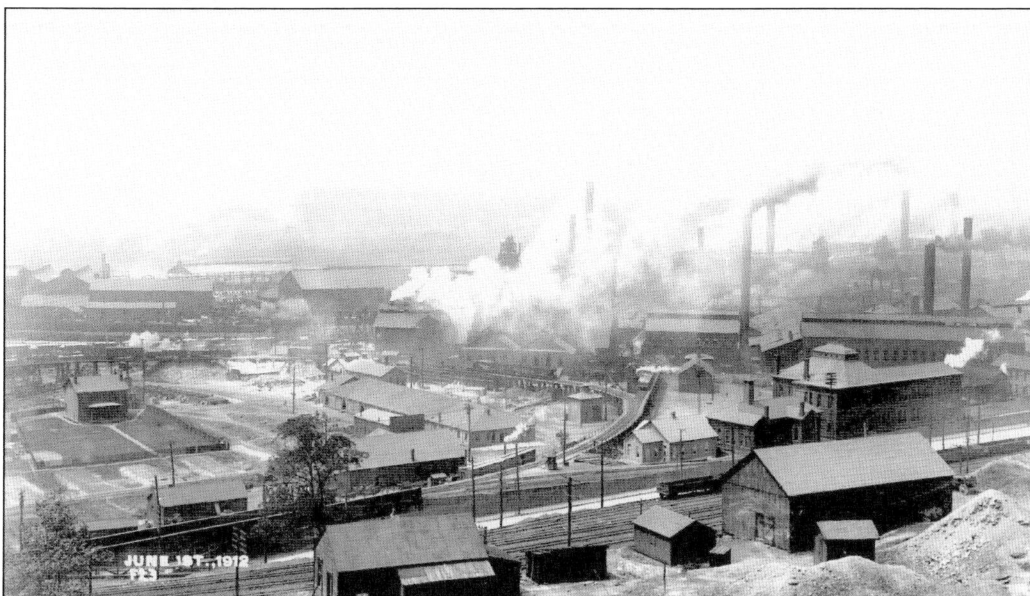

EDGAR THOMSON MILL, JUNE 1912. In May 1912, newspapers reported that officials from the Carnegie Steel Company announced plans to invest between $8 and $10 million in the Edgar Thomson mill and that 3,000 men would be hired to make extensive improvements. Plans called for the erection of 14 modern open-hearth furnaces and major renovations to the rail mills. (Courtesy of the Rivers of Steel National Heritage Area.)

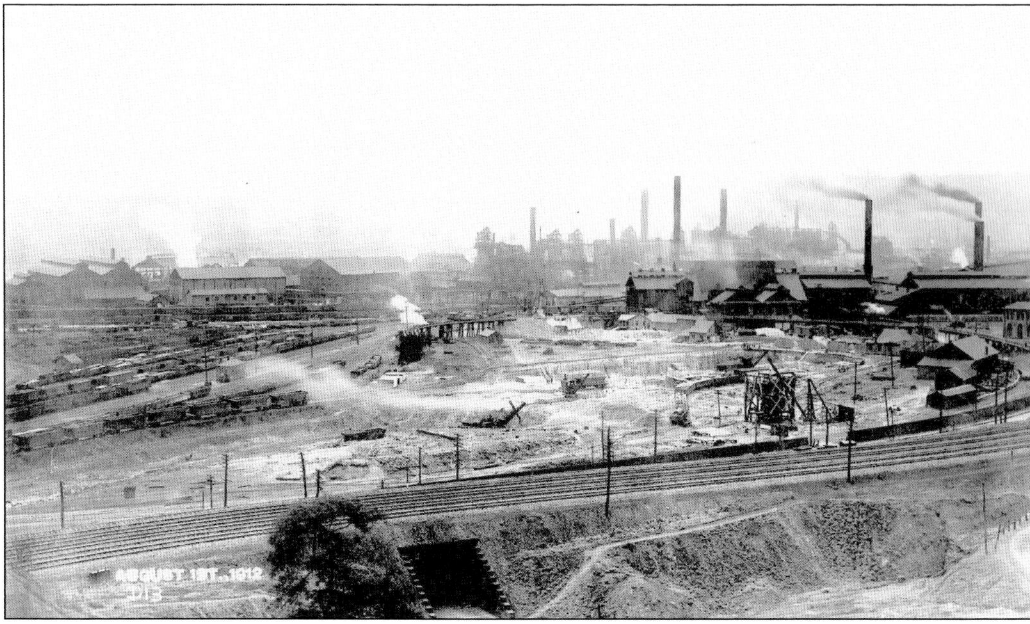

EDGAR THOMSON MILL, AUGUST 1912. During the month of June 1912, the old McKinney Club House, the superintendents meeting place and dining hall, was razed to make room for a new plant. Stocking and shipping yards for Mills No. 1 and No. 2 were constructed, and one of the old rail mills was remodeled. (Courtesy of the Rivers of Steel National Heritage Area.)

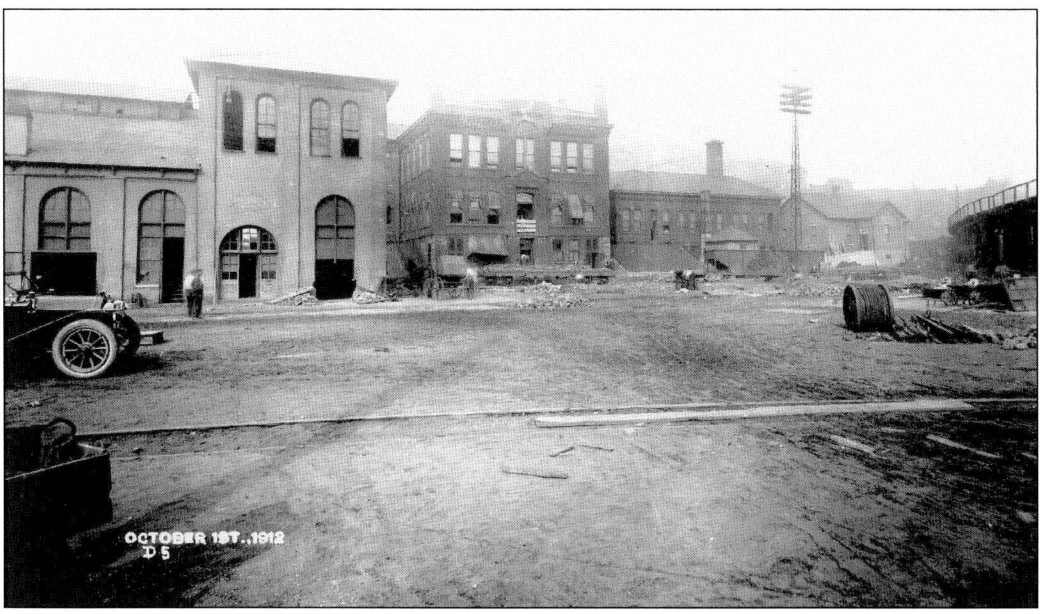

EDGAR THOMSON MILL, OCTOBER 1912. A number of Edgar Thomson's buildings and offices are seen in this image. Among the many improvements planned for the mill, a new emergency hospital was one of the most valued. Ground had been broken in December 1911 and the hospital was completed in September 1912. (Courtesy of the Rivers of Steel National Heritage Area.)

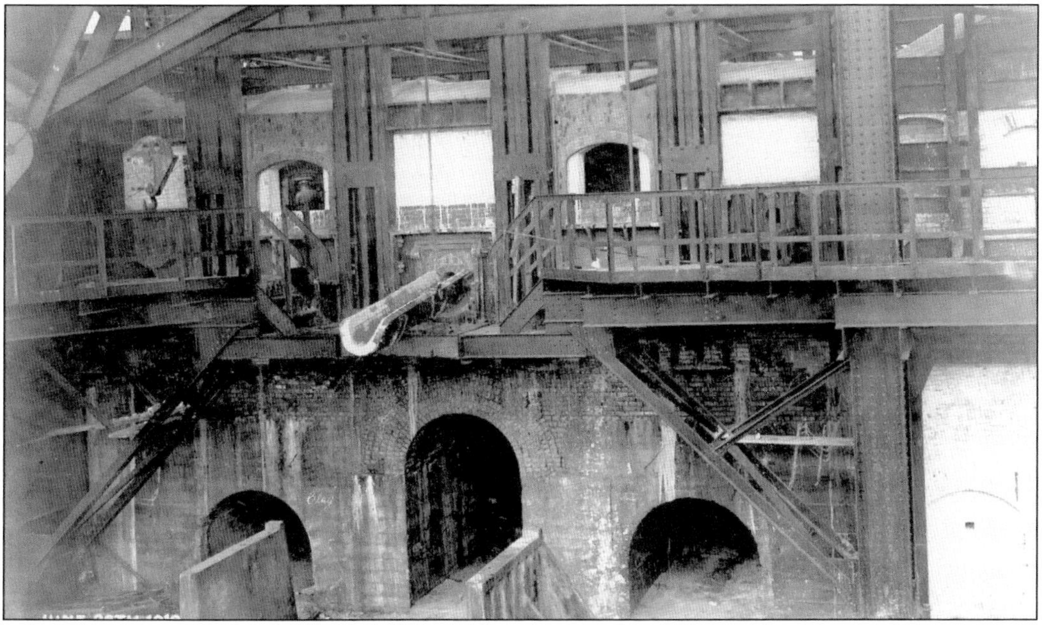

EDGAR THOMSON MILL, JUNE 1913. In May 1912, the good news was announced throughout the plant that funds for improvements to the mill would finally come to pass with a massive new appropriation. Ground was broken on May 31, 1913. The improvements that were being made would significantly boost production as the new 14-furnace basic open-hearth plant came on line. (Courtesy of the Rivers of Steel National Heritage Area.)

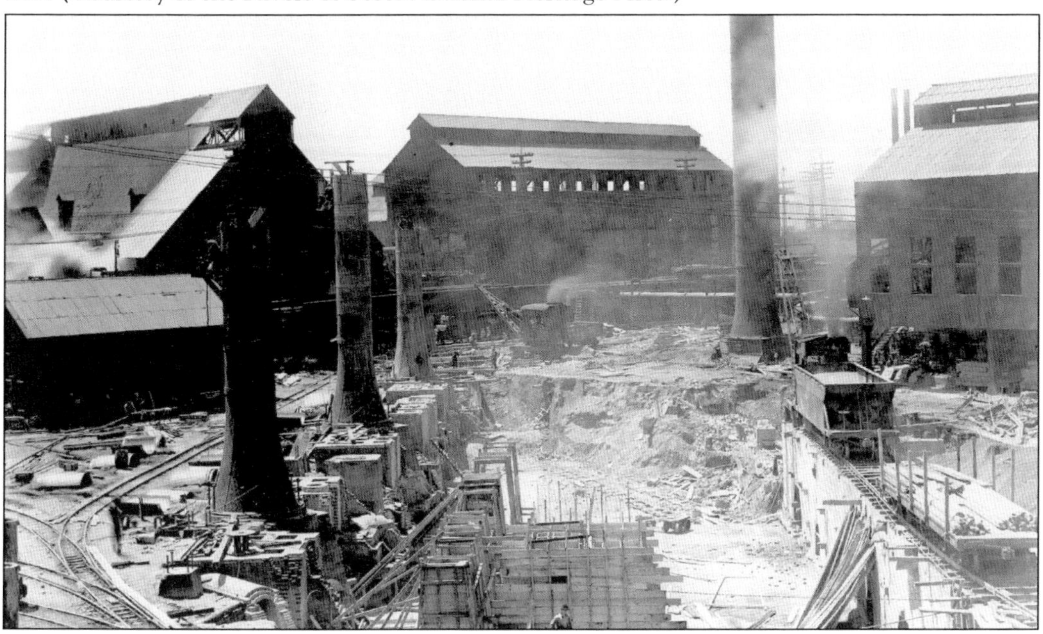

EDGAR THOMSON MILL, JULY 1913. During the height of the mill's renovation work, construction materials were seemingly everywhere. There were few mill buildings that were not impacted by the monumental rebuilding phase. The new employment office was opened in October. It had been operating in the basement of the general office since early June. (Courtesy of the Rivers of Steel National Heritage Area.)

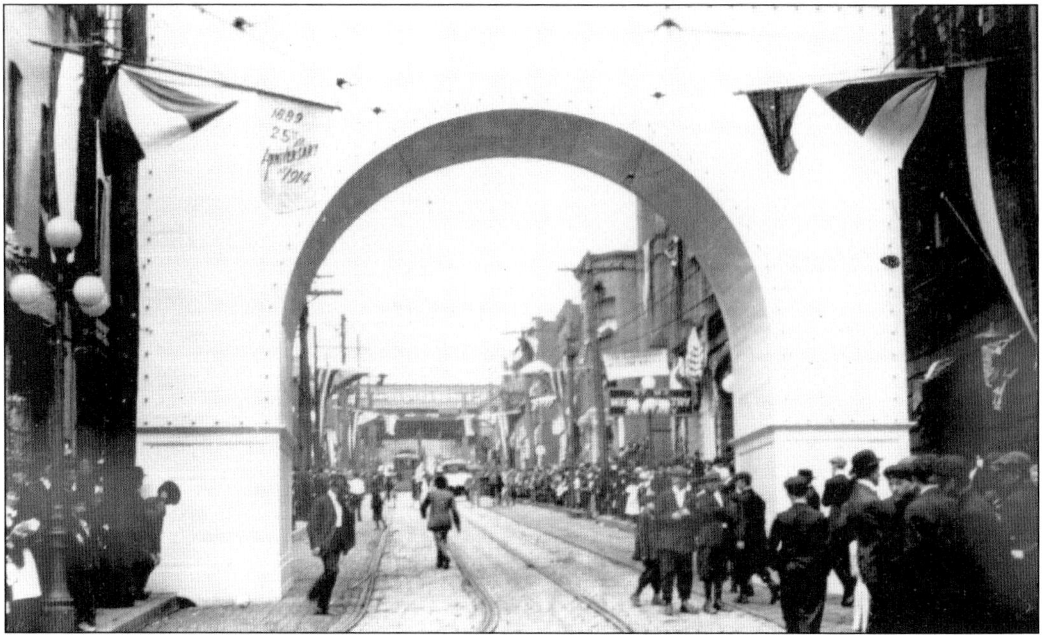

BRADDOCK CARNEGIE LIBRARY 25TH ANNIVERSARY PARADE. In honor of its 25 years of service and in recognition of Braddock's unique stature in the fast-growing world of Carnegie libraries in America, a special anniversary party was held in 1914. The party was held on April 29, and the master of philanthropy, Andrew Carnegie, came back for the festivities. The town was decorated for the party and three arches of triumph were constructed along Braddock's main thoroughfare. (Courtesy of Braddock Carnegie Library.)

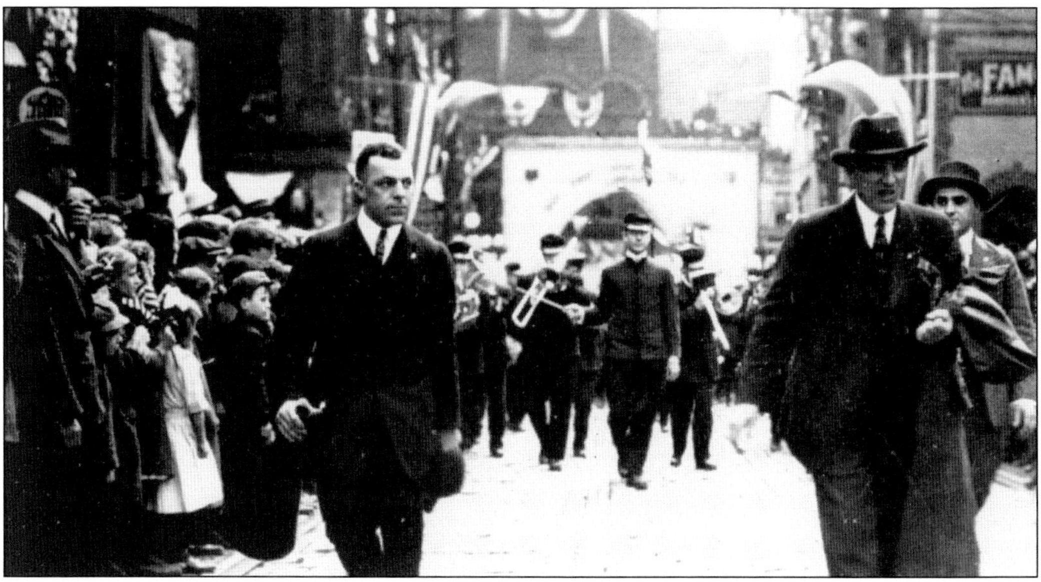

FLAGS FLYING AND PORTRAITS HUNG. This view of the parade looks down Library Street toward Braddock Avenue. Local businesses joined in the celebration by outfitting their storefronts with flags and bunting. Portraits of Andrew Carnegie were displayed everywhere. On the afternoon of the event, schools and businesses were closed in order that everyone might participate in the festivities. (Courtesy of Braddock Carnegie Library.)

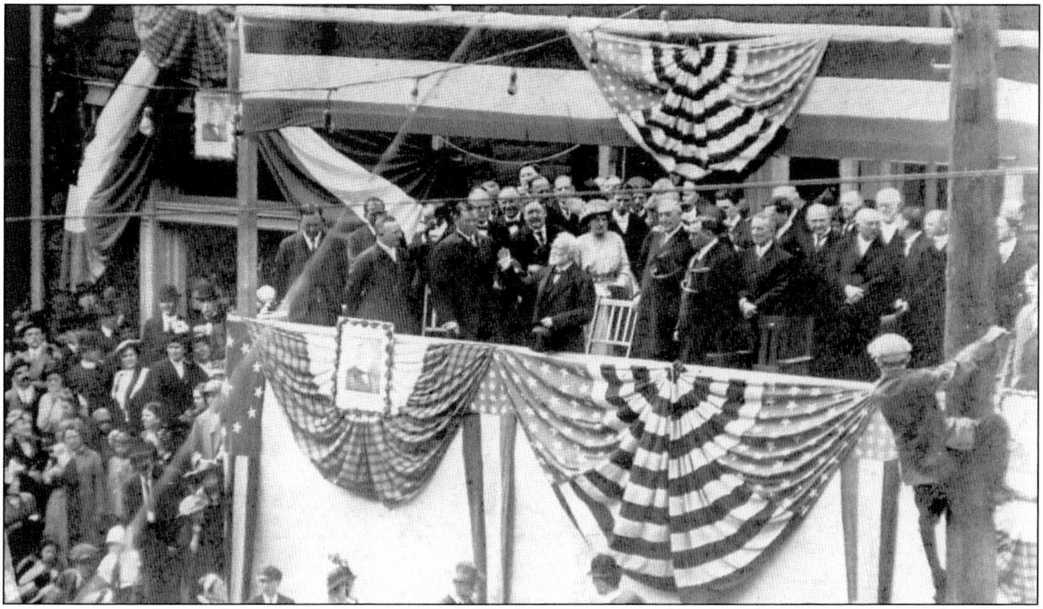

ANDREW CARNEGIE ON REVIEWING STAND. Everyone wanted to catch a glimpse of Andrew Carnegie, so a large reviewing stand was constructed in front of the library. Wave after wave of bands and marchers comprised of schoolchildren, workers, war veterans, and police and fire departments passed. Andrew Carnegie and countless dignitaries crowded the reviewing stage. This was Carnegie's last visit to the area; he died four years later in 1919. (Courtesy of Braddock Carnegie Library.)

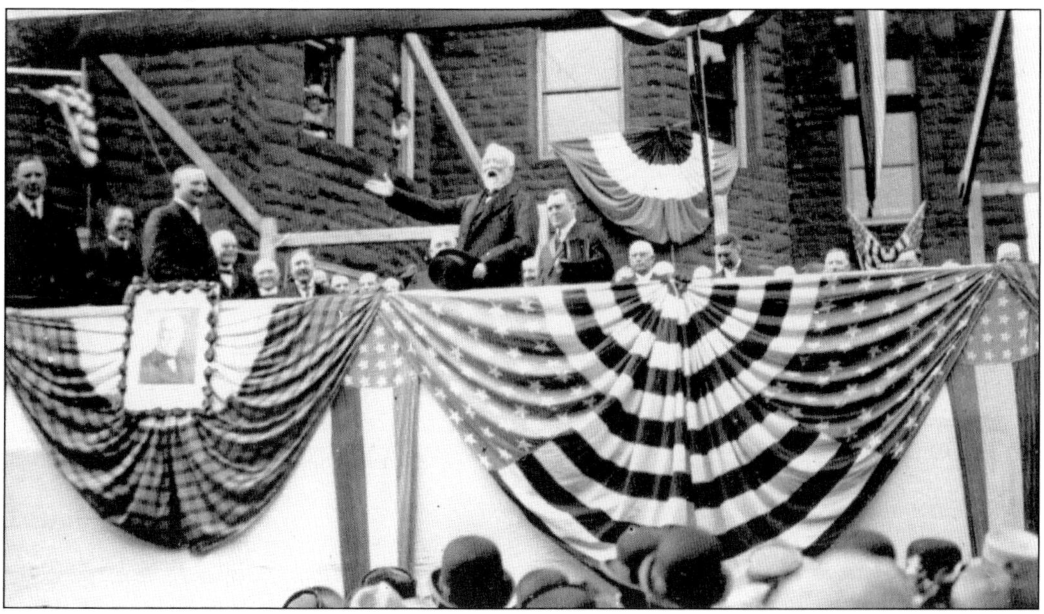

"BRADDOCK HAS BEEN MY CRY." Carnegie is seen here speaking to an enthusiastic crowd. Carnegie's remarks were filled with recollections of the mill's early days and those of his friend Capt. William R. (Bill) Jones. Carnegie is quoted to have stated in his remarks that "I am proud to be a man of Braddock, and in my travels through Europe and every other continent, Braddock has been my cry." (Courtesy of Braddock Carnegie Library.)

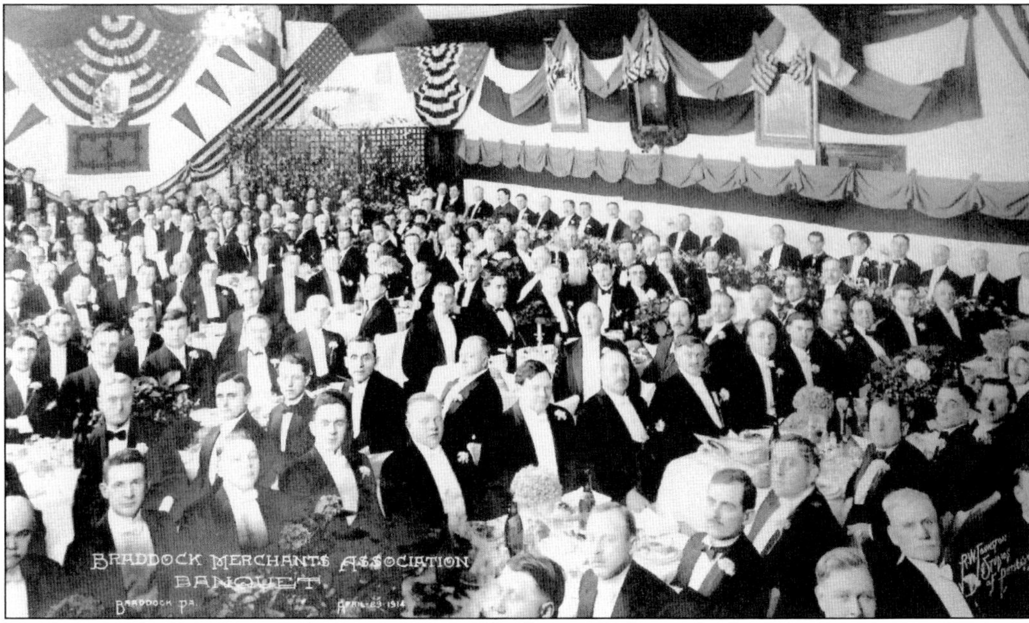

BRADDOCK MERCHANT'S ASSOCIATION BANQUET. Later in the evening of the 25th anniversary celebration the Braddock Merchant's Association sponsored a banquet for Andrew Carnegie and 250 special guests. Held in the Braddock Carnegie Library Gym, many more speeches of tribute were delivered by the area's leading business, government, and educational leaders. (Courtesy of Braddock Carnegie Library.)

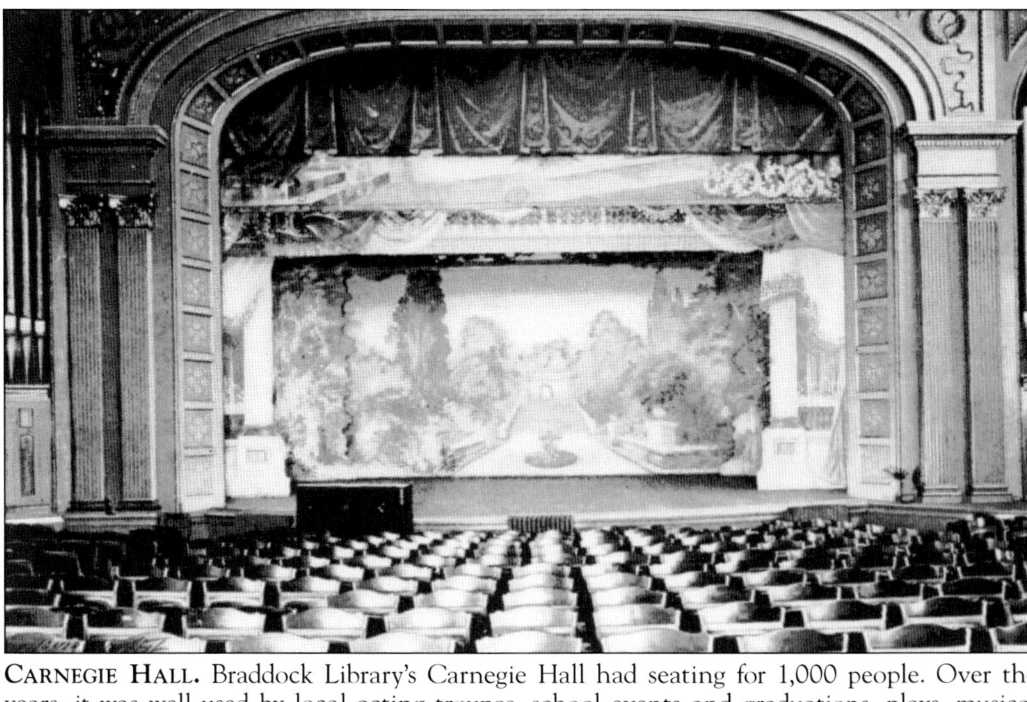

CARNEGIE HALL. Braddock Library's Carnegie Hall had seating for 1,000 people. Over the years, it was well used by local acting troupes, school events and graduations, plays, musical events, and guest lectures. (Courtesy of Braddock Carnegie Library.)

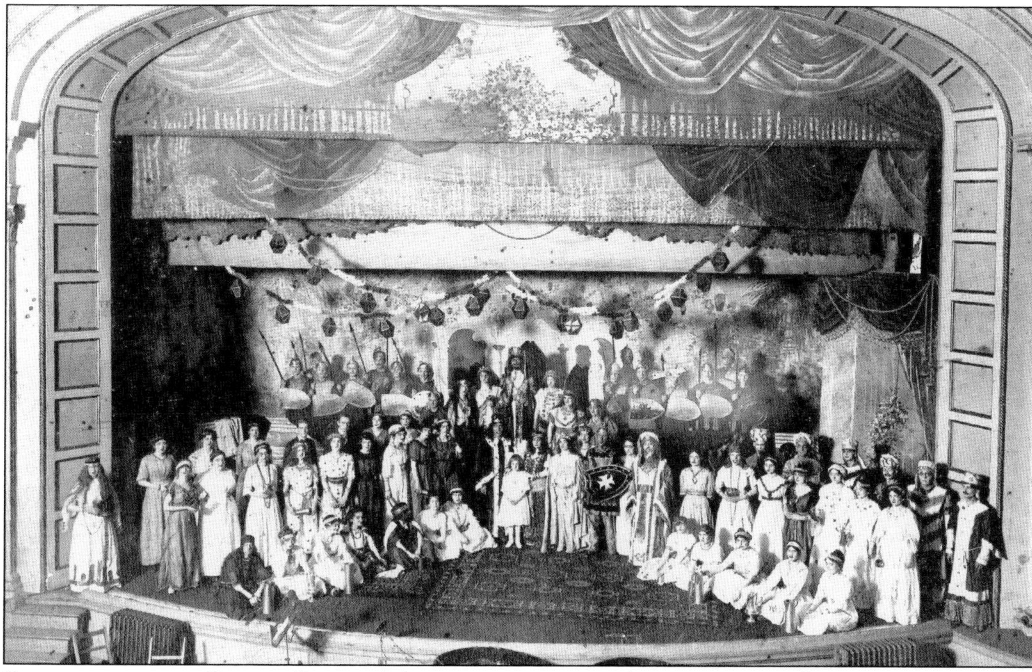

Pageantry on a Grand Scale. A large cast is seen on the Carnegie Hall stage in this undated photograph. This group's spectacular costumes reflect the singular status of the hall and its stage in high-level performance arts. (Courtesy of Braddock Carnegie Library.)

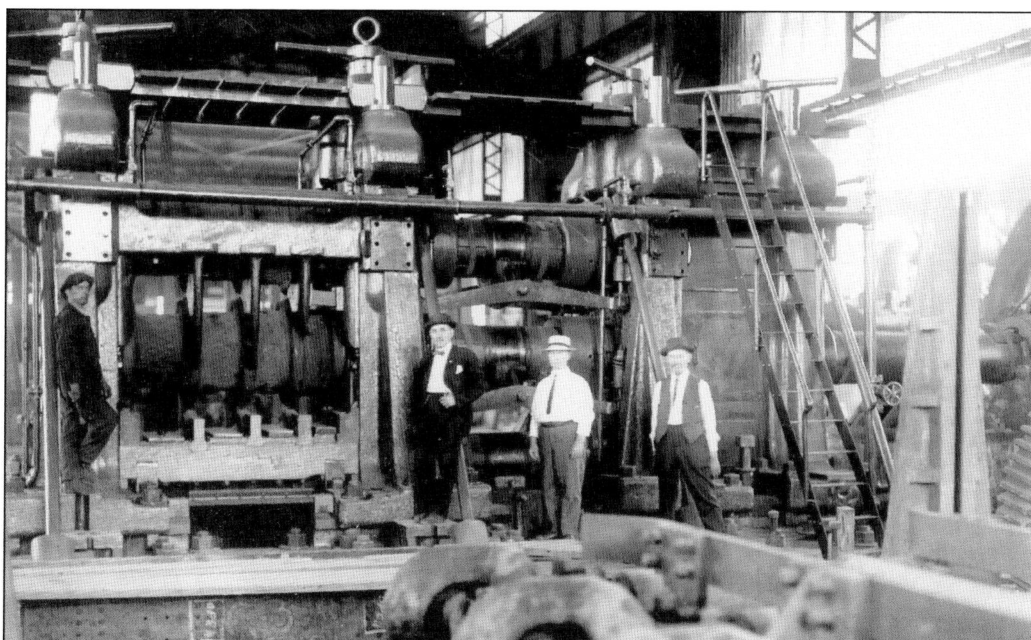

Men and Machinery. The scale and mass of the Edgar Thomson mill's machinery can be seen. This image was taken during August 1914, during one of the most intensive periods of mill improvement and expansion that had occurred in more than 20 years. (Courtesy of the Rivers of Steel National Heritage Area.)

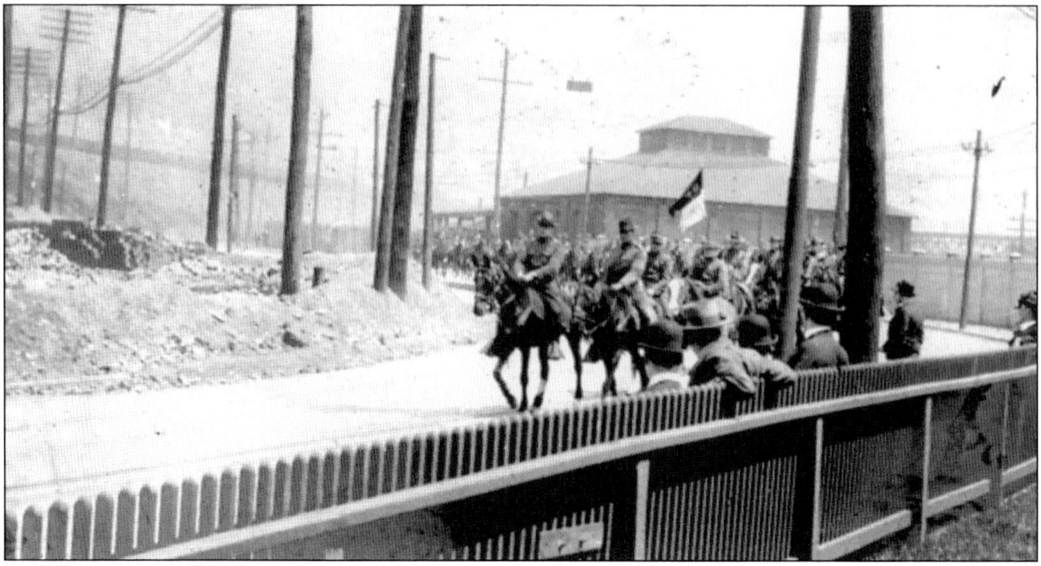

EIGHT-HOUR DAY LABOR RIOTS OF 1916. As World War I progressed, demand for munitions and machine tools grew dramatically. When pressure mounted on factories, workers were forced into making concessions on the number of hours per day that they worked. It was not long before labor unrest started to create strikes and work stoppages. In May 1916, local labor organizations marched and rioted over working conditions and the eight-hour day. Pictured here are Pennsylvania National Guard troops as they march into Braddock from East Pittsburgh. (Courtesy of Braddock Carnegie Library.)

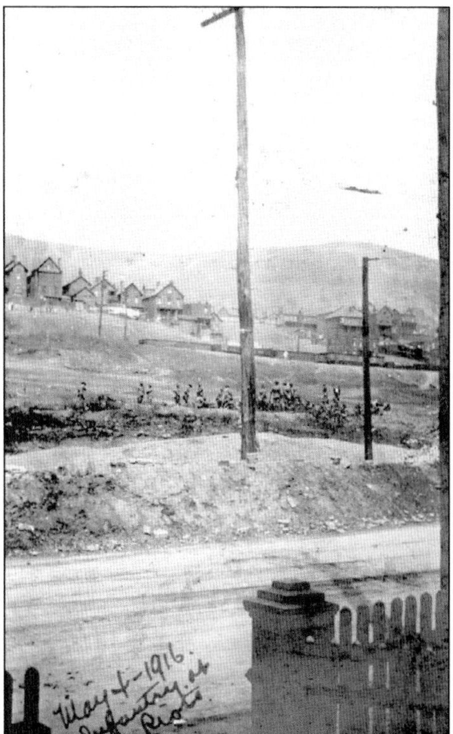

"ALL WE WANT IS AN EIGHT-HOUR DAY." Pennsylvania National Guard troops encamped on a hillside outside Braddock's Edgar Thomson plant maintaining a vigil of the mill and main streets. The striker's slogan was "All we want is an eight-hour day / With nine and one–half hours' pay." By the time that this image was recorded, the strike involved almost 36,000 employees from four of Westinghouse's area plants and many more from mills and factories in Braddock and Rankin. (Courtesy of Braddock Carnegie Library.)

STRIKING WORKERS FILLED THE STREETS. Striking workers and area residents gather outside the Edgar Thomson mill. On May 1, 1916, the marchers were led by a Lithuanian band and carried red flags as they weaved their way from East Pittsburgh's Westinghouse plants to Braddock and Rankin. By the end of the march they had succeeded in bringing together an estimated 36,000 workers. (Courtesy of Braddock Carnegie Library.)

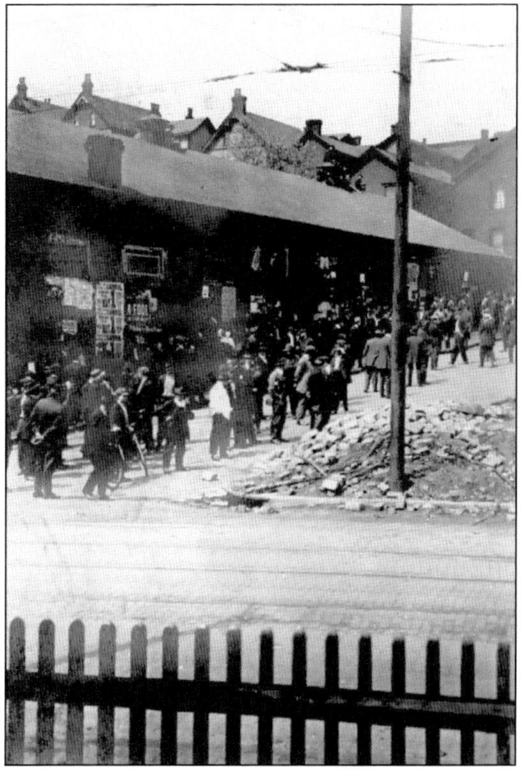

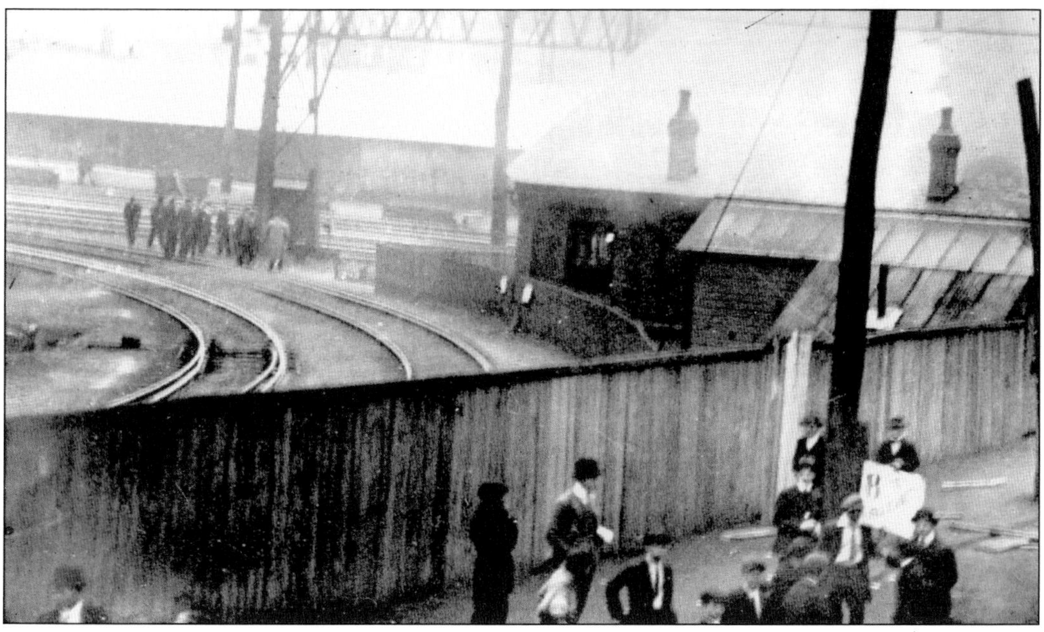

"SHARE THE PROFITS!" Striking workers with signs promoting an eight-hour day gather outside the Edgar Thomson Steel Works mill while police huddle inside the plant's gates. Braddock resident Katherine Bell, a 21-year-old Irishwoman, emerged as a highly energized and vocal strike leader. Besides the eight-hour day, she also demanded a "share of the company's wartime profits." (Courtesy of the Library of Congress.)

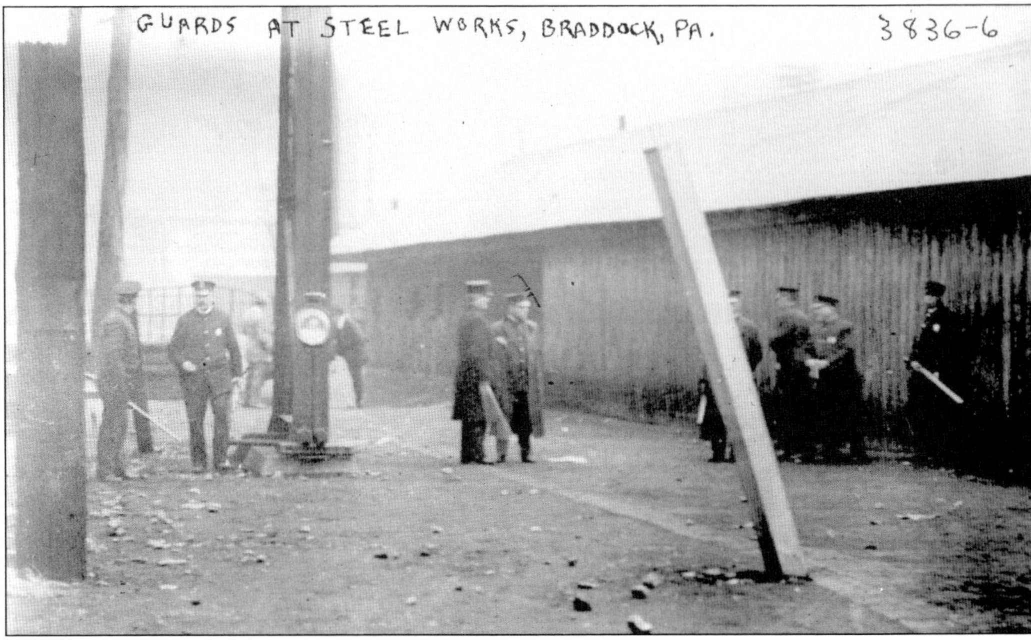

PROTECT THE MILLS! Local streets are filled with striking workers and union supporters. In response, U.S. Steel Company's managers closed their plants and amassed a force of guards, railroad detectives, and police armed with clubs, rifles, shotguns, and machine guns to protect the mills. (Courtesy of the Library of Congress.)

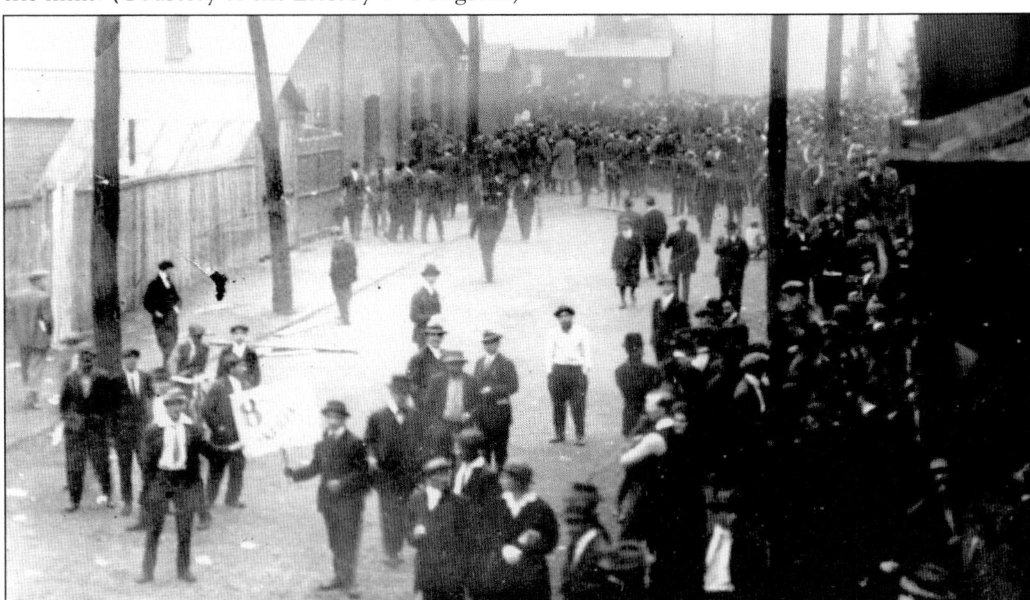

SLOVAK AND RUSYN RIOTERS ARRESTED. On May 2, anger reached fever level and the strikers' actions became more threatening. The guards amassed at the Edgar Thomson plant reacted violently by shooting into the crowd. Three Braddock residents were killed and dozens wounded. Gov. Martin Brumbaugh declared martial law and called out National Guardsman to quell the unrest. Nearly 30 strike leaders were soon arrested and dozens of "Slovak and Rusyn" residents were charged with rioting. (Courtesy of the Library of Congress.)

Five

Dry Goods and Sundries

After Gen. Edward Braddock's defeat it took many years for the Braddock area to be settled. Fifty years after the battle, only a handful of farms had been established. At the century mark, however, new industry began to emerge, and much like a strong magnet, these industries lured an ethnically diverse pool of workers to them. It began with the Dutch, English, Scotch, and Irish who were attracted to Braddock's strategic river location and fertile farmlands. As industry materialized, they frequently required coal for production. As a result, a need for coal miners attracted immigrants of Welsh heritage, who brought with them the skills necessary to mine the area's coal deposits.

As industry grew so too did the need for increasingly higher levels of mechanical and engineering skills. This seemingly unquenchable demand attracted skilled workers from Germany, Norway, and Sweden, all thirsting for higher wages and American-style freedom. Not long after these artisans were attracted, however, their demand for higher wages created much anxiety among the industrial elite. In turn, the industrialists began wholesale recruitment of "more plentiful" and less wage demanding workers from Italy, Hungary, Poland, Russia, many other eastern European countries, and African Americans from the southern states. A commemorative booklet prepared for North Braddock's golden jubilee in 1947 adeptly noted that time and generations of "living together" had now allowed for the real American to be born.

As industry grew during the latter part of the 19th century, it consumed land along the riverfronts. Demand for land for housing and commercial activity followed. Residential housing, whether privately owned or built by the corporations to house newly recruited labor from Europe, was constructed around the factories and mills. As workers and their families were drawn to the area, they needed food, clothing, and the other articles necessary for day-to-day living. Such demand drew sundry shopkeepers who came seeking to satisfy these basic needs. Between the mid-1920s and 1960, annual commercial business sales volume increased from $12 million per year to $40 million. During the same period, the number of commercial businesses in the area increased from approximately 200 to more than 760.

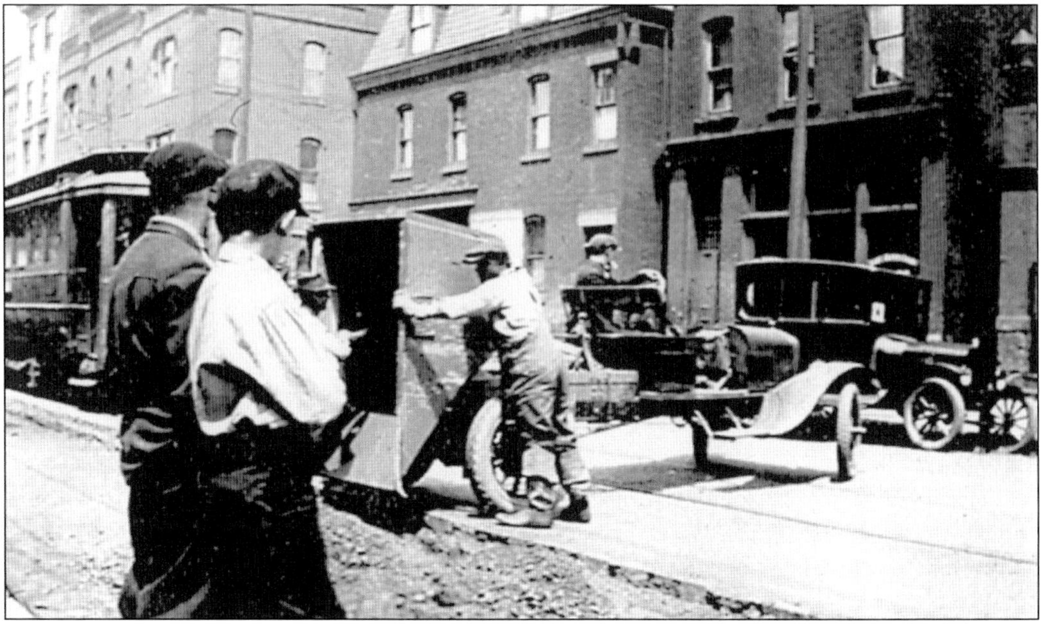

BRADDOCK ROAD CONSTRUCTION. Not long before World War I, automobile ownership became more common as Henry Ford's Model T became more available and affordable. As automobile ownership grew, the need for improved roadways became urgent. This early-1920s Braddock street scene includes elements of both rail and automobile traffic, as workers are improving the roadway. (Courtesy of Braddock Carnegie Library.)

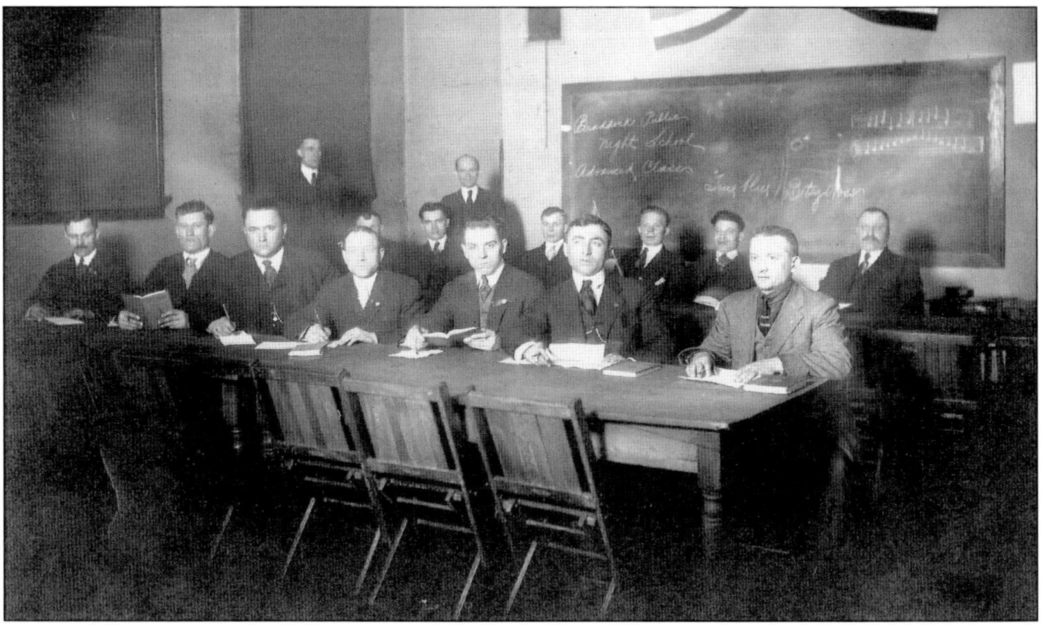

OUT OF THIS AMALGAM. Evening schools for teaching English language, explaining naturalization laws, and citizenship responsibilities became increasingly common. Braddock Carnegie Library was among the first organizations in the area to offer such service. Between 1900 and 1920, Braddock, North Braddock, and Rankin boroughs each offered classes through their public schools or social organizations. (Courtesy of Braddock Carnegie Library.)

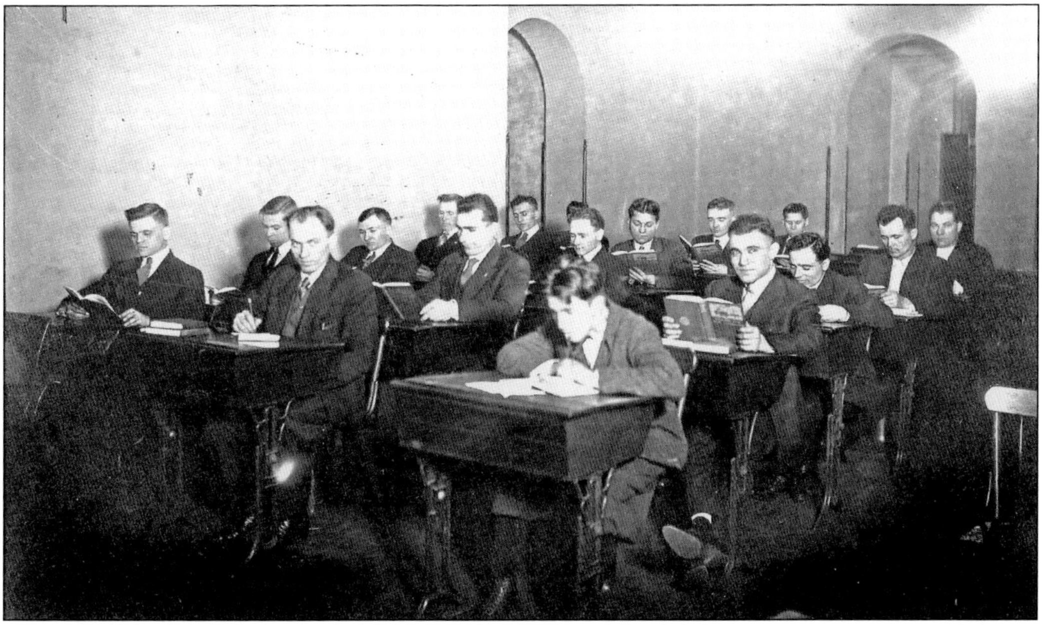

AN AMERICAN EMERGES. Americanization classes meant learning English and grasping the fundamental rules of America's political and economic systems. Social agencies, settlement houses, churches, libraries, and public schools offered most of these classes. They were developed as the result of a positive interest in helping immigrants; other times as a result of fear of those that were different. (Courtesy of Braddock Carnegie Library.)

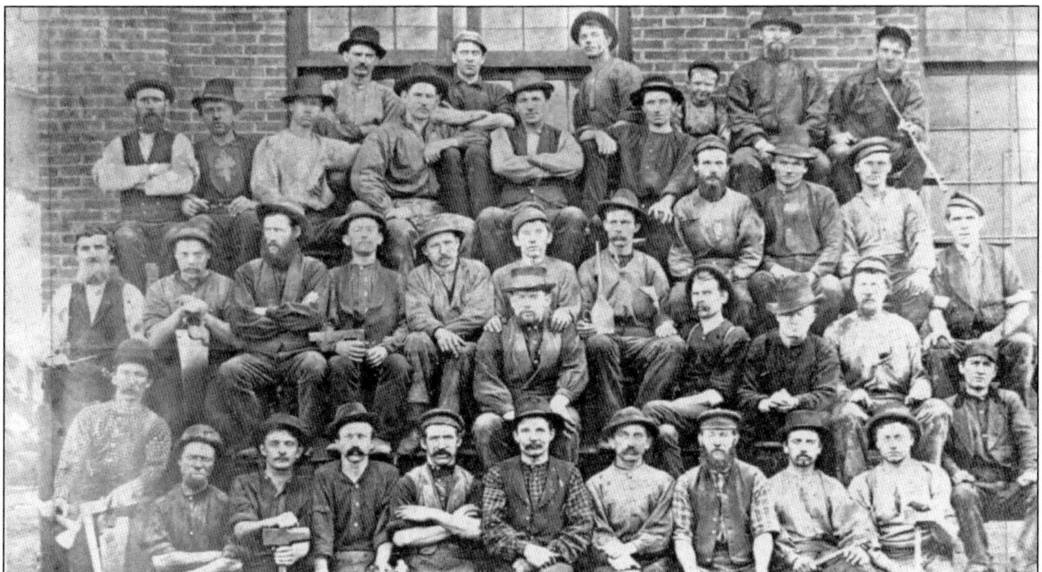

THE MELTING POT. In 1908, playwright Israel Zangwill introduced the term *melting pot*. It became a familiar metaphor used to describe the mixing of people of multiple ethnicities. The local communities understood the blessings and the challenges of the mixtures that were occurring in the local crucible. As everything began to change, work conditions, living conditions, and social convention all were being transformed from the old into the new. The concept of what constituted an American had changed dramatically. (Courtesy of Braddock Carnegie Library.)

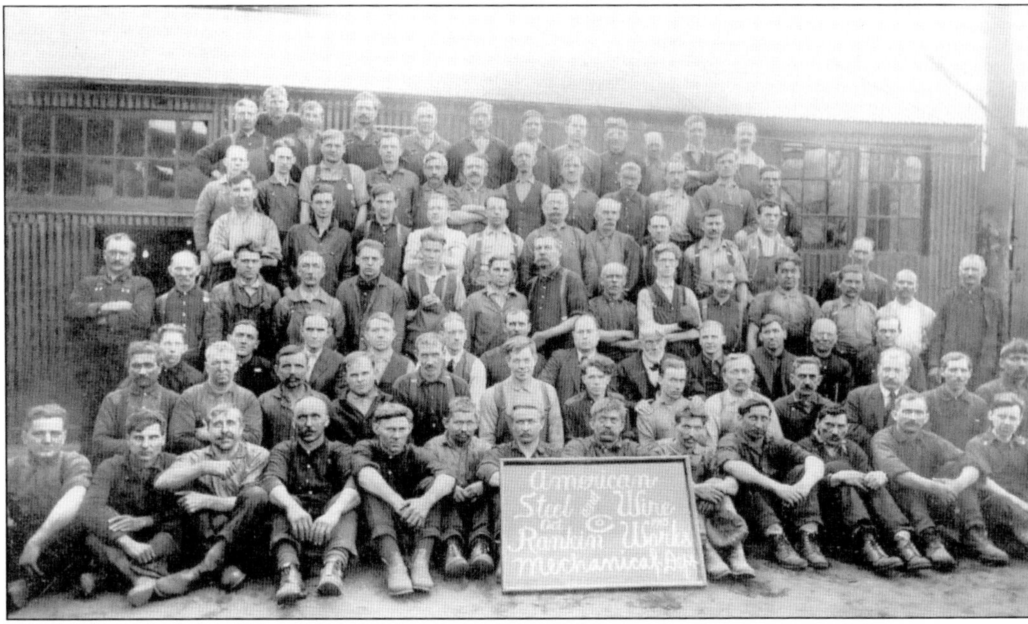

AMERICAN STEEL AND WIRE MECHANICAL DEPARTMENT. In 1886, Col. Thomas Fitch and William Edenborn purchased land in Rankin and built the first Rankin Wire Company. Initially a rod mill was developed and later a galvanizing department, nail mill, fence department, and cooper shop. The image shown here was taken in 1915. By 1916, the firm employed almost 1,250 men and by then had become the Rankin Works of the American Steel and Wire Company, a subsidiary of the U.S. Steel Corporation. (Courtesy of Braddock Carnegie Library.)

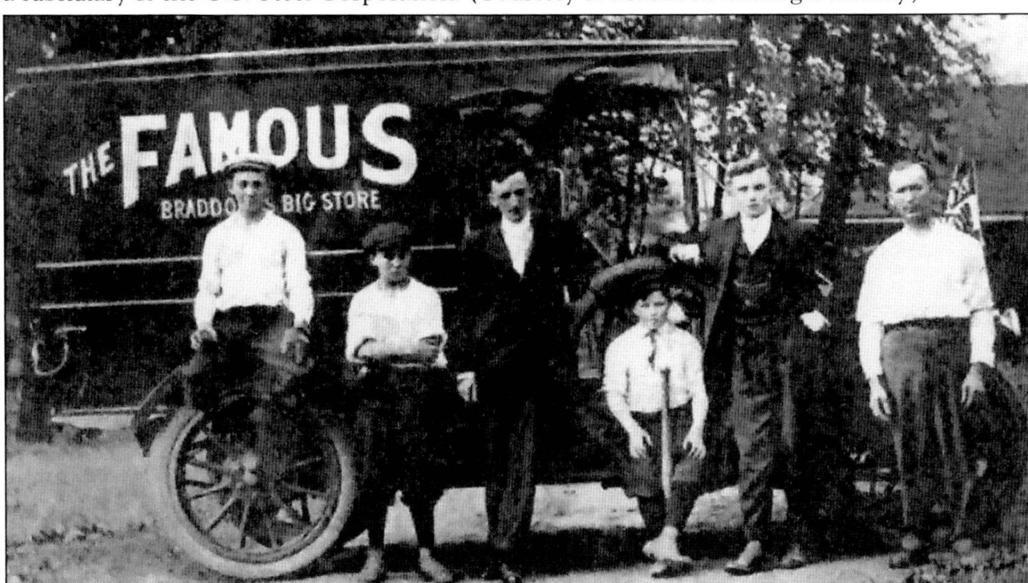

BRADDOCK'S BIG STORE. Braddock's first department store grew from humble beginnings. When it was founded in 1881, the town of Braddock contained only a handful of inhabitants and a new steel mill, Andrew Carnegie's Edgar Thomson Steel Works. During its heyday, the store was a "teeming beehive" operating six days a week and offering the region's first "one-price-for-all" standard. (Courtesy of Kenneth Goldsmith.)

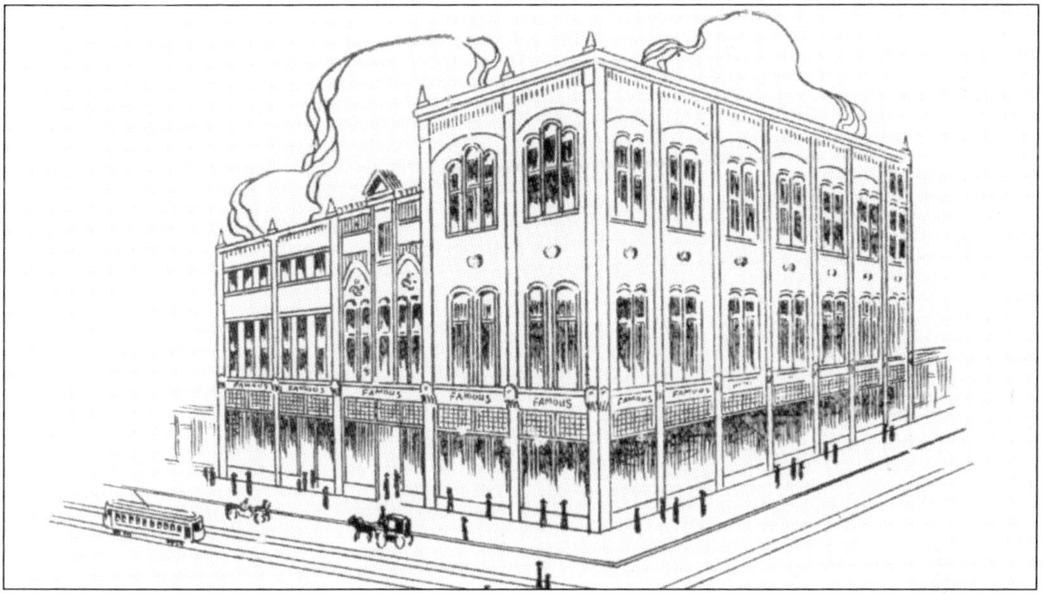

The Famous Department Store. The firm of Katz and Goldsmith, composed of Leo A. Katz and Louis J. Goldsmith, opened the store the Famous on Braddock Avenue in 1881. The store prospered from the beginning as employment from Andrew Carnegie's Edgar Thomson mill dramatically improved the local economy. The store soon became Braddock's largest and "best-lighted" store, boasting the largest plateglass window in the region. (Courtesy of *The Unwritten History of Braddock's Field.*)

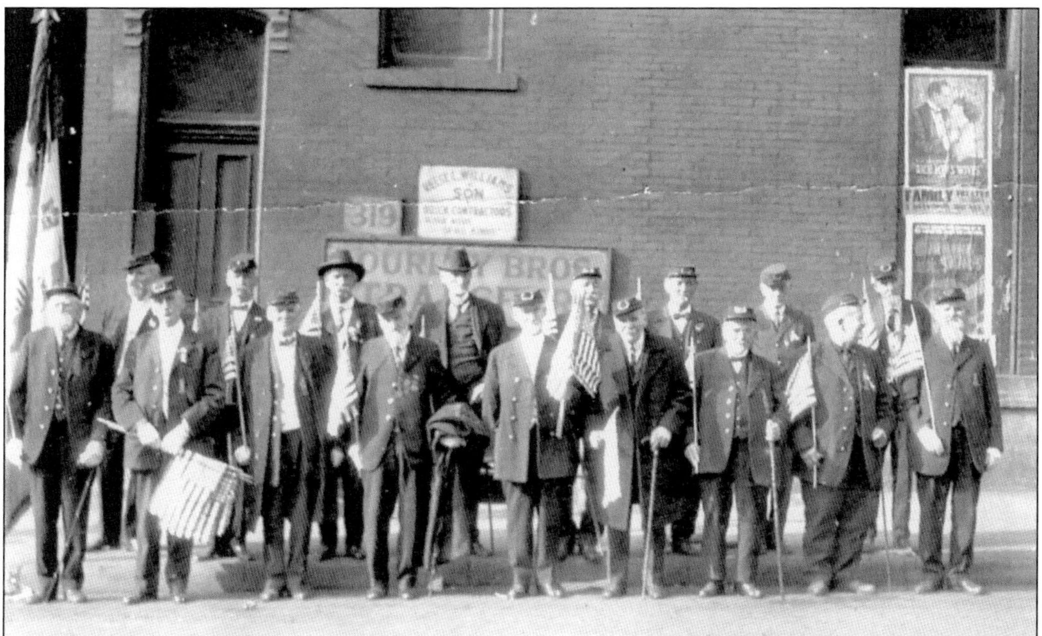

The Boys of the Sixties. Civil War veterans muster for one more call. Beginning with John Frazier, the Braddock area contributed both men and materials to the nation's military efforts. This image of a small group of Civil War veterans was taken in Braddock around 1922. (Courtesy of Braddock Carnegie Library.)

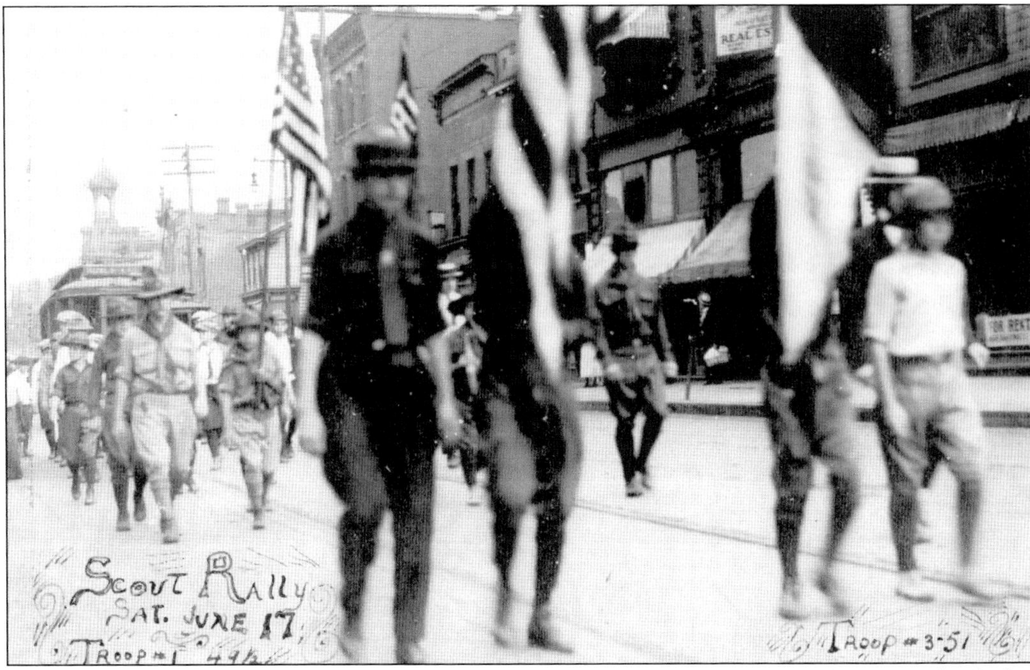

Boy Scouts on Braddock Avenue. Scouting was widely embraced nationally before World War I. Military pride and a civic-minded disposition often came together in Braddock; it citizens became exceptionally adept at staging parades along Braddock Avenue as this early Boy Scout marching scene from the 1920s depicts so well. (Author's collection.)

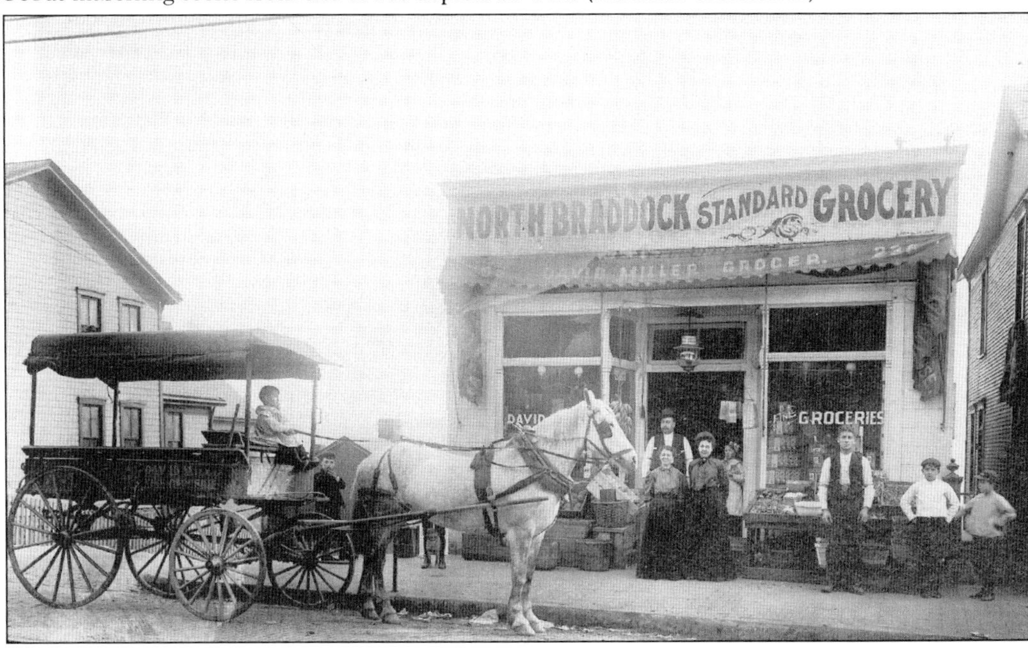

Miller's Grocery in North Braddock. As residential housing flowed from Braddock up the hills to North Braddock and beyond, shopkeepers followed. Beginning with small storefronts and often delivering their goods by wagon, the shopkeeper was critical to community growth. (Courtesy of John Katz.)

MILLER'S MARKET. As workers and their families were drawn to the area, they needed food, clothing, and the other articles necessary for day-to-day living. Such demand drew shopkeepers who were willing and able to satisfy these demands. When business was good, additional space was added or new stores were acquired or built. (Courtesy of John Katz.)

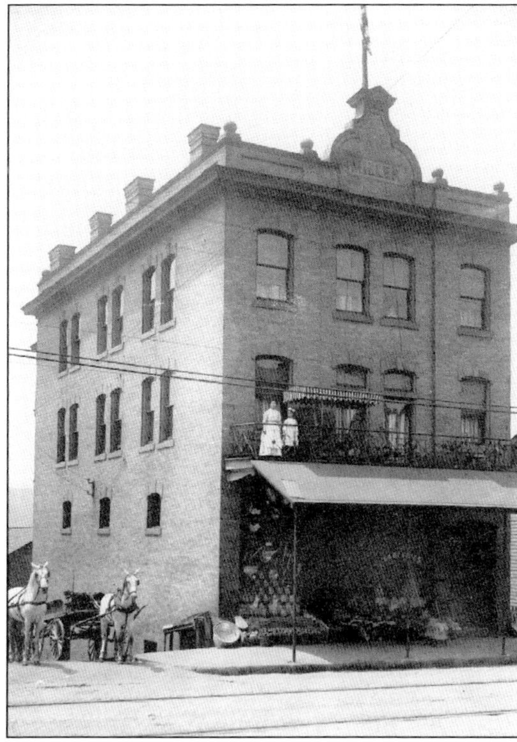

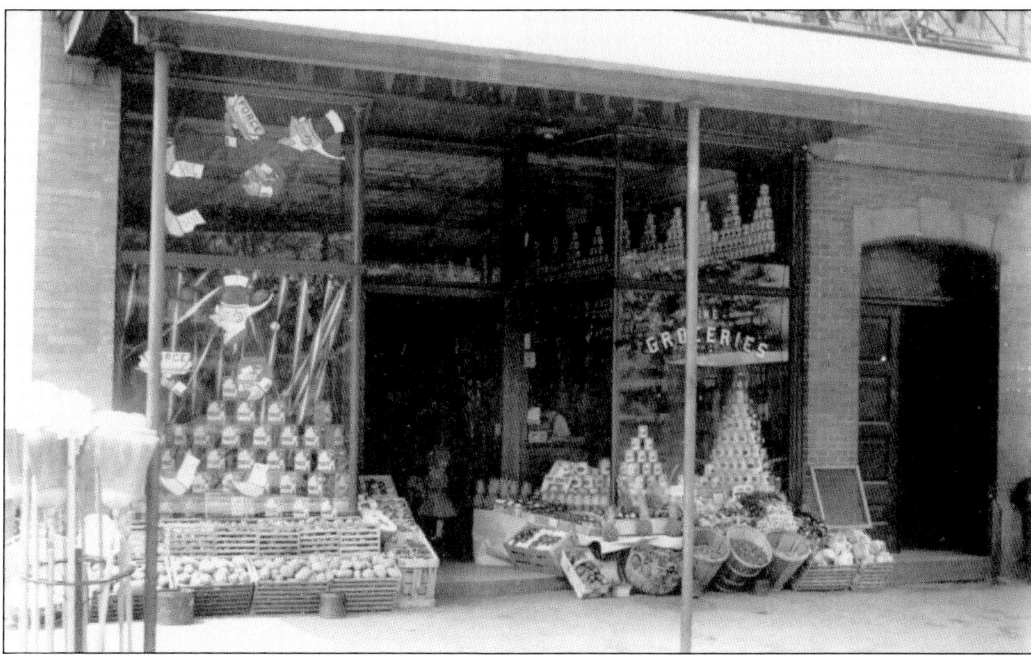

THE NEIGHBORHOOD GROCER. During World War I and into the postwar period, dry goods and department stores continued to build or expand; bars, pool halls, hotels, ethnic clubs, and banks proliferated, but the neighborhood grocery was still among the most important community asset. As business and prosperity grew, larger storerooms were needed to meet the demand. (Courtesy of John Katz.)

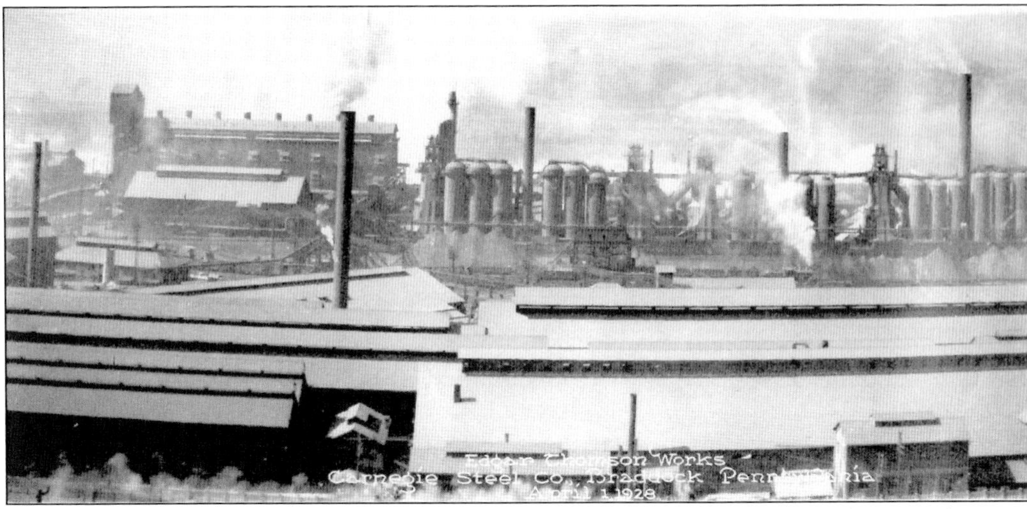

EDGAR THOMSON WORKS. The Edgar Thomson Steel Works mill is seen here in this 1928 image as viewed from the hillside of North Braddock. A description of the area written around the time of this photograph described it as "particularly cheerless." Even then it was recognized that the clouds of smoke and fumes emerging from the plant resulted in an almost total lack of trees, grass, or anything green. (Courtesy of Braddock Carnegie Library.)

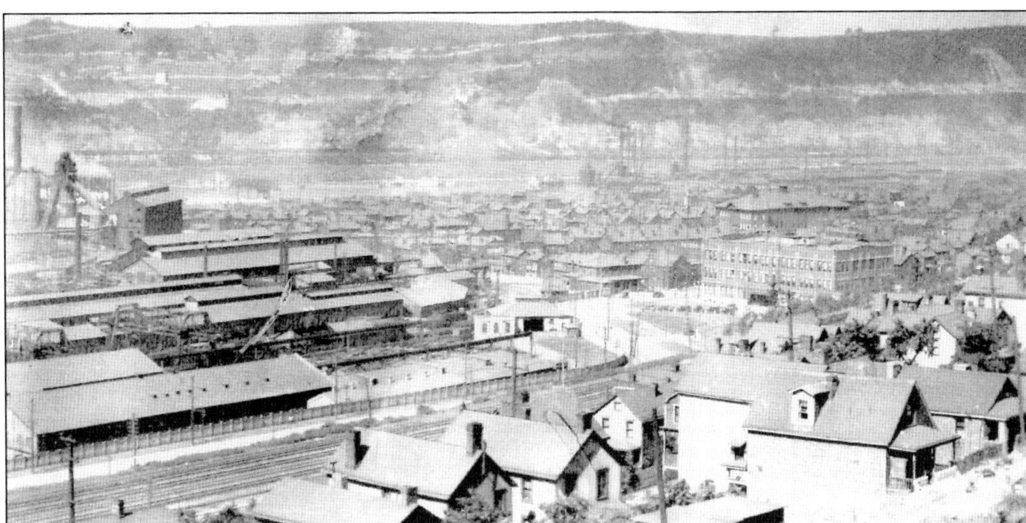

EDGAR THOMSON WORKS, LOOKING SOUTHWEST. Looking southwest from above the Edgar Thomson mill, privately built and corporately owned residential housing can be seen as it was constructed in areas closest to the mills. While North Braddock hosted most of the mill, Braddock was thought to be the epicenter of the world's steel-making industry. (Courtesy of Braddock Carnegie Library.)

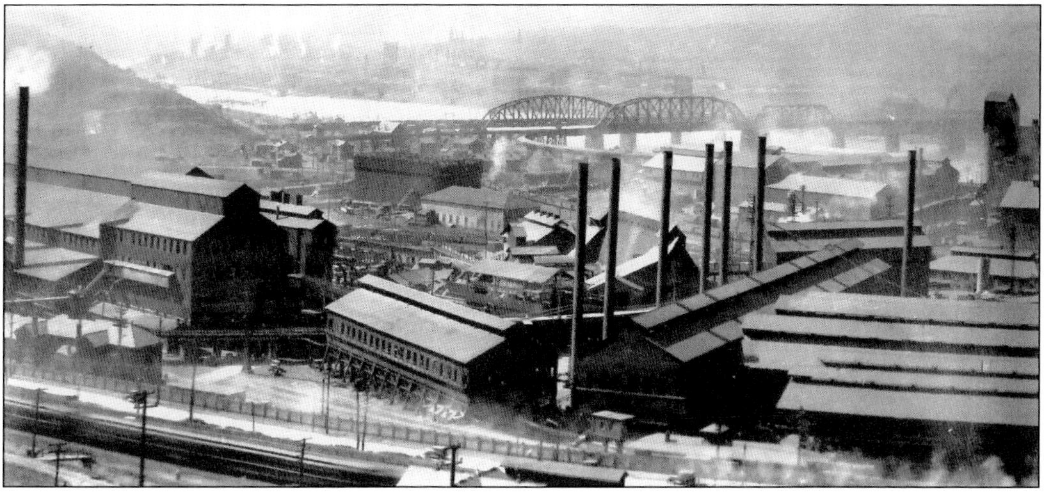

EDGAR THOMSON WORKS, LOOKING SOUTHEAST. In the distance above and to the left of the Edgar Thomson mill, the stacks of the Duquesne mills can be seen in this April 1928 photograph. A local axiom suggested much about how area residents felt, proclaiming, "what Braddock makes the world takes." (Courtesy of Braddock Carnegie Library.)

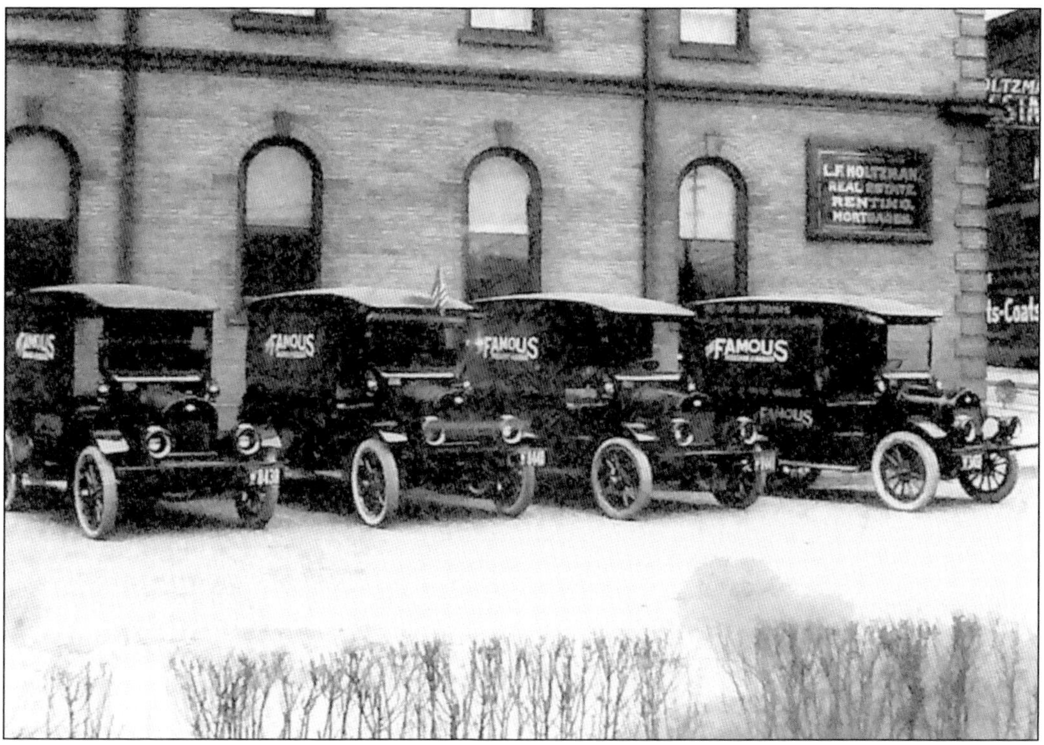

THE FAMOUS. From the time of the Famous's opening in 1881 it grew, prospered, and continually expanded, eventually opening an additional store in McKeesport in 1915. It offered the finest department store goods in the area and attracted shoppers from throughout the region. The delivery fleet for the Famous department stores of Braddock and McKeesport is seen in this 1920s photograph. (Courtesy of Kenneth Goldsmith.)

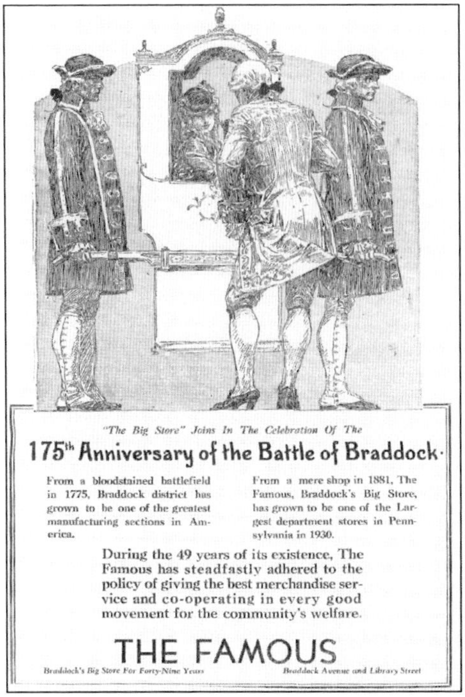

THE FAMOUS DEPARTMENT STORE ADVERTISEMENT. During the 175th anniversary celebration of the Battle of Braddock's Field, the Famous advertised its 49-year commitment to the community. (Courtesy of Braddock Carnegie Library.)

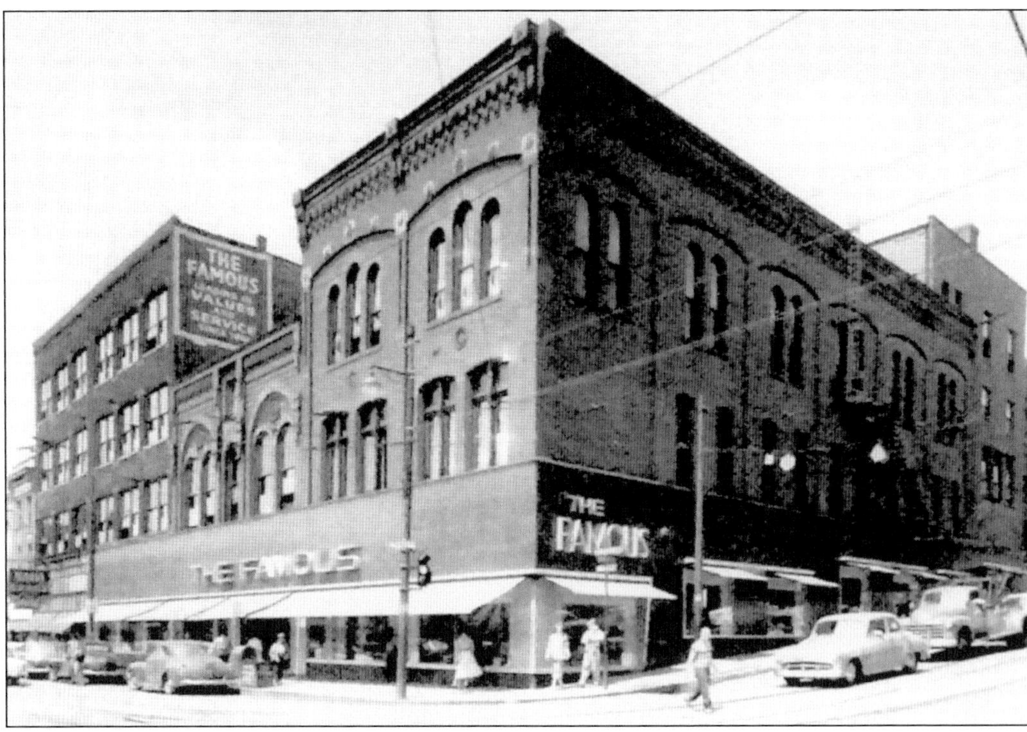

BRADDOCK'S "MODERN" DEPARTMENT STORE. The Braddock store continued to prosper, and in the 1950s, it remodeled its facade with aluminum and black tile. Designed by the architectural firm of Mitchell and Ritchey, the renovations made it one of the most modern-looking stores in the region. (Courtesy of Kenneth Goldsmith.)

COLONEL WASHINGTON MONUMENT. On Wednesday, July 9, 1930, Braddock's tribute to George Washington was expressed through the unveiling of a new monument. Dedicated at Jones and Bell Avenues in North Braddock, the statue was created by noted sculptor Frank Vittor. This period image shows Vittor in his studio working on the Washington statue. (Courtesy of Braddock Carnegie Library.)

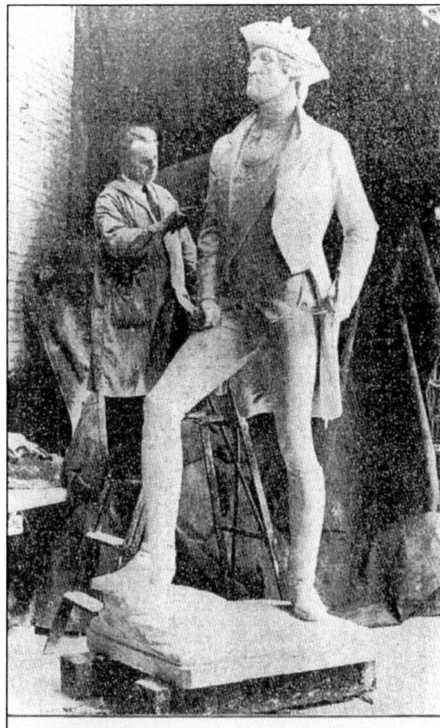

SCULPTOR VITTOR AT WORK ON MONUMENT

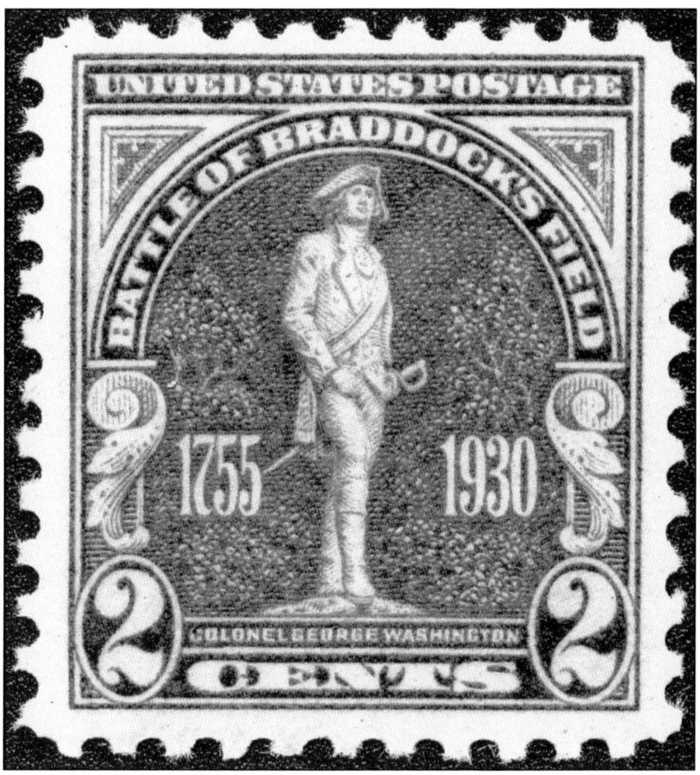

BATTLE OF BRADDOCK'S FIELD U.S. POSTAGE STAMP OF 1930. Considered purely as a political inspiration of Pennsylvania Representative and Braddock native M. "Clyde" Kelly, the Battle of Braddock's Field, a 2¢ U.S. postage stamp of 1930, was developed to promote the 175th anniversary celebration. The stamp was only available in Braddock on July 9; no other location in the country had it available until the following day. (Author's collection.)

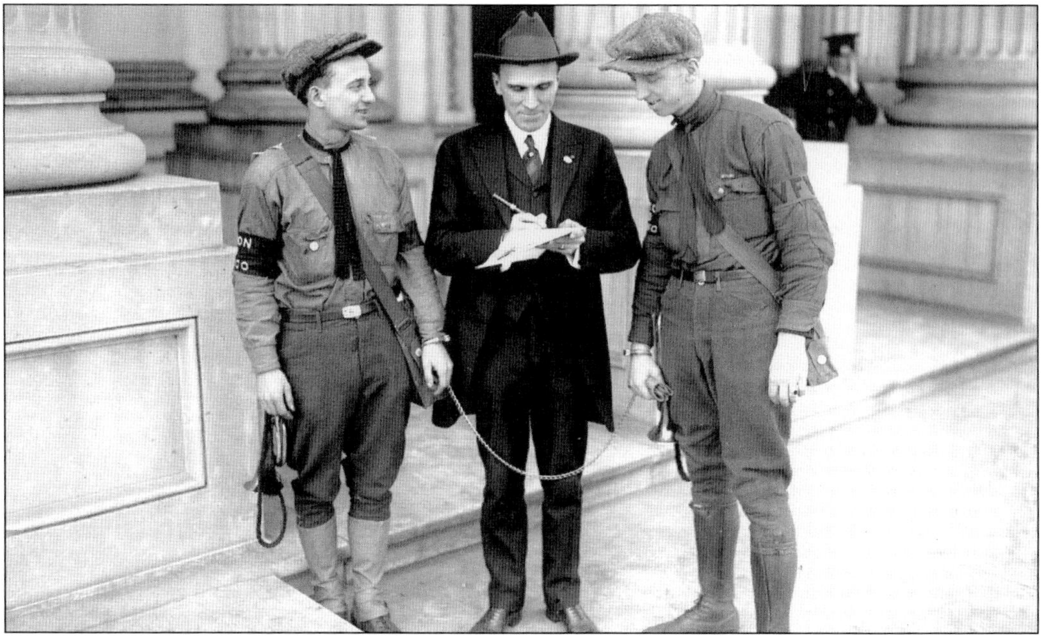

MELVILLE "CLYDE" KELLY. Melville "Clyde" Kelly was born in 1883 in Ohio. In 1904, he founded the *Braddock Leader* newspaper and later acquired the *Daily News* and the *Evening Herald*. He subsequently merged all three into the *Daily News-Herald*. In 1910, he was elected to the Pennsylvania House of Representatives, and in 1913, he won election to Congress. Kelly maintained a home on Corey Avenue while running his newspaper and serving in Congress. He is seen here at center interviewing Robert H. White (left) and Harry E. Dow (right). (Courtesy of the Library of Congress.)

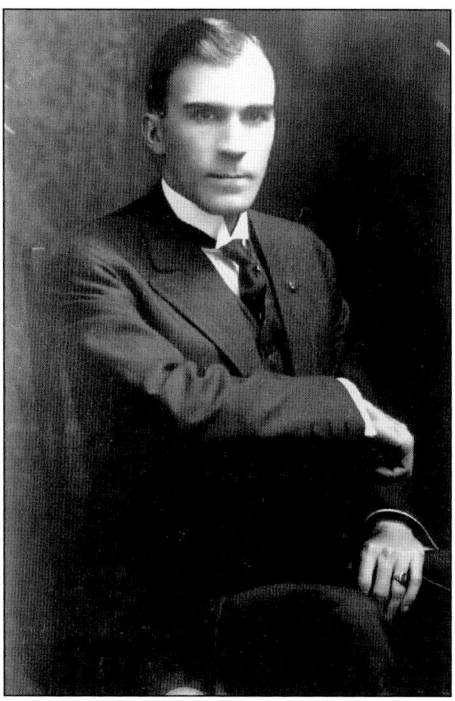

THE KELLY ACT. Clyde entered the 1916 congressional race as a Progressive Party candidate and won. He next ran for reelection as a Republican and won handily, a feat that was to recur for another eight elections. Kelly sponsored the Contract Air Mail Act, which he shepherded through Congress in 1925. The "Kelly Act" provided for airmail transportation to be transferred to the private sector, thereby creating the modern commercial airline industry. (Courtesy of the Library of Congress.)

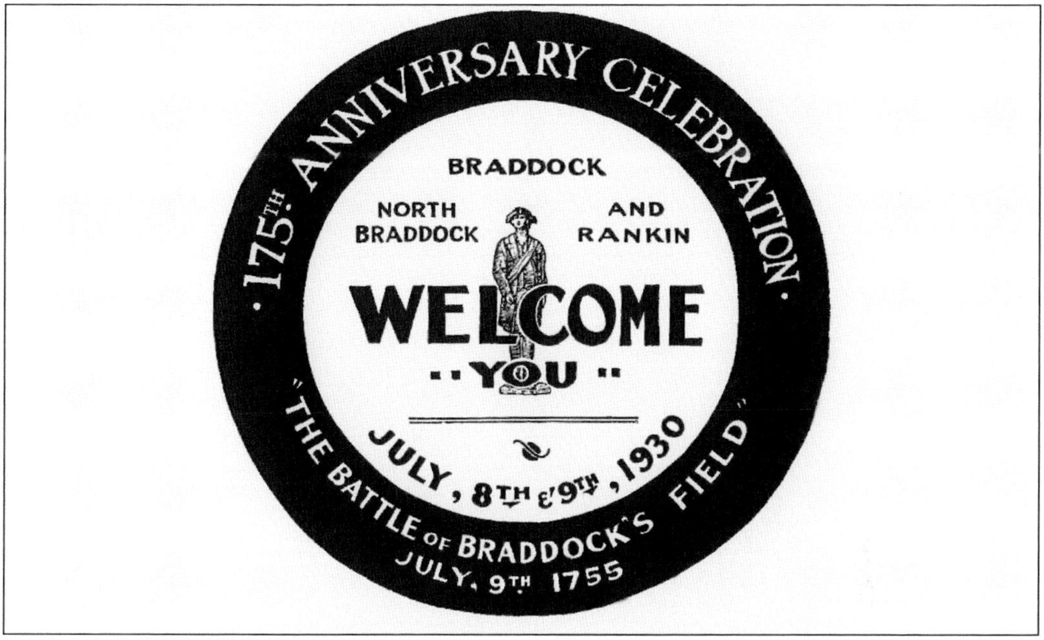

BATTLE OF BRADDOCK'S FIELD 175TH CELEBRATION PLANNED. Earlier in 1930, local newspapers reported that Congress had unanimously approved Congressman Clyde Kelly's proposed bill for the organization of a commission for the celebration of the Battle of Braddock's Field to be held in Braddock on July 8–9, 1930. Pres. Herbert Hoover signed the bill, designating that two members each from the Senate and House of Representatives and one presidential appointment would participate in the commemorative event. Hoover's appointment was treasury secretary Andrew W. Mellon. (Courtesy of Braddock Carnegie Library.)

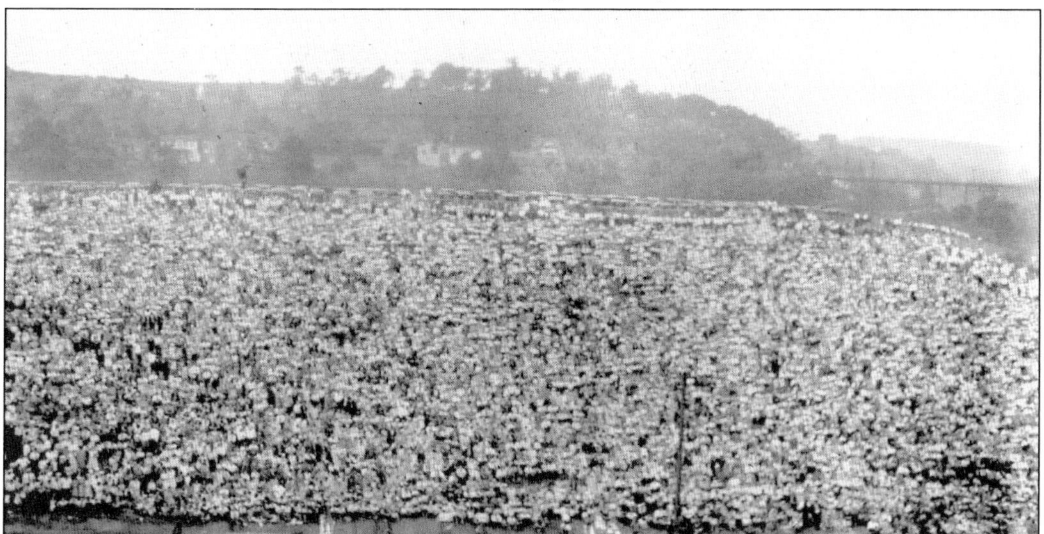

VICTORY PAGEANT ANNOUNCED. Local newspapers reported that the John B. Rogers Producing Company had signed a contract to produce a *Battle of Braddock's Field* pageant as part of the anniversary celebration. More than 1,000 cast members were drawn from the local schools and community. The pageant was performed in Rankin in what was described as a "natural amphitheater" near the Hawkins School. (Author's collection.)

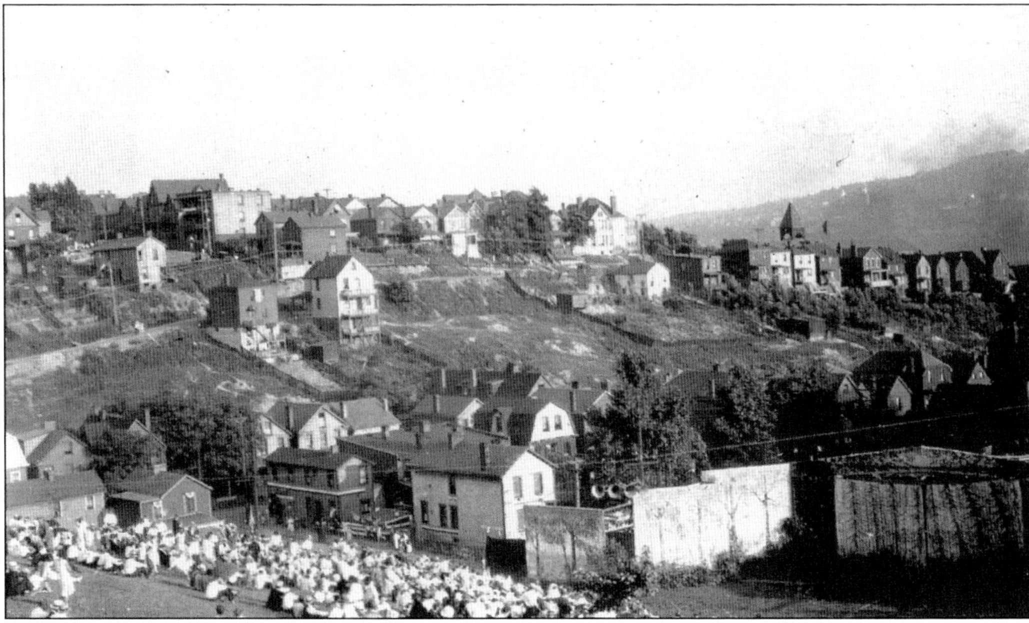

RANKIN'S "NATURAL AMPHITHEATER." Seen here are houses dotting the hillside of Rankin as the crowd gathers in anticipation of the anniversary pageant. The community was well prepared to receive the crowds by the time of the pageant. Reports stated that 35,000 people attended the pageant on the evening of July 8. A crowd of more than 45,000 attended the following evening. (Author's collection.)

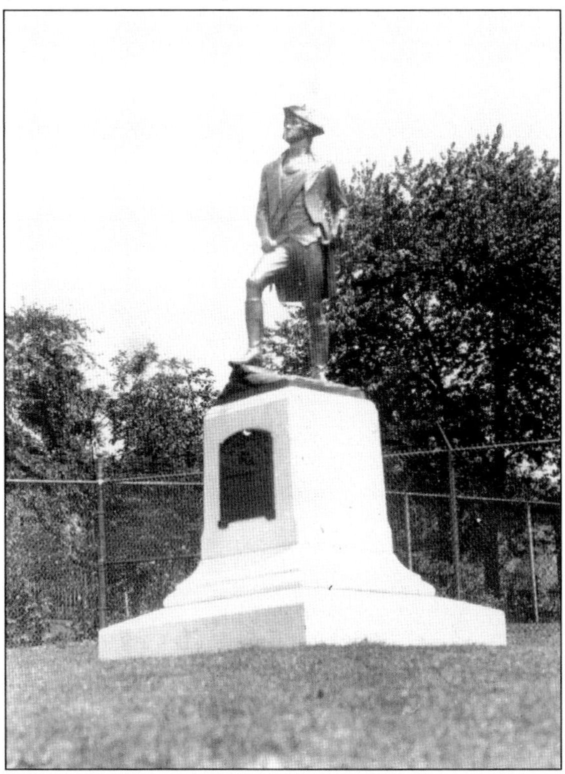

COLONEL WASHINGTON MONUMENT UNVEILED. A special postage stamp had been approved to commemorate the Battle of Braddock's Field's 175th anniversary celebration. The stamp included an engraving of Frank Vittor's sculpture of Col. George Washington. During the anniversary celebration, Margaret Jane Keagy, granddaughter of Mr. and Mrs. Alexander M. Scott, unveiled the statue. The statue was placed on property that was donated by Mrs. A. M. Scott, at a location above the entrance of the Scott High School athletic field. (Author's collection.)

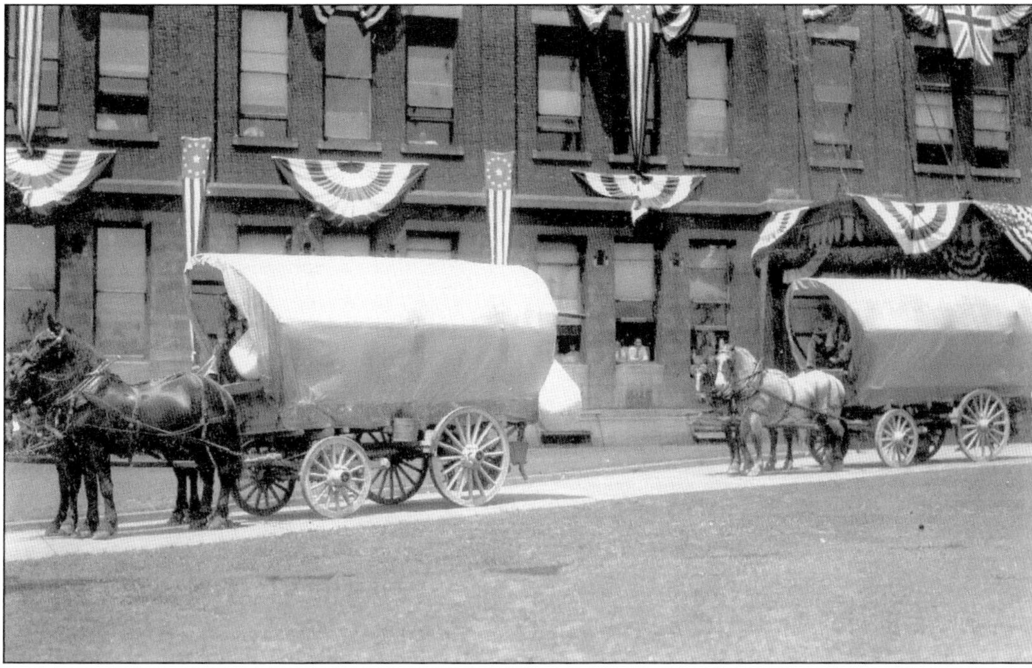

Conestoga Wagons Lead Parade. Conestoga Wagons are seen here preparing to lead the anniversary parade from the second position, directly behind Nirella's Marching Band. (Author's collection.)

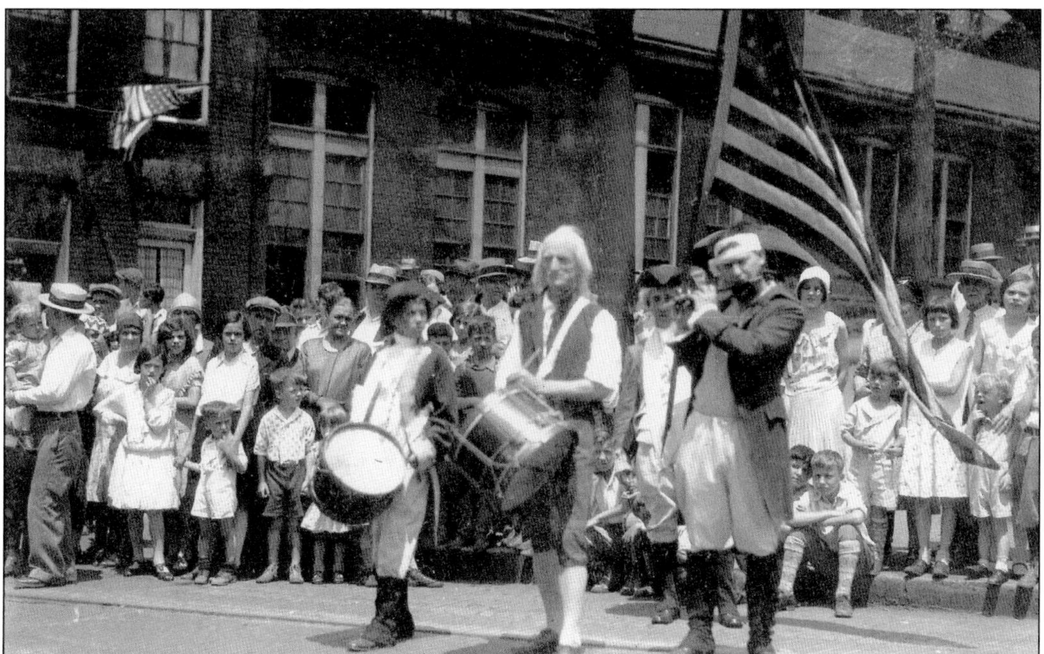

Fife and Drum Actors. Fife and drum actors line up for the parade as they prepare to show the colors. The parade route was four miles long and took almost two hours to pass through Braddock, North Braddock, and Rankin. Crowds reportedly stood five and six deep along the route. (Author's collection.)

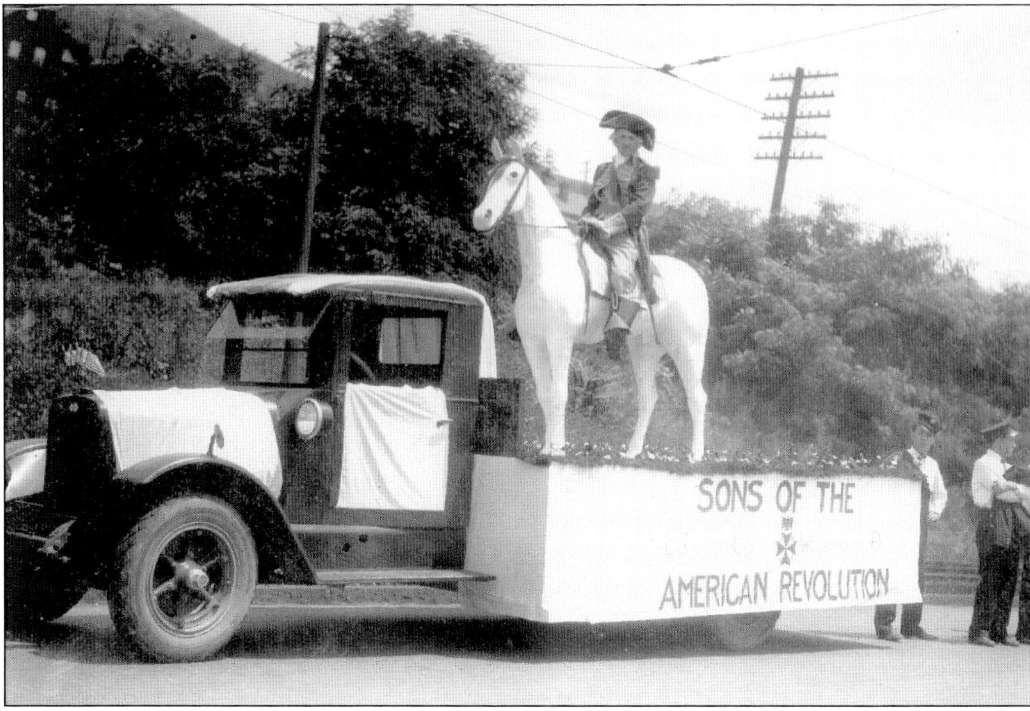

GEORGE WASHINGTON RETURNS. As was the case in 1755, George Washington returned to Braddock; this time as part of the Sons of the American Revolution float. (Author's collection.)

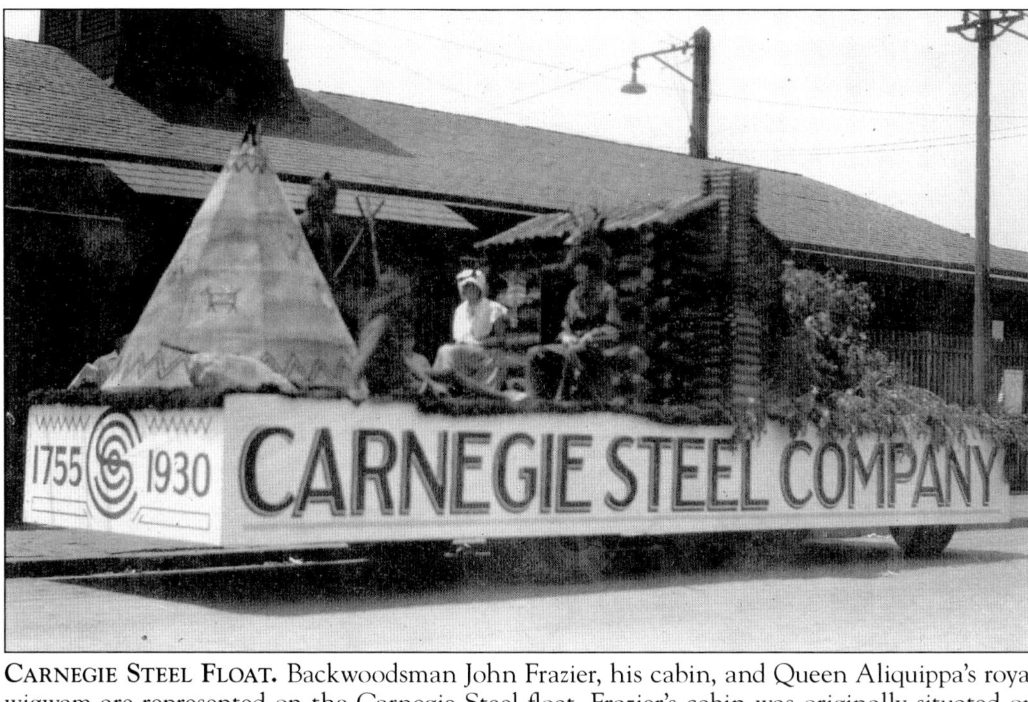

CARNEGIE STEEL FLOAT. Backwoodsman John Frazier, his cabin, and Queen Aliquippa's royal wigwam are represented on the Carnegie Steel float. Frazier's cabin was originally situated on property owned by Carnegie Steel. (Author's collection.)

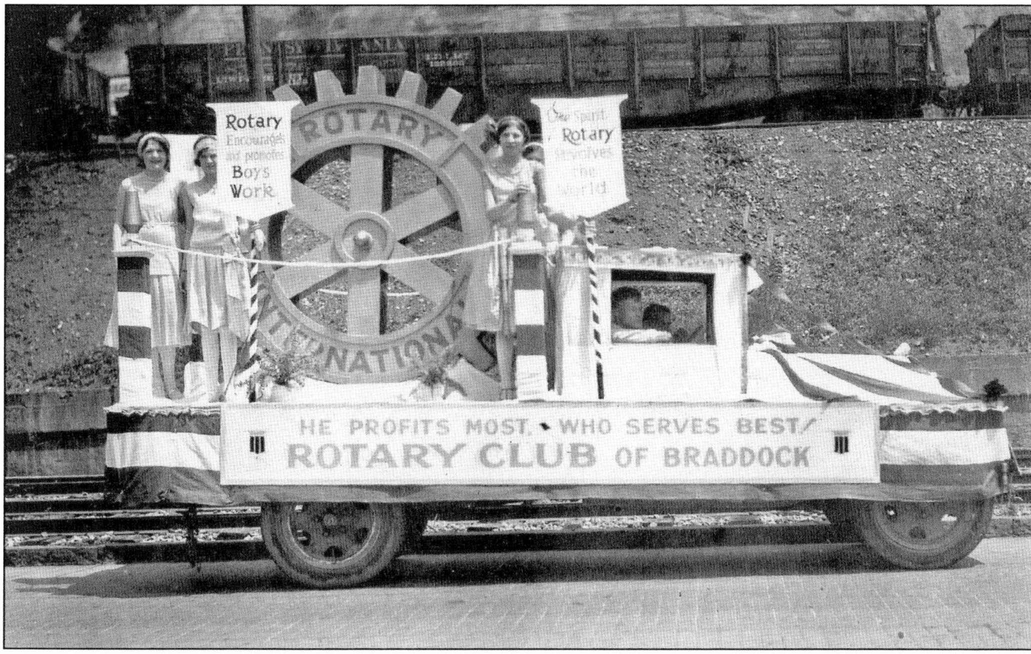

BRADDOCK ROTARY CLUB. The Braddock Rotary Club float is seen getting ready to enter the parade. The club was chartered on January 26, 1928, being sponsored by the McKeesport Rotary Club. There were 28 charter members and William C. Roderus served as president until June 1929. (Author's collection.)

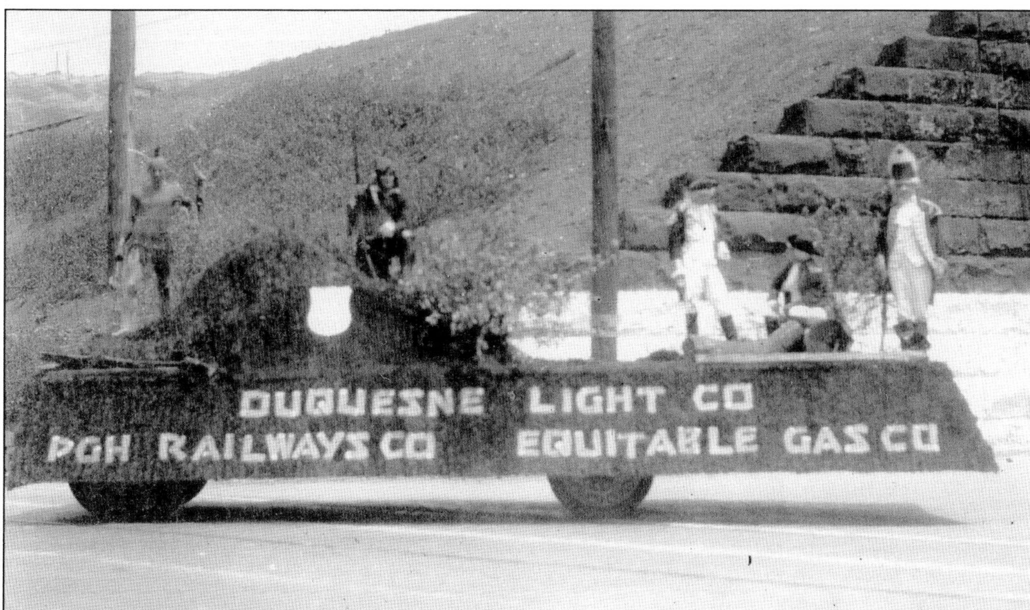

DUQUESNE LIGHT, PITTSBURGH RAILWAYS, EQUITABLE GAS FLOAT. Duquesne Light, Equitable Gas, and Pittsburgh Railways's joint float won the $100 gold first prize for best float. The float was designed to represent an outdoor scene of the Braddock area prior to the battle, with Gen. Edward Braddock and George Washington consulting as a Native American scout watches them from a mound. (Author's collection.)

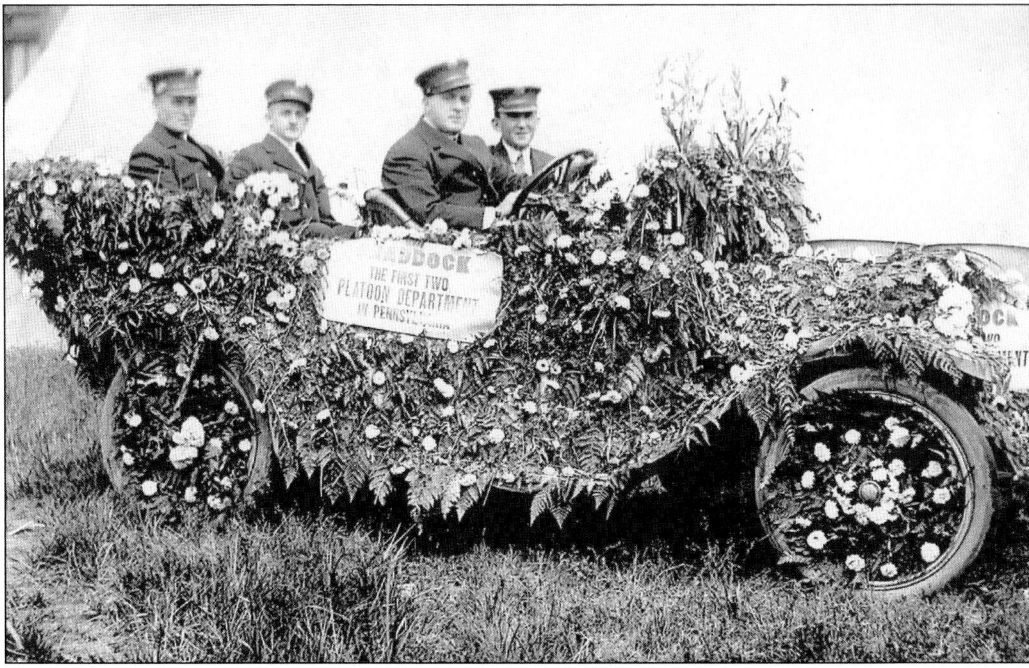

BRADDOCK POLICE CAR. This real-photo postcard image shows a Braddock police car decorated with flowers and a sign noting that the department was the first two-platoon department in Pennsylvania. (Author's collection.)

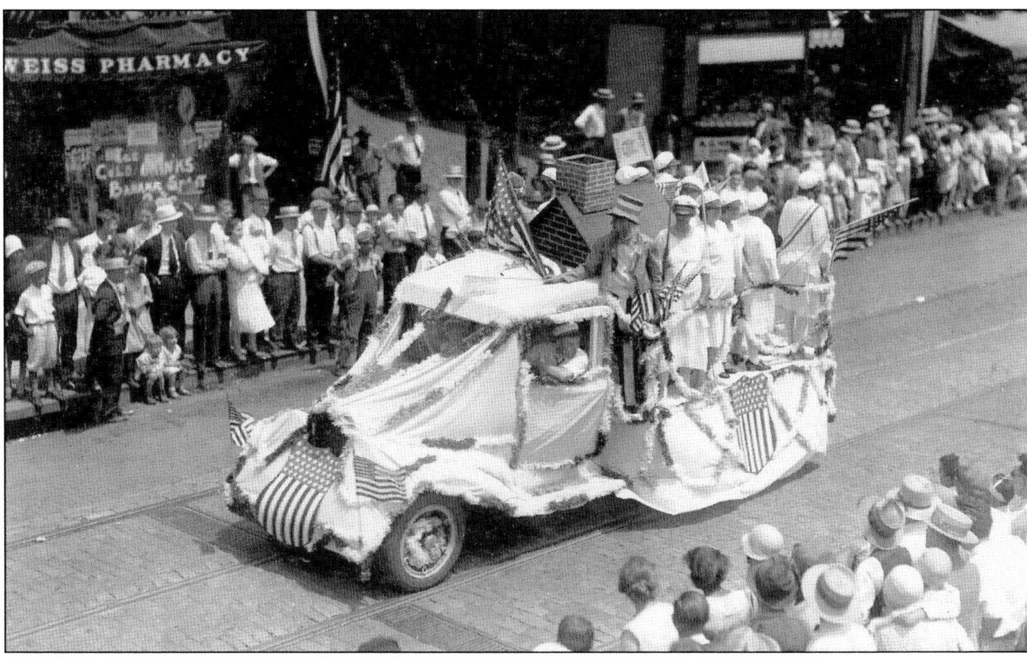

DAUGHTERS OF THE AMERICAN REVOLUTION FLOAT. Uncle Sam joined the Daughters of the American Revolution on this patriotic float. Enthusiastic crowds lined the streets while many other residents and business owners took to the windows to obtain a good view of the procession. (Author's collection.)

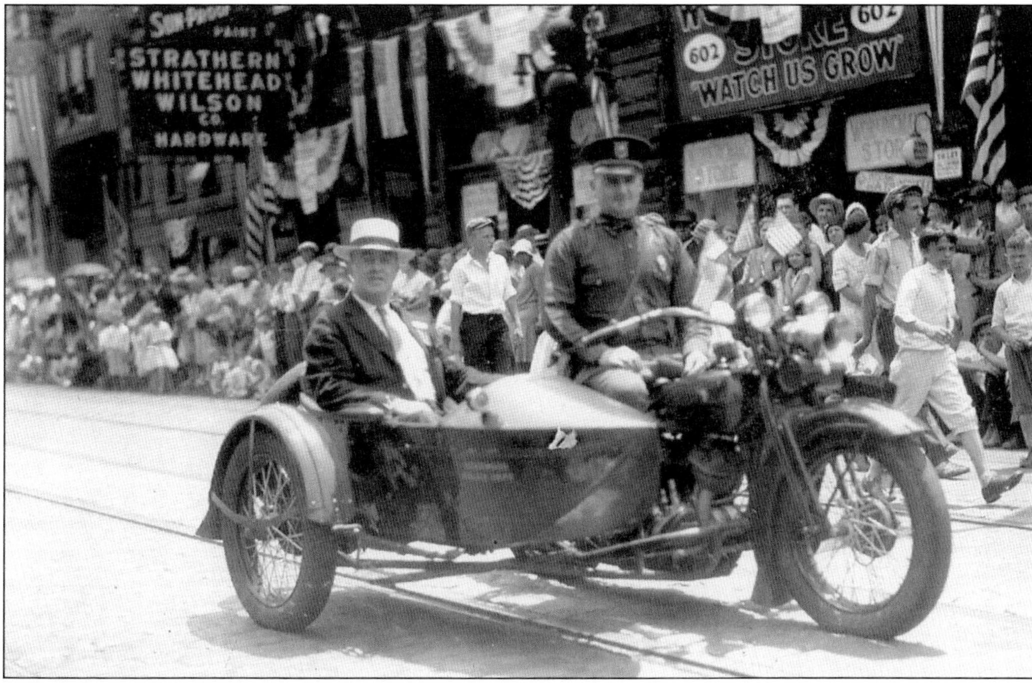

Motorcycle Police. Braddock's motorcycle police are seen driving along the parade route. The sidecar offered an interesting conveyance that attracted much attention from the crowd. (Author's collection.)

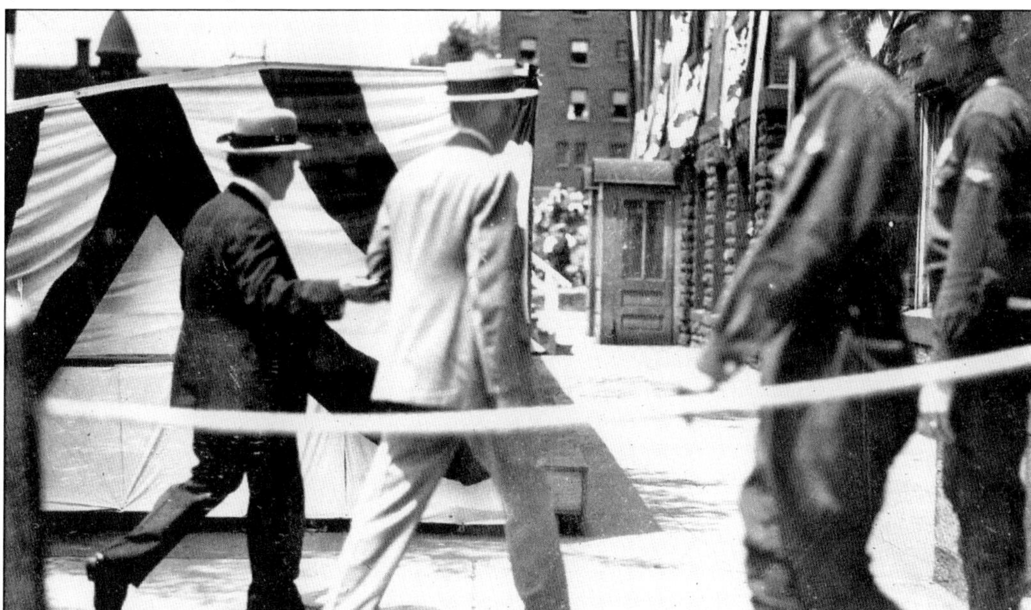

U.S. Treasury Secretary Andrew W. Mellon. Pres. Herbert Hoover appointed Secretary of the Treasury Andrew W. Mellon as chairman of the 175th anniversary of the Battle of Braddock Anniversary Commission. Mellon (center) and Braddock National Bank cashier George A. Todd are seen here making their way through the crowds. Pres. Warren G. Harding had appointed Mellon as treasury secretary in 1921. (Author's collection.)

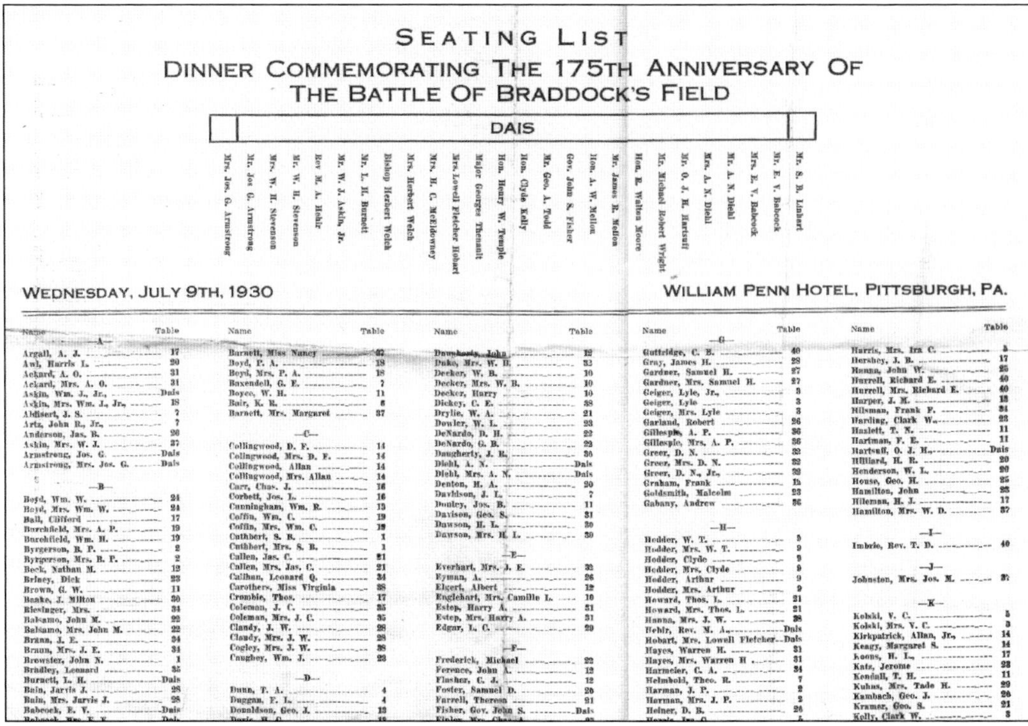

SEATING LIST

DINNER COMMEMORATING THE 175TH ANNIVERSARY OF THE BATTLE OF BRADDOCK'S FIELD

DAIS

Mrs. Jos. G. Armstrong
Mr. Jos G. Armstrong
Mrs. W. H. Stevenson
Mr. W. H. Stevenson
Rev M. A. Hehir
Mr. W. J. Askin, Jr.
Mr. L. H. Burnett
Bishop Herbert Welch
Mrs. Herbert Welch
Mrs. H. C. McEldowney
Mrs. Lowell Fletcher Hobart
Major Georges Thenault
Hon. Henry W. Temple
Hon. Clyde Kelly
Mr. Geo. A. Todd
Gov. John S. Fisher
Hon. A. W. Mellon
Mr. James R. Mellon
Hon. E. Walton Moore
Mr. Michael Robert Wright
Mr. O. J. H. Hartsuff
Mrs. A. N. Diehl
Mr. A. N. Diehl
Mrs. E. V. Babcock
Mr. E. V. Babcock
Mr. S. B. Linhart

WEDNESDAY, JULY 9TH, 1930 — WILLIAM PENN HOTEL, PITTSBURGH, PA.

Name	Table
—A—	
Argall, A. J.	17
Awl, Harris L.	20
Ackard, A. O.	31
Ackard, Mrs. A. O.	31
Askin, Wm. J., Jr.,	Dais
Askin, Mrs. Wm. J., Jr.,	18
Aldisert, J. S.	7
Artz, John R., Jr.,	7
Anderson, Jas. B.	26
Askin, Mrs. W. J.	37
Armstrong, Jos. G.	Dais
Armstrong, Mrs. Jos. G.	Dais
—B—	
Boyd, Wm. W.	24
Boyd, Mrs. Wm. W.	24
Ball, Clifford	17
Burchfield, Mrs. A. P.	19
Burchfield, Wm. H.	19
Byrgerson, B. P.	2
Byrgerson, Mrs. B. P.	2
Beck, Nathan M.	12
Briney, Dick	23
Brown, G. W.	11
Baake, J. Milton	30
Biesinger, Mrs.	34
Balsamo, John M.	22
Balsamo, Mrs. John M.	22
Brann, J. E.	34
Braun, Mrs. J. E.	34
Brewster, John N.	1
Bradley, Leonard	35
Burnett, L. H.	Dais
Bain, Jarvis J.	28
Bain, Mrs. Jarvis J.	28
Babcock, E. V.	Dais
Barnett, Miss Nancy	[illegible]
Boyd, P. A.	18
Boyd, Mrs. P. A.	18
Baxendell, G. E.	7
Boyce, W. H.	11
Bair, K. R.	6
Barnett, Mrs. Margaret	37
—C—	
Collingwood, D. F.	14
Collingwood, Mrs. D. F.	14
Collingwood, Allan	14
Collingwood, Mrs. Allan	14
Carr, Chas. J.	16
Corbett, Jos. L.	16
Cunningham, Wm. R.	13
Coffin, Wm. C.	19
Coffin, Mrs. Wm. C.	19
Cuthbert, S. B.	1
Cuthbert, Mrs. S. B.	1
Cullen, Jas. C.	21
Cullen, Mrs. Jas. C.	21
Callhan, Leonard Q.	34
Carothers, Miss Virginia	38
Crombie, Thos.	17
Coleman, J. C.	35
Coleman, Mrs. J. C.	35
Clandy, J. W.	28
Claudy, Mrs. J. W.	28
Cogley, Mrs. J. W.	38
Caughey, Wm. J.	23
—D—	
Dunn, T. A.	4
Duggan, F. L.	4
Donaldson, Geo. J.	13
Dunphoody, John	12
Duke, Mrs. W. B.	33
Decker, W. B.	10
Decker, Mrs. W. B.	10
Decker, Harry	10
Dickey, C. E.	38
Drylie, W. A.	21
Dowler, W. L.	23
DeNardo, D. H.	22
DeNardo, G. B.	22
Daugherty, J. R.	36
Diehl, A. N.	Dais
Diehl, Mrs. A. N.	Dais
Denton, H. A.	20
Davidson, J. L.	7
Donley, Jos. B.	11
Davison, Geo. S.	31
Dawson, H. L.	30
Dawson, Mrs. H. L.	30
—E—	
Everhart, Mrs. J. E.	32
Eyman, A.	26
Elgert, Albert	12
Englehart, Mrs. Camille L.	10
Estep, Harry A.	31
Estep, Mrs. Harry A.	31
Edgar, L. C.	29
—F—	
Frederick, Michael	22
Ference, John A.	12
Flasher, C. J.	12
Foster, Samuel D.	26
Farrell, Theresa	21
Fisher, Gov. John S.	Dais
—G—	
Guttridge, C. B.	40
Gray, James H.	28
Gardner, Samuel H.	27
Gardner, Mrs. Samuel H.	27
Geiger, Lyle, Jr.,	3
Geiger, Lyle	3
Geiger, Mrs. Lyle	3
Garland, Robert	26
Gillespie, A. P.	36
Gillespie, Mrs. A. P.	36
Greer, D. N.	32
Greer, Mrs. D. N.	32
Greer, D. N., Jr.,	32
Graham, Frank	15
Goldsmith, Malcolm	23
Gabany, Andrew	36
—H—	
Hodder, W. T.	9
Hodder, Mrs. W. T.	9
Hodder, Clyde	9
Hodder, Mrs. Clyde	9
Hodder, Arthur	9
Hodder, Mrs. Arthur	9
Howard, Thos. L.	21
Howard, Mrs. Thos. L.	21
Hanna, Mrs. J. W.	38
Hehir, Rev. M. A.	Dais
Hobart, Mrs. Lowell Fletcher	Dais
Hayes, Warren H.	31
Hayes, Mrs. Warren H	31
Harmeier, C. A.	34
Helmbold, Theo. R.	7
Harman, J. P.	2
Harman, Mrs. J. P.	2
Heiner, D. B.	26
Harris, Mrs. Ira C.	[illegible]
Hershey, J. B.	17
Hanna, John W.	25
Hurrell, Richard E.	40
Hurrell, Mrs. Richard E.	40
Harper, J. M.	13
Hilsman, Frank F.	34
Harding, Clark W.	23
Hazlett, T. N.	11
Hartman, F. E.	11
Hartsuff, O. J. H.	Dais
Hilliard, H. R.	20
Henderson, W. L.	20
House, Geo. H.	25
Hamilton, John	23
Hileman, H. J.	17
Hamilton, Mrs. W. D.	37
—I—	
Imbrie, Rev. T. D.	40
—J—	
Johnston, Mrs. Jos. M.	37
—K—	
Kolski, V. C.	5
Kolski, Mrs. V. C.	5
Kirkpatrick, Allan, Jr.,	14
Keagy, Margaret S.	14
Koons, H. L.	17
Katz, Jerome	23
Kendall, T. H.	11
Kuhns, Mrs. Tade H.	29
Kambach, Geo. J.	26
Kramer, Geo. S.	21
Kelly, Clark W.	[illegible]

SEATING CHART FOR DINNER CELEBRATION. This banquet-seating list shows the seating arrangements for the dinner banquet that followed the day's events. Gov. John S. Fisher and treasury secretary Andrew W. Mellon and many other dignitaries made congratulatory speeches. The guest list contained the names of many of the region's most noted government, business, and civic leaders. (Author's collection.)

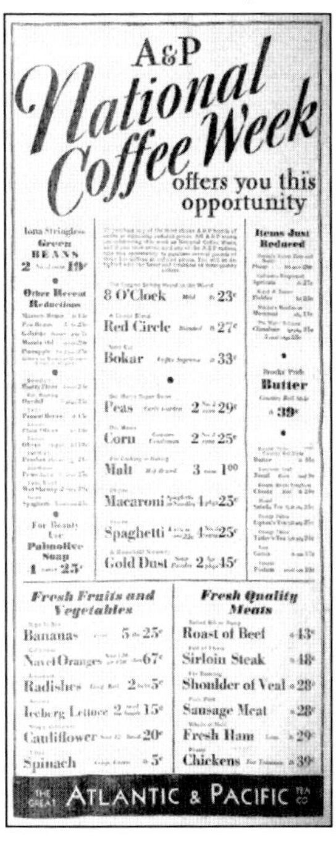

A&P GROCERY STORE ADVERTISEMENT. Braddock continued to draw commercial activity even during the Depression. The Great Atlantic and Pacific Tea Company had several stores in the area. In 1936, it created history in Braddock when the national food chain opened its very first self-serve market. (Courtesy of Braddock Carnegie Library.)

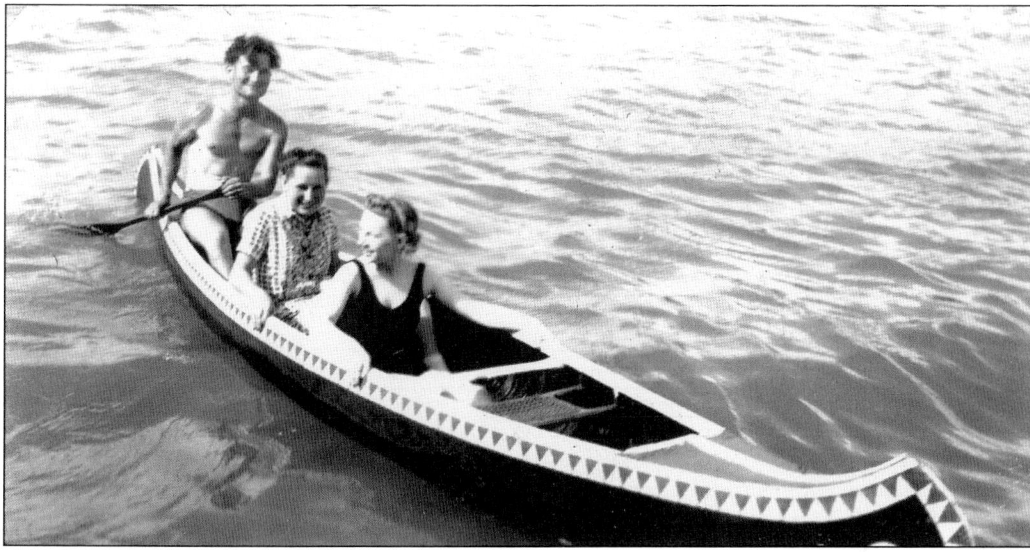

Recreation on the Mon River. Braddock's proximity to the Monongahela River offered many opportunities for sport and recreation. Before mining, industry, and pollution negatively impacted the quality of the area's waterways, fishing offered a rich source of food and recreation. Even after fishing declined, the water afforded ample opportunity for recreational boating, like this 1938 canoe trip. (Courtesy of Victoria Hruska.)

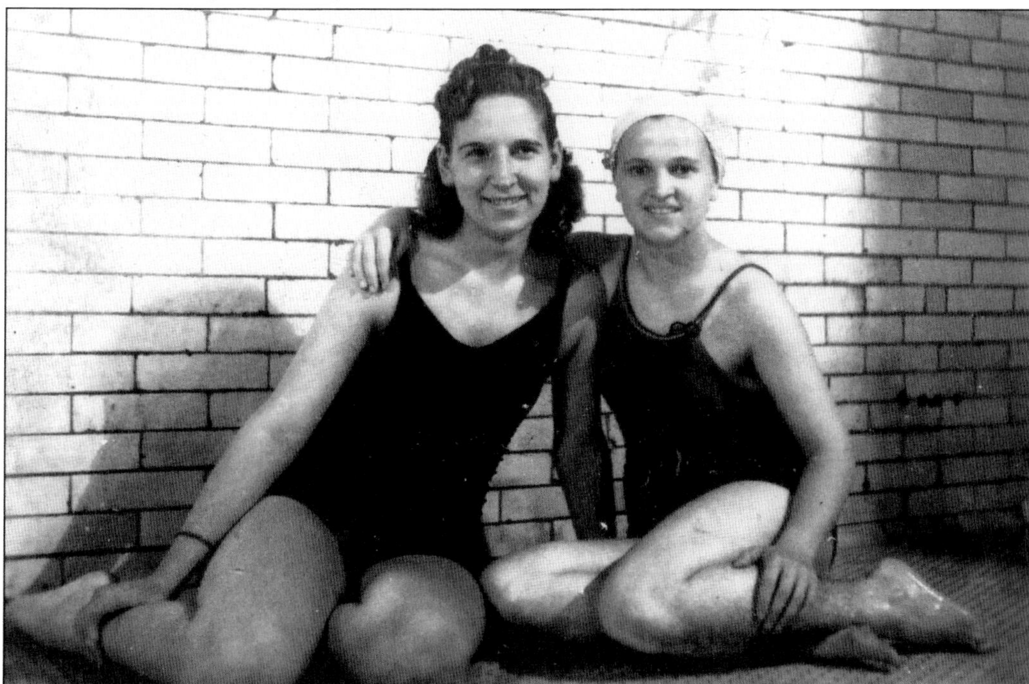

Carnegie Club Swimming Pool. In 1893, Barbara Mosellin was named as the first "lady attendant" of the newly opened swimming pool in the Carnegie Community Center. Swimming at the Carnegie Club's swimming pool was always an attraction for local residents. Bea Ciesielski (left) and Mary Radziwon Ciesielski are seen poolside in this 1938 image. (Courtesy of Victoria Hruska.)

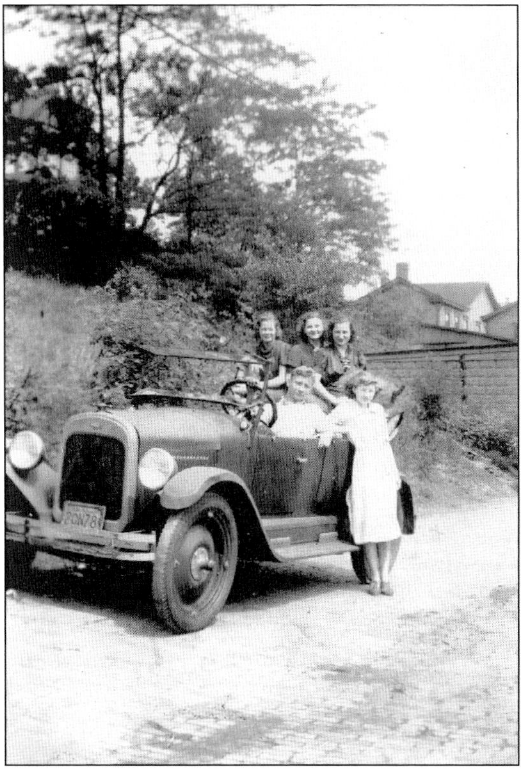

LEISURE TIME AND AUTOMOBILES. As work became more plentiful after the Depression, the number of working days and work hours were reduced. Take-home pay began to climb, and it was not long before leisure time was being filled with many new opportunities for social interaction. Growing numbers of residents were now able to own an automobile—and they were having fun! (Courtesy of Victoria Hruska.)

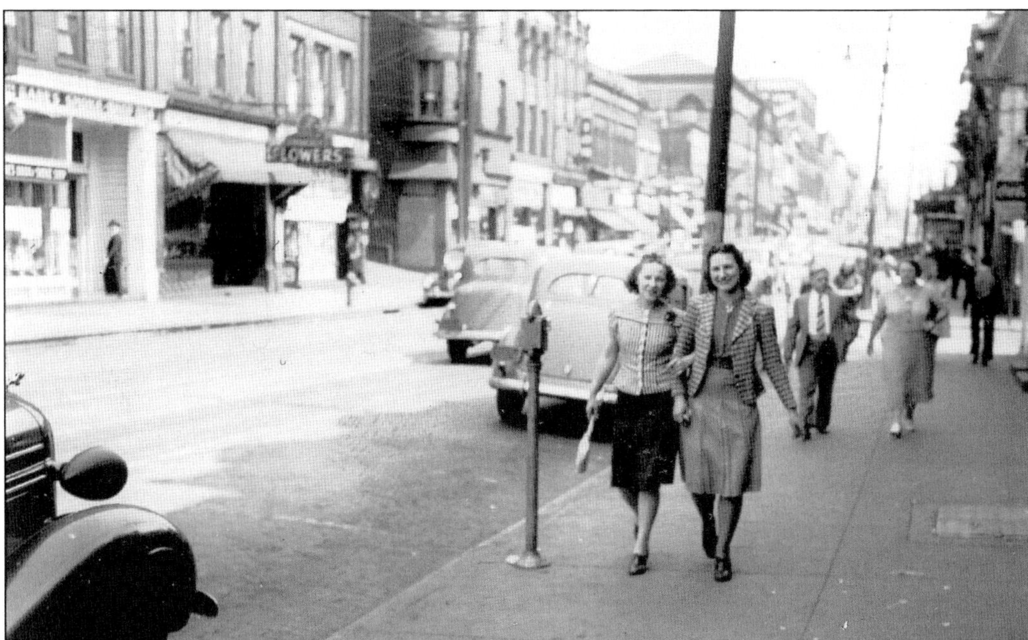

BRADDOCK AVENUE SHOPPING SCENE. As automobile ownership grew, so too did the need for parking spaces along Braddock Avenue. As parking meters became prevalent they represented a significant source of income for Braddock borough. Business owners often kept pockets full of change ready to feed the meters of their customers. (Courtesy of Victoria Hruska.)

WOMEN AT AMERICAN STEEL AND WIRE. Local mills and factories hummed with activity during World War II. Many residents recall how the Monongahela Valley's steel products helped win the war. While the men were off to war, however, it was the women who were operating the machinery and producing much of the product. This 1943 plant magazine highlights Braddock resident Margaret Ciesielski's work as a machine operator in the Rankin Works. (Courtesy of Margaret Szulc.)

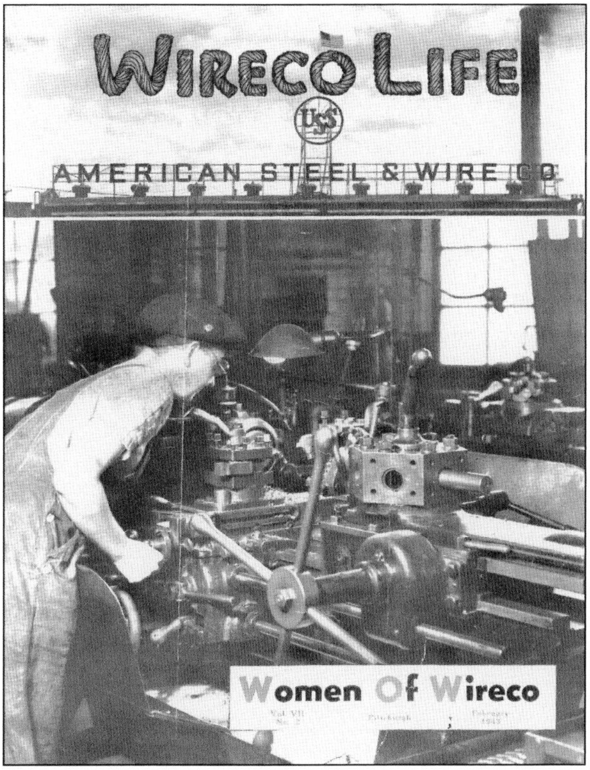

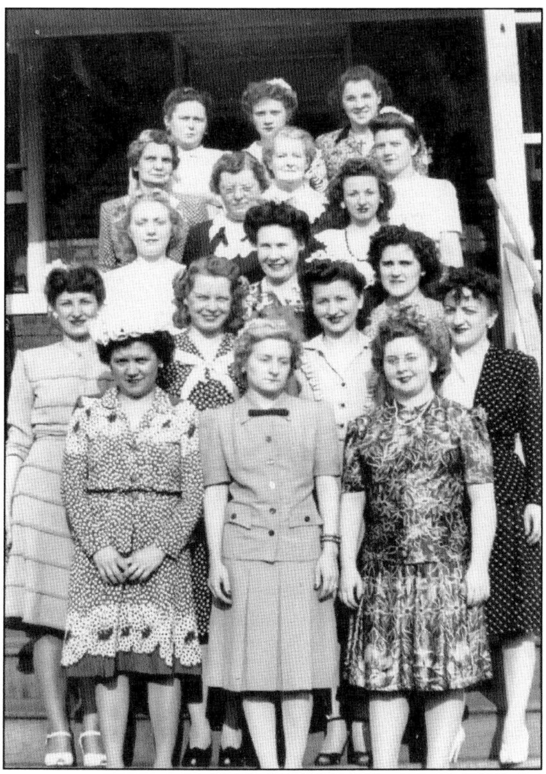

AMERICAN STEEL AND WIRE OFFICE WORKERS. U.S. Steel's American Steel and Wire Company needed qualified workers and recognized the impact that women were having on business. During the war years, women employees were running front offices, back offices, and factory floors—all in an effort to keep production at full throttle. Some of the office staff appearing in this picture include: Mary Sharp, Honey Kennedy, Estelle Mulligan, Victoria Ciesielski, Mary Urban, Mabel Maluty, Catherine Nickel, Mildred Anderson, Nellie Taylor, Pat O'Hare, Janet Patterson, and Mildred Plavetich. (Courtesy of Victoria Hruska.)

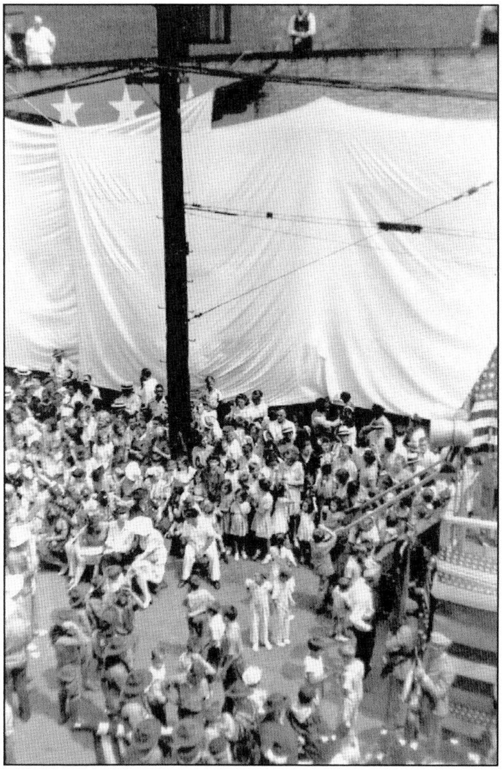

VETERANS HONOR ROLL DEDICATED. Like many towns across the United States, local communities lost many of their citizens in war. During the war years, many parades were held and numerous monuments unveiled. Large crowds often came together to celebrate victory and to unveil monuments constructed to recognize the valor of fallen soldiers, like this dedication that took place on Eighth Street on July 5, 1943. (Courtesy of Braddock Carnegie Library.)

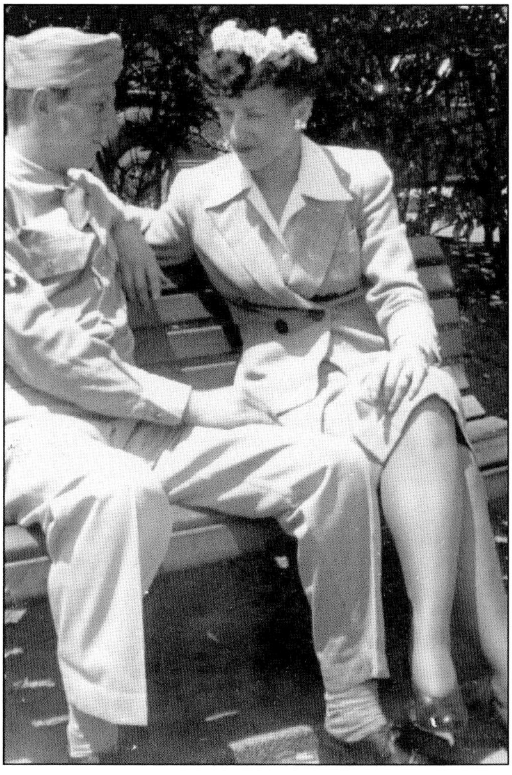

PAUL T. AND VICTORIA HRUSKA. During World War II, military leave was a time to visit home and to make sure that the girl who was left behind understood just how important she was to the man fighting in the war. As leaves were short, courtships and marriage decisions were greatly abbreviated. Paul Hruska was an army corporal stationed at Fort Meade, Maryland, while Victoria worked in Rankin's American Steel and Wire Company as receptionist and PBX telephone operator. (Courtesy of Victoria Hruska.)

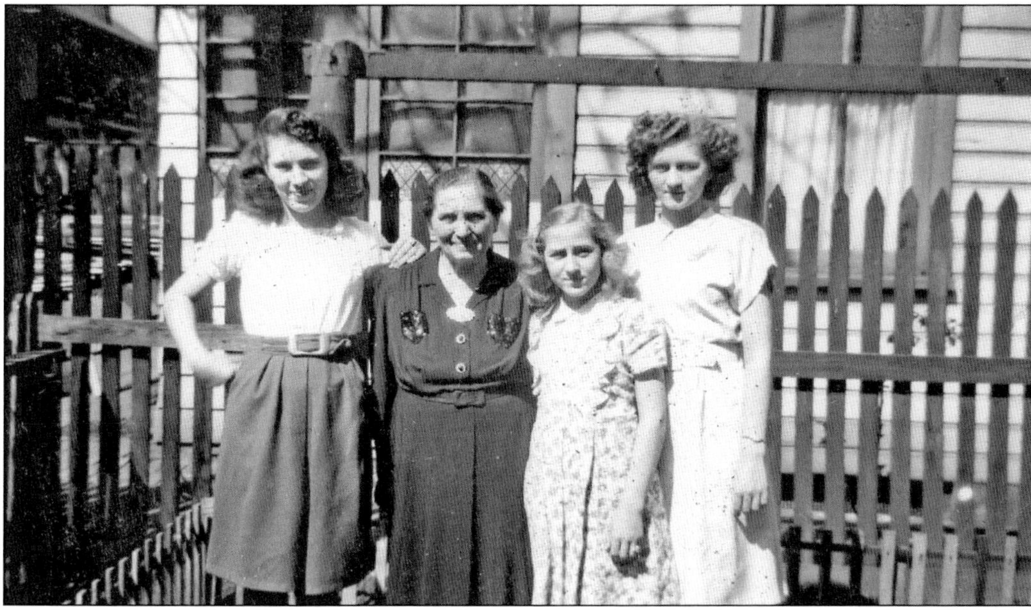

FAMILIES TOGETHER. In May 1947, from left to right, Theresa Kobylanski, Catherine Gilarski, Josephine Pallotta, and Anna Szwarc gathered for this backyard photograph. Family life had rapidly returned to normal after the end of the war. In the Braddock area, it was a time of change. Women were now part of the workforce; love was in the air, new families were started, and demand for cars, houses, and consumer goods began to expand dramatically. (Courtesy of Anna [Gilarski] Szwarc.)

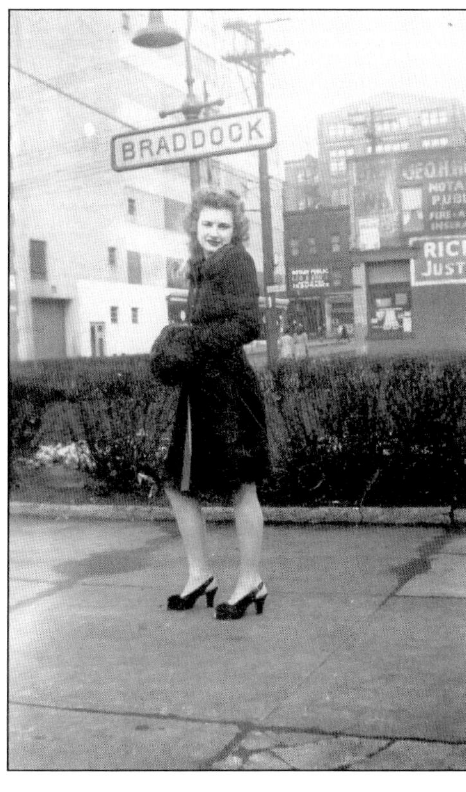

MEETING AT THE TRAIN STATION. While automobiles were all the rage, railroads and train stations continued to draw considerable passenger traffic. Areas just outside the train stations gained renewed life as meeting places for young people like Eleanor Oleniczak, seen here. (Courtesy of Anna [Gilarski] Szwarc.)

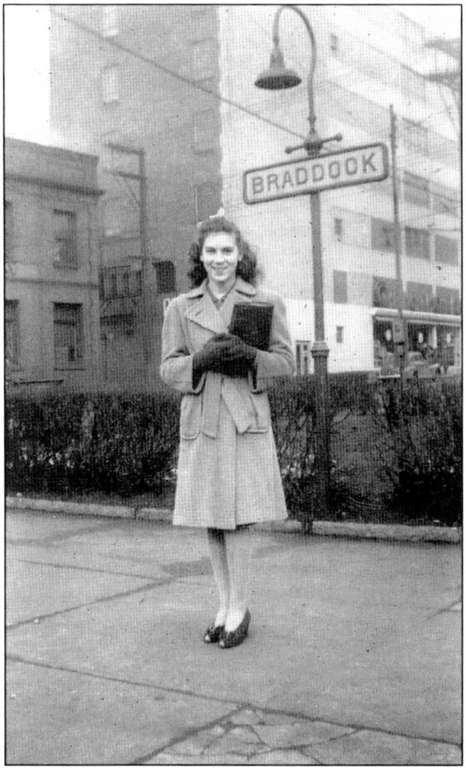

TRAIN STATION MEMORIES. Everyone knew the locations of Braddock's many train stations. Areas around the stations were places that friends and loved ones would gather to take pictures. This one of Theresa (Gilarski) Kobylanski did just that, as there were few better places in Braddock that could be more instantly recognized than this area just outside the Baltimore and Ohio station. (Courtesy of Anna [Gilarski] Szwarc.)

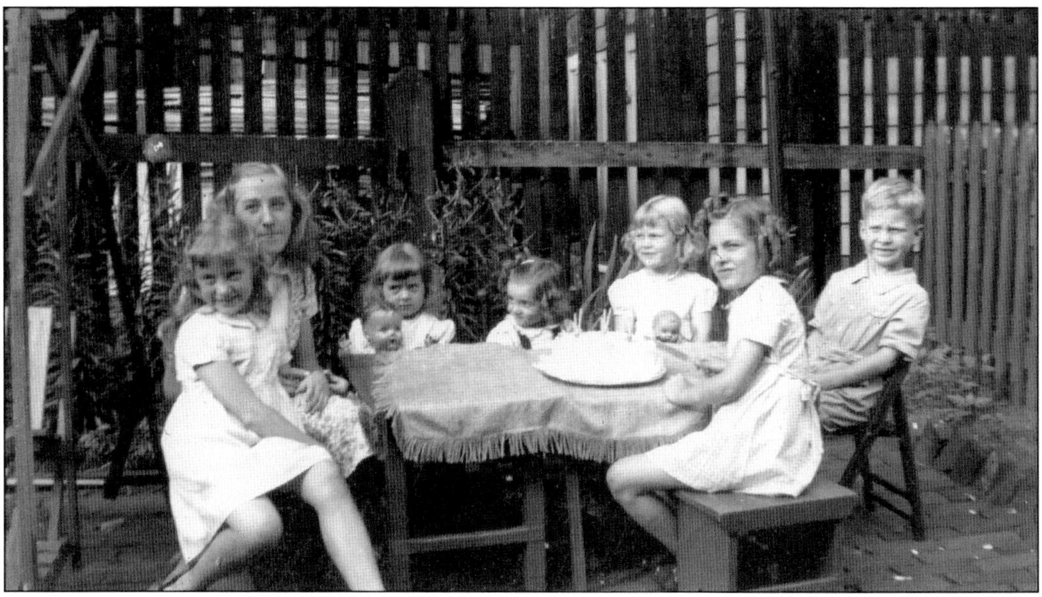

LET'S PLAY. Postwar holidays and birthday celebrations were wonderful events as the number of children living in the community grew dramatically. These were the days of full employment, neighborhood parties, ethnic celebrations, and religious fervor. From left to right, Dolly Stafiej, Josephine Gilarski Pallotta, Terry Sidor Mikolajczyk, JoAnn Novak Baacke, Mary Jane Szwarc Zablocki, Jackie Szwarc and Connie Szwarc Schartner celebrate a birthday on July 2, 1948. (Courtesy of Anna [Gilarski] Szwarc.)

LET'S RIDE. Children were everywhere and every sidewalk, side yard, and common space became a playground. The baby boom was in full swing in the early 1950s as Braddock area communities saw the largest birth rate increases in the town's history. Connie Szwarc is enjoying her bicycle on a sidewalk near her home on this particular summer day. (Courtesy of Anna [Gilarski] Szwarc.)

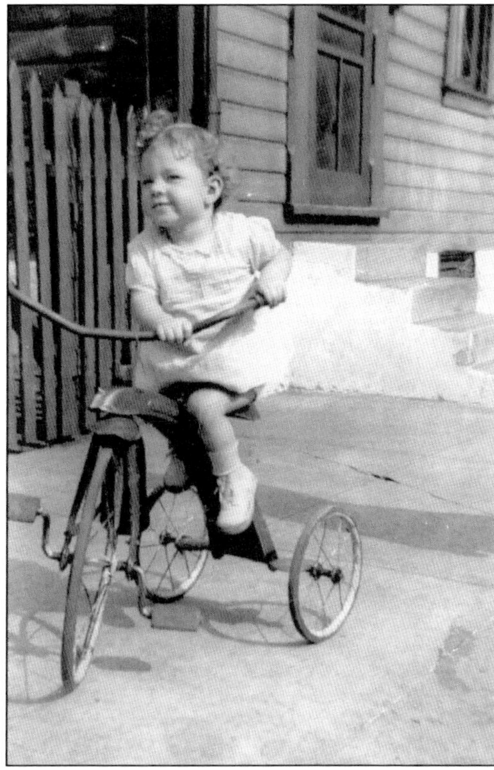

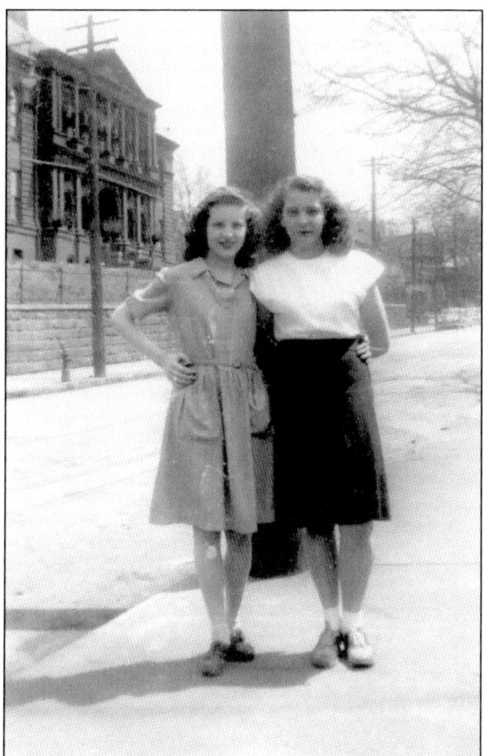

HIGH SCHOOL FRIENDS. Schools around the district were flourishing with growing numbers of students. Friends Mary Zubac (left) and Anna Trasky Sullivan are seen here in front of Scott High School in North Braddock around 1947. (Courtesy of Anna [Trasky] Sullivan.)

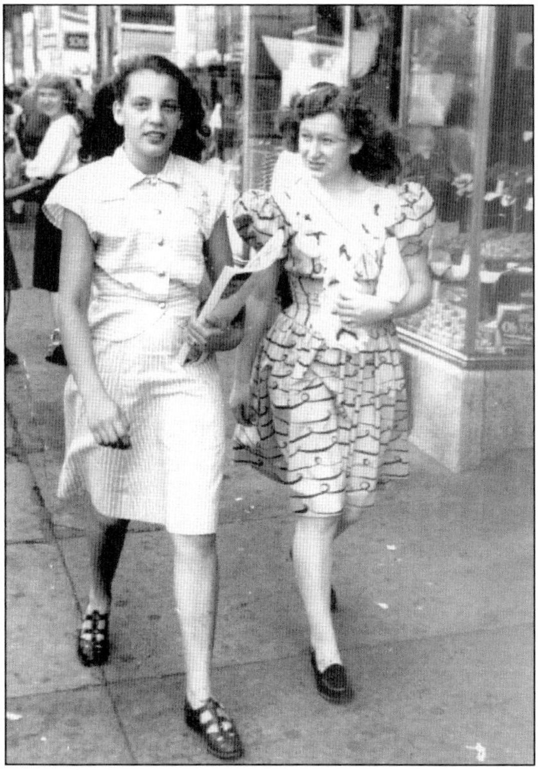

BRADDOCK AVENUE BUSTLE. Anna Trasky Sullivan (left) is seen here walking along Braddock Avenue between Eighth and Ninth Streets with her friend Bernice Toth (Sotak), on the way to Sullivan's job at the Braddock Isaly's store. (Courtesy of Anna [Trasky] Sullivan.)

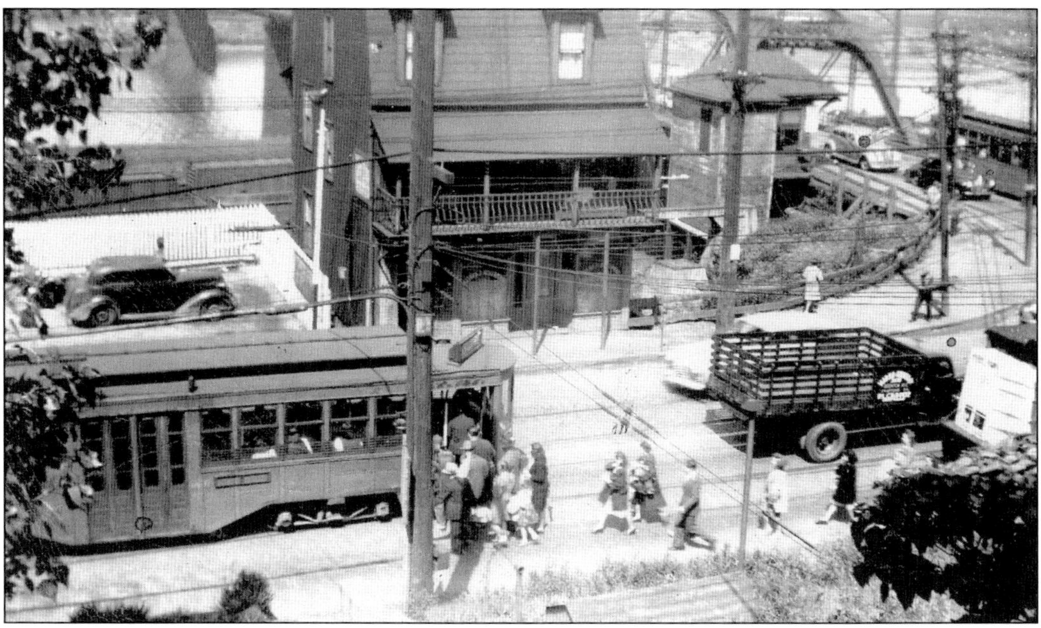

WEST BRADDOCK BRIDGE AT DUQUESNE JUNCTION. The year 1951 was an important one for local communities as the Braddock bridge was to be replaced by the George Rankin Jr. Bridge. The old bridge had served the Monongahela Street Railway Company well over the years by connecting its rail traffic with Kenny's Grove in Mifflin Township and numerous housing communities along the river. (Courtesy of Victoria Hruska.)

DUQUESNE JUNCTION. Viewed from the Whitaker side of the Monongahela River, the George Rankin Jr. Bridge is seen while under construction around 1950–1951. The new 505-foot bridge was designed as a steel cantilever spandrel-braced bridge and built by Bethlehem Steel under contract with Allegheny County. Bethlehem Steel and Carrie Furnace can be seen in the background. (Courtesy of Victoria Hruska.)

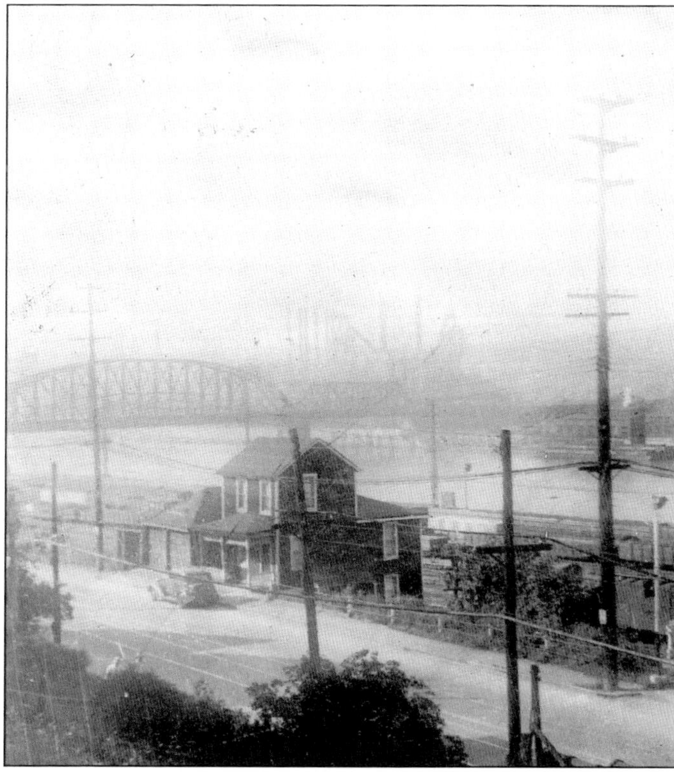

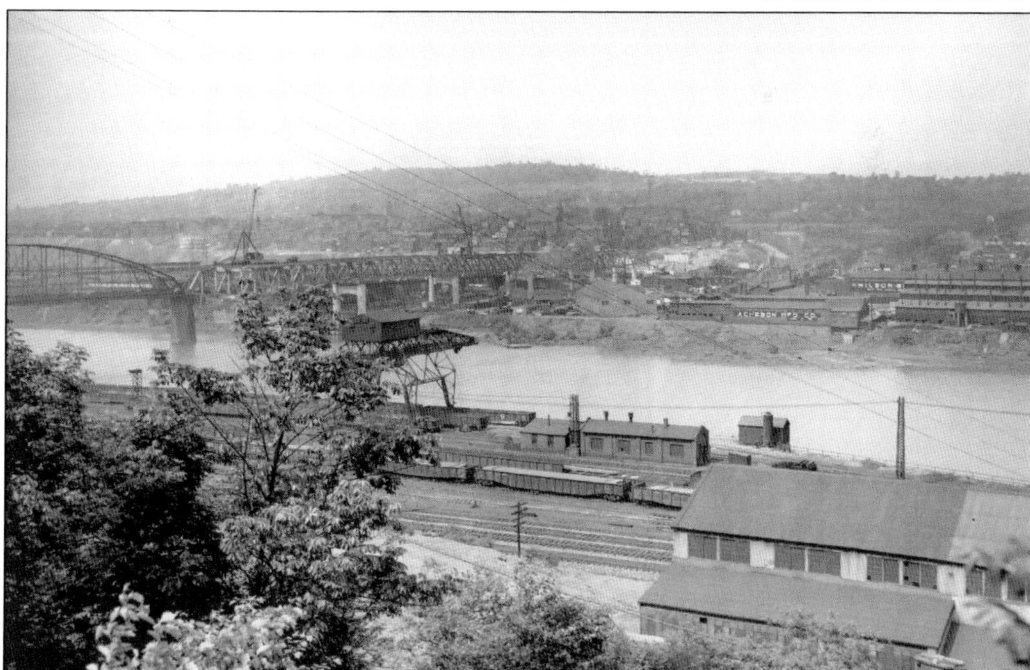

RANKIN BRIDGE. The George Rankin Jr. Bridge is under construction in this *c.* 1950 view from the Whitaker side of the Monongahela River. The communities of Braddock and Rankin are seen in the background. (Courtesy of the Rivers of Steel National Heritage Area.)

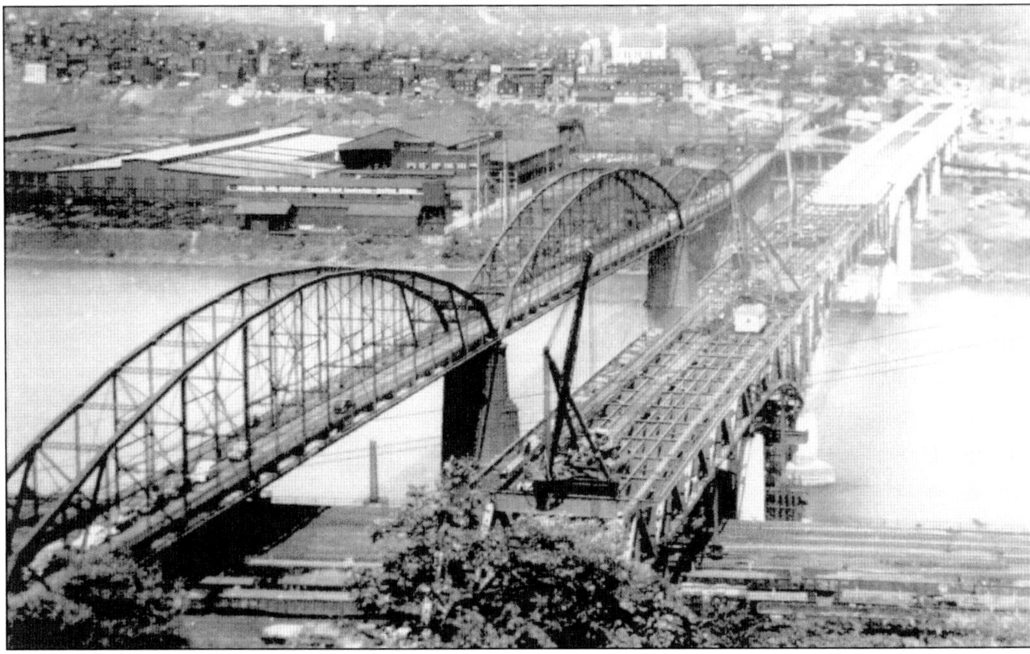

TWIN BRIDGES. The West Braddock bridge was constructed in 1897 connecting the Monongahela Street Railway for use in connecting its trolley line to that of the Braddock Electric Line that began business in 1893. Bethlehem Steel Corporation and the Rankin community can be seen in the upper left area of this *c.* 1950 image. (Courtesy of the Rivers of Steel National Heritage Area.)

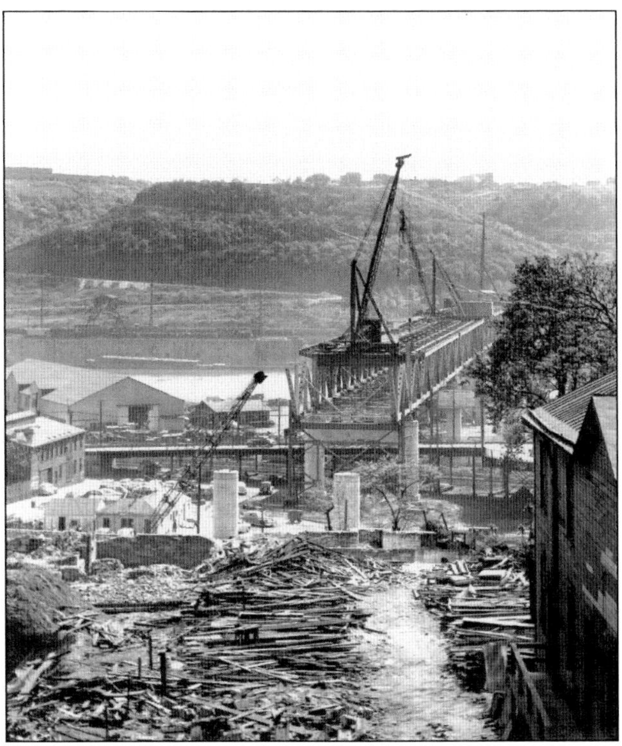

RANKIN VIEW OF BRIDGE CONSTRUCTION. This view of construction of the Rankin bridge is seen from the Rankin side, around 1950. (Courtesy of the Rivers of Steel National Heritage Area.)

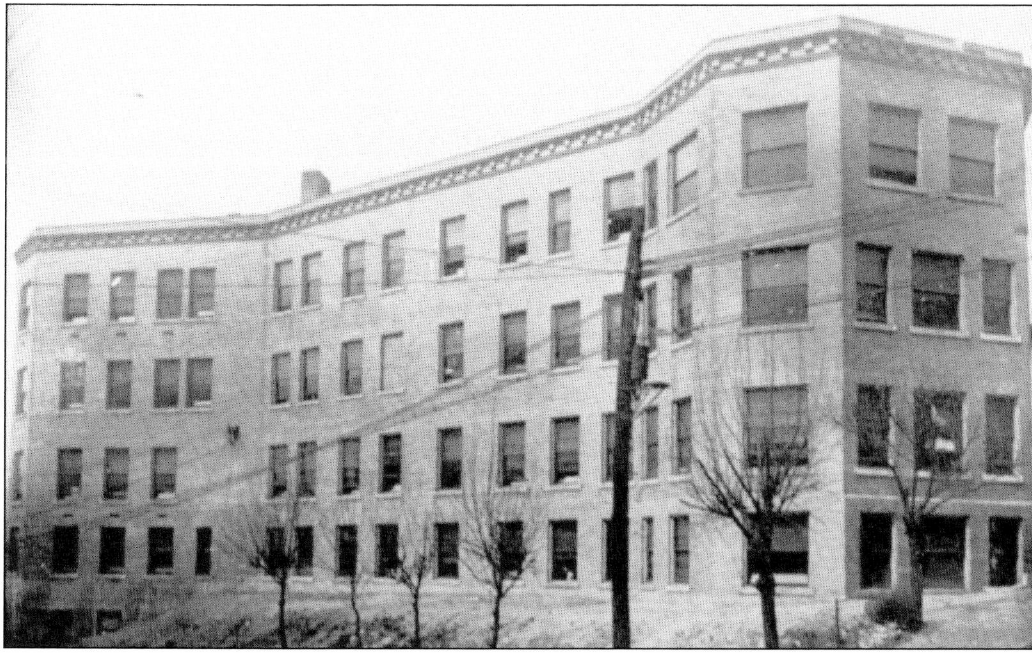

BRADDOCK GENERAL HOSPITAL EAST WING. In 1917, the hospital was able to open its new east wing, adding another 60 beds. The hospital now had 130 beds total and it was much better equipped to meet the demands of the community and businesses that were growing around it. Some of the other improvements gained in the new wing included new kitchen facilities, operating rooms, and pathology laboratories. (Courtesy of *The Unwritten History of Braddock's Field.*)

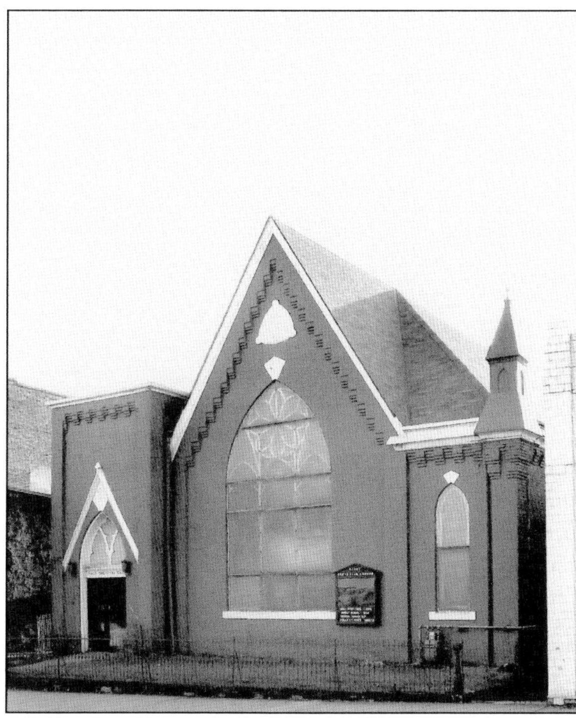

CITY OF CHURCHES. The First Christian Church is recorded as the oldest church in the Braddock area. Church services began in the home of Isaac Mills in 1830 and a preacher walked from Pittsburgh to deliver services each week. The current church building is located along Braddock Avenue on property once owned by the Mills family. Between 1830 and 1917, 44 churches were established in Braddock, and for many years, Braddock was recognized as the "City of Churches." (Author's collection.)

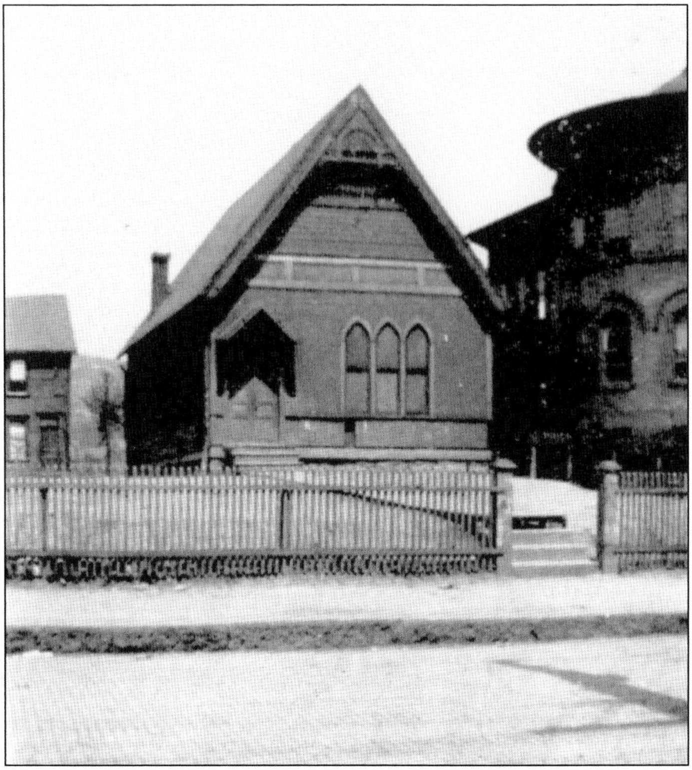

EARLY BEGINNINGS. Upon its formation in 1891, Rankin found itself without a single church. Rankin resident members of the First Baptist Church of Braddock were convinced of the need for a mission chapel in Rankin due to the many families of mixed nationality and language residing within the community. In 1893, the chapel was opened, and in 1900, it was converted to church status as the First Baptist Church of Rankin. (Courtesy of Rankin Christian Center.)

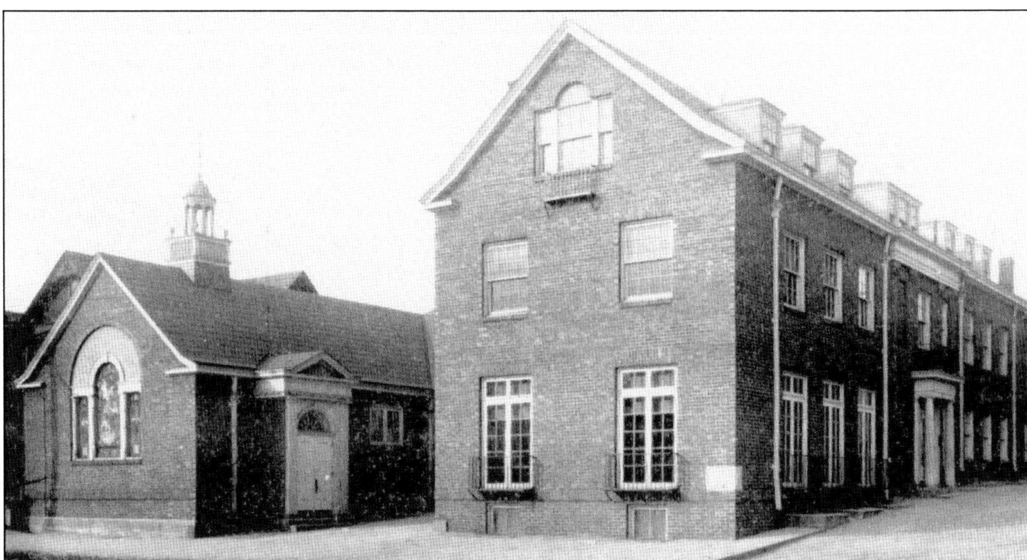

RANKIN CHRISTIAN CENTER. It was not long before the mission-type work needed to support the Rankin community became obvious. Planned as a social-religious experiment by the northern convention of the Baptist Church, establishment of the Rankin Christian Center became a primary objective. A site near the center of Rankin Borough was selected to build a facility. Completed in October 1923, the center included a chapel, library, social rooms, meeting hall, gymnasium, public laundry, and "shower baths." (Courtesy of Rankin Christian Center.)

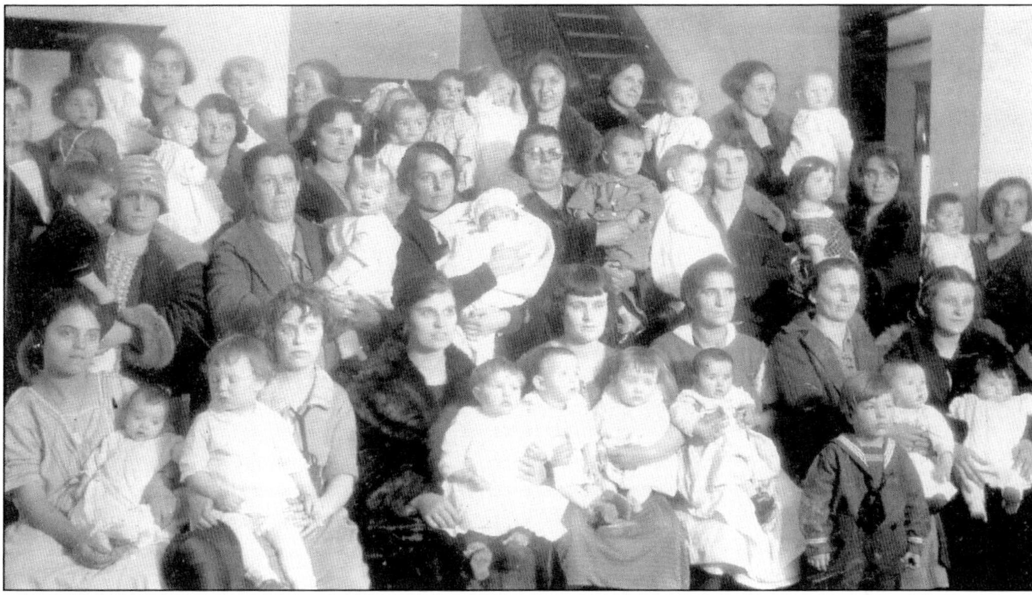

BABY SHOWS. Not long after opening its doors, Rankin Christian Center administrators worked with the Public Health Nursing Association to open a clinic and soon began offering "baby welfare work." A "Baby Show" was developed to initiate the clinic's services, and 66 babies were entered after being weighed and registered. The first group of mothers and babies to attend the clinic in 1924 are seen in the image. (Courtesy of Rankin Christian Center.)

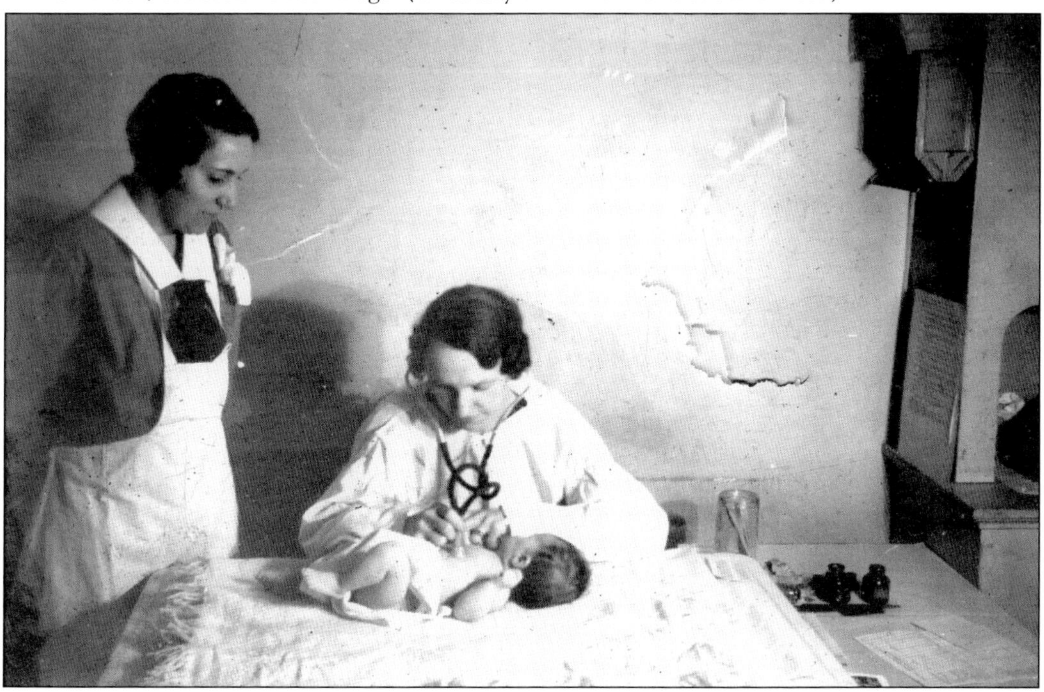

BABY CLINIC. Local physicians Dr. O. I. Polk and Dr. M. B. Weber, along with two public health nurses, began the service that presented mothers with information on raising healthy children. A doctor and nurse are seen here examining a baby during one of the center's early clinic visits. (Courtesy of Rankin Christian Center.)

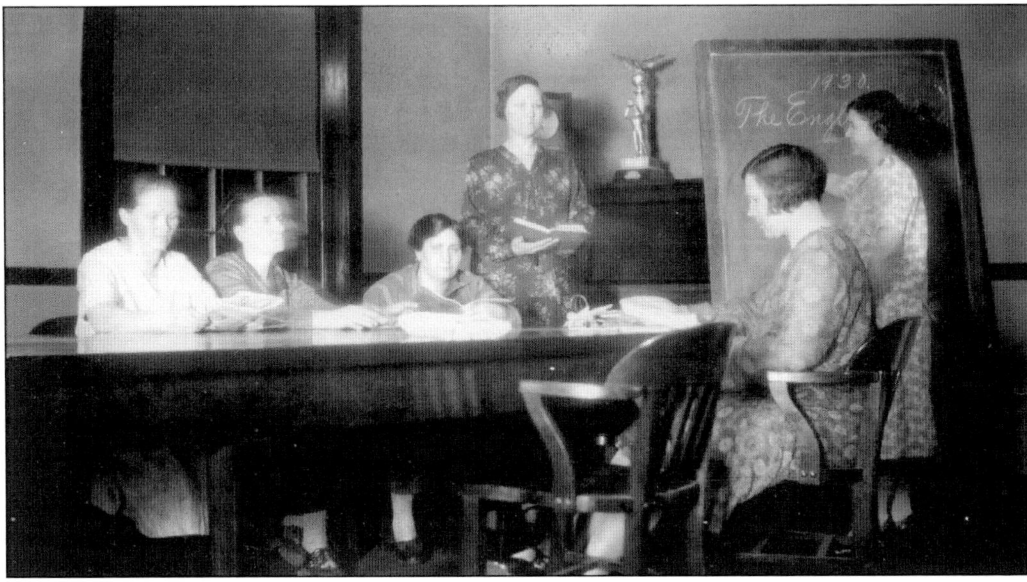

Americanization Classes. During the 1920s and 1930s, Americanization classes were held at the Rankin Christian Center to assist new residents in learning the English language and preparing them for U.S. citizenship. The classes were sponsored and supported by the Braddock Women's Christian Temperance Union (WCTU). Classes for women were held each Wednesday; men's classes were held on Fridays. (Courtesy of Rankin Christian Center.)

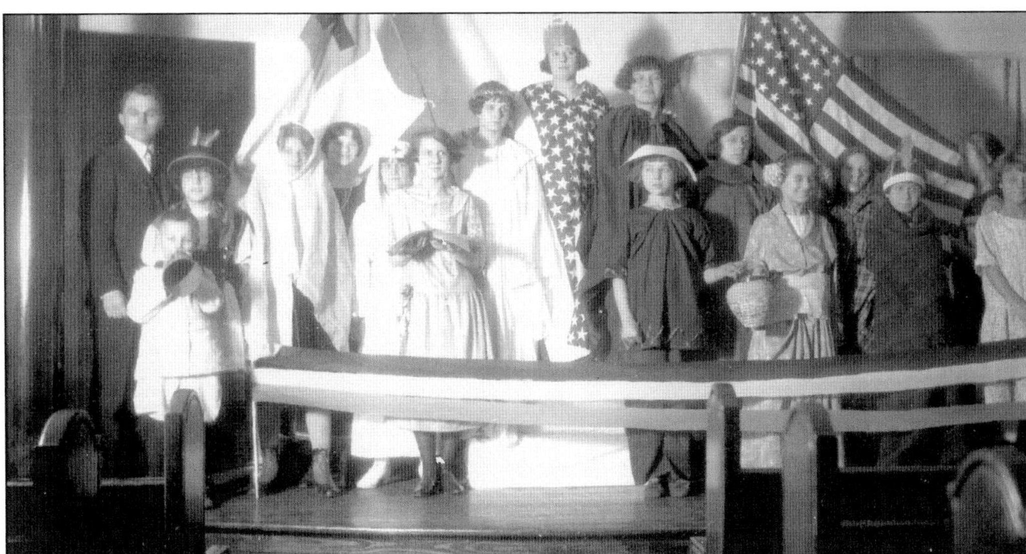

"The Tie that Binds." During the mid-1920s, members of the Rankin Christian Center's World Wide Guild are shown here preparing to stage a pageant called "The Tie that Binds." Girls who participated in the guild told missionary stories in the Rankin Christian Center's Sunday school program that was comprised of 15 or more classes each week. (Courtesy of Rankin Christian Center.)

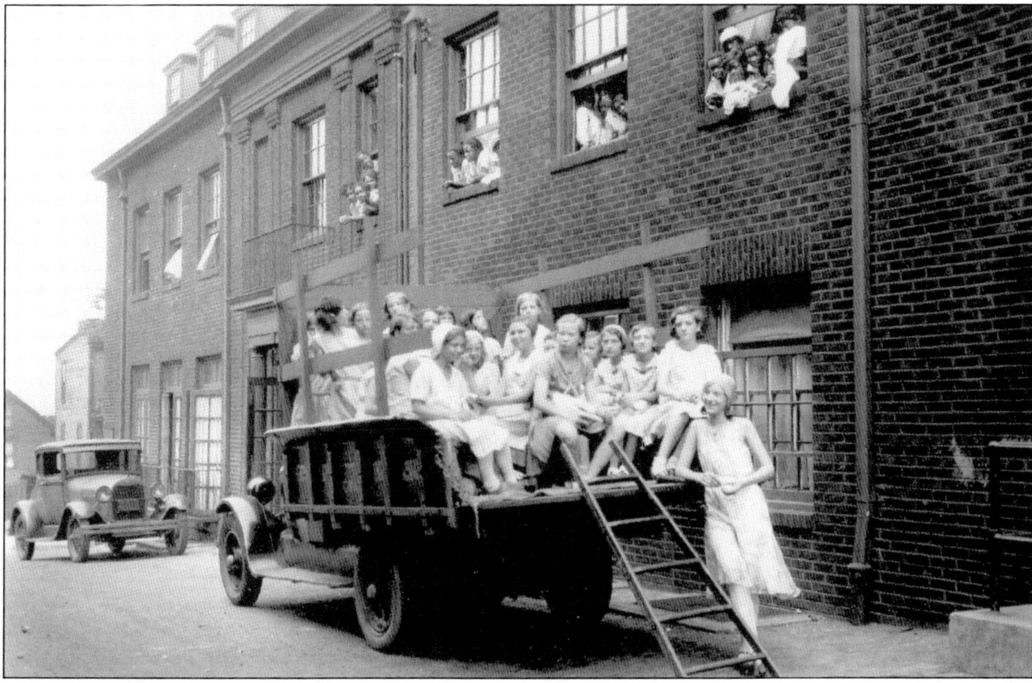

CITY OF UNDERSTANDING. In 1926, the Rankin Christian Center's annual report described Rankin as a "city of understanding, friendly, helpful folk," acknowledging that major changes were occurring throughout the community. By then, the center had created a wealth of opportunities for children of all races and nationalities to come together at the center for educational and recreational activities. (Courtesy of Rankin Christian Center.)

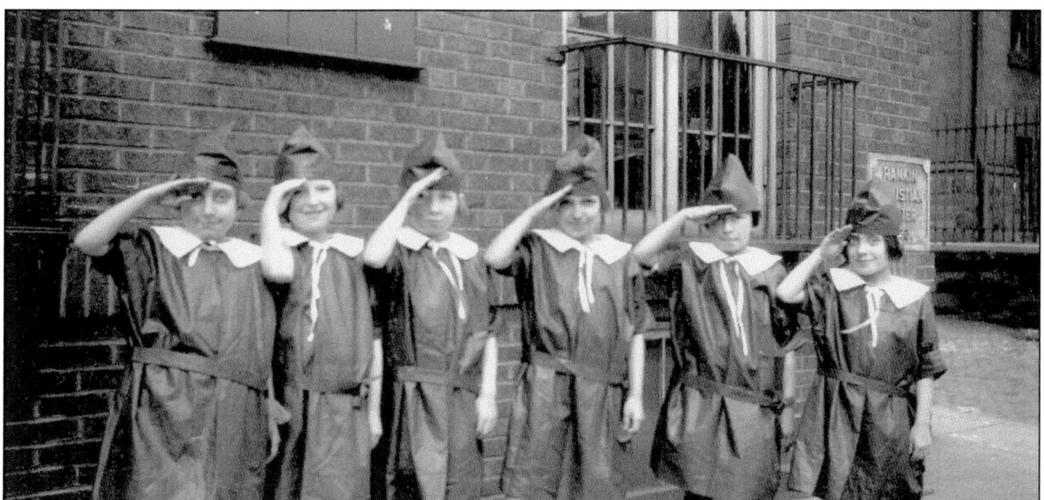

BROWNIES, BLUE BIRDS, AND BUSY BEES. Under the direction of center director Luella Adams, a diverse range of activities and clubs were created. During the mid-1920s, it was reported that six clubs were held each Tuesday, including the Brownies I, Brownies II, Pathfinders, Heralds, Blue Birds, and Busy Bees. Song, stories, handwork, and gymnasium were among the various activities that were lead by volunteers from Wilkinsburg High School. (Courtesy of Rankin Christian Center.)

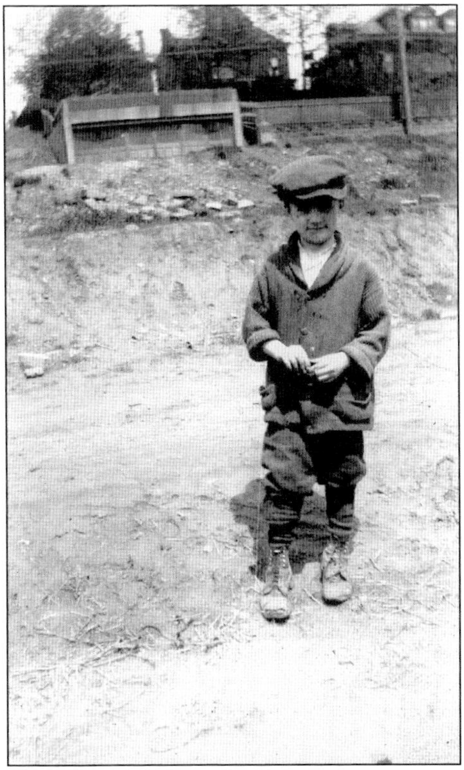

NO PLAYGROUNDS. Until the summer of 1920 there were few opportunities for sport or recreation in Rankin, leaving young children to their own devices. When the Rankin Christian Center opened, it could now actively engage them in constructive activity. (Courtesy of Rankin Christian Center.)

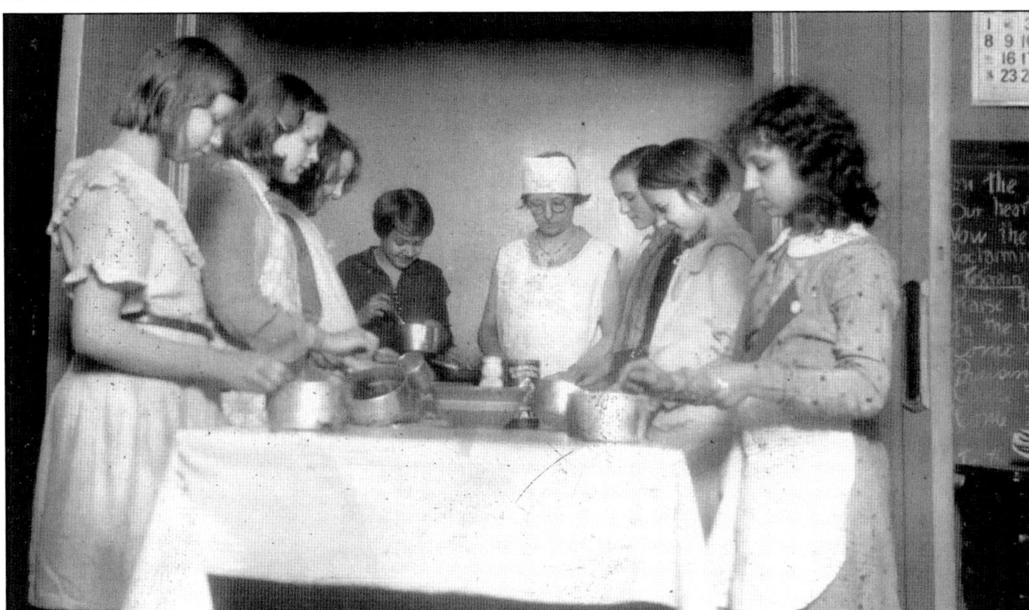

DOMESTIC ARTS. Shown here in this 1927 image, young girls participate in a household arts class where they are taught that *art* is comprised of things other than pictures or music. According to the curriculum, they were taught that art included such things as cooking, menu planning, table setting and serving, sanitation, interior decorating, and economy. (Courtesy of Rankin Christian Center.)

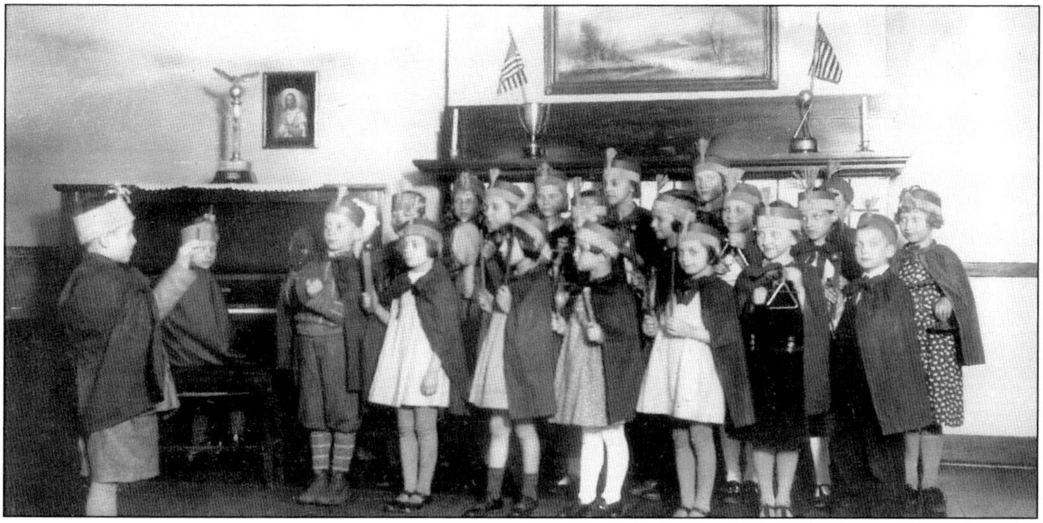

PRETTY THINGS. Young children were engaged in many activities, including healthy play, making "pretty things" with their hands, learning how to be helpful around the home, and of course, the value of obedience. (Courtesy of Rankin Christian Center.)

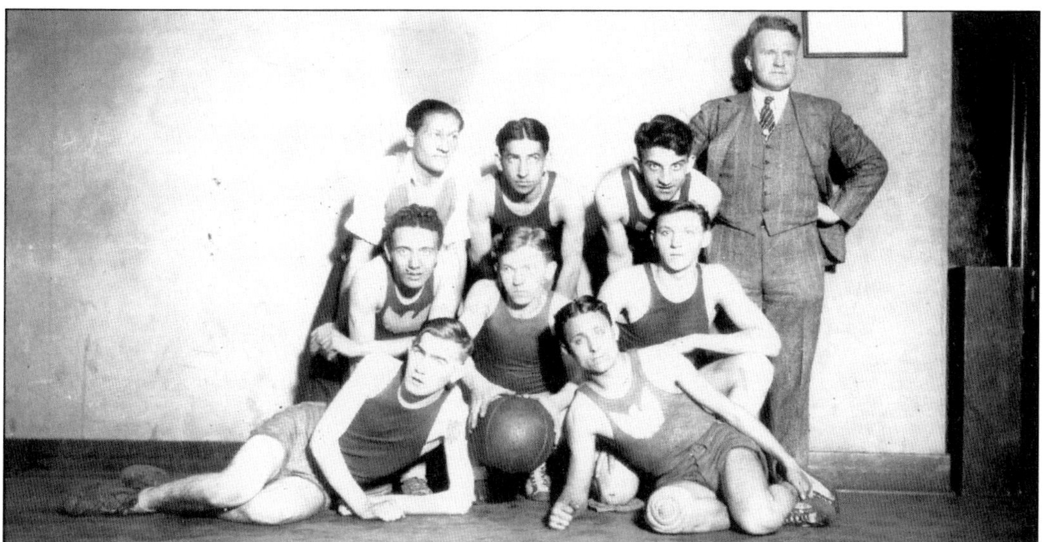

THE EAGLES SOARED. In 1930, it was reported that there were 16 teams participating in Rankin Christian Center supported league play. Shown here is the 1930 Senior Press League Championship team "the Eagles." C. D. Jeffrey served as Rankin Christian Center gymnasium supervisor. (Courtesy of Rankin Christian Center.)

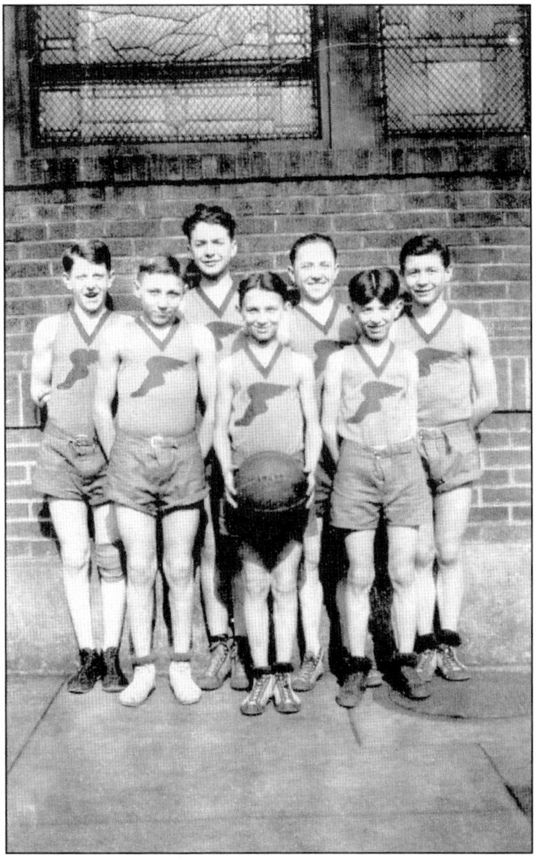

WINGFOOT BASKETBALL. During the mid-1920s there were eight basketball teams representing Rankin Christian Center. Among the teams were the Harmony Team, the Crescents, Center Big Five (reportedly the African American team), Nuzzo Tailors, and the Wingfoot Club. The Wingfoot Club was champion of the Tri-Borough Junior League. (Courtesy of Rankin Christian Center.)

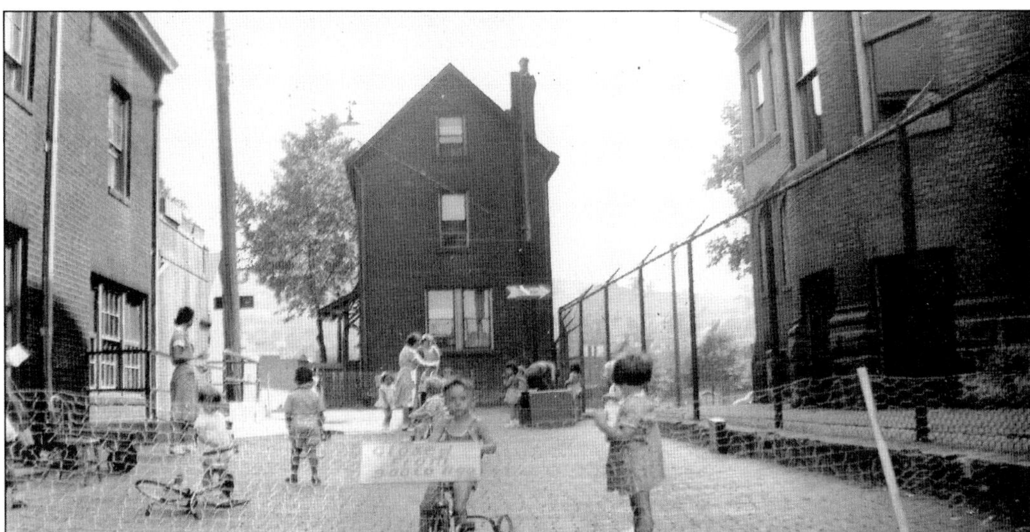

BIG SISTERS AND SECOND MOTHERS. The Rankin Christian Center Day Nursery was approved by the Allegheny County Day Nursery Association. The nursery served as a "second mother" or "big sister" to those women who were forced to work in order to feed and clothe their children. (Courtesy of Rankin Christian Center.)

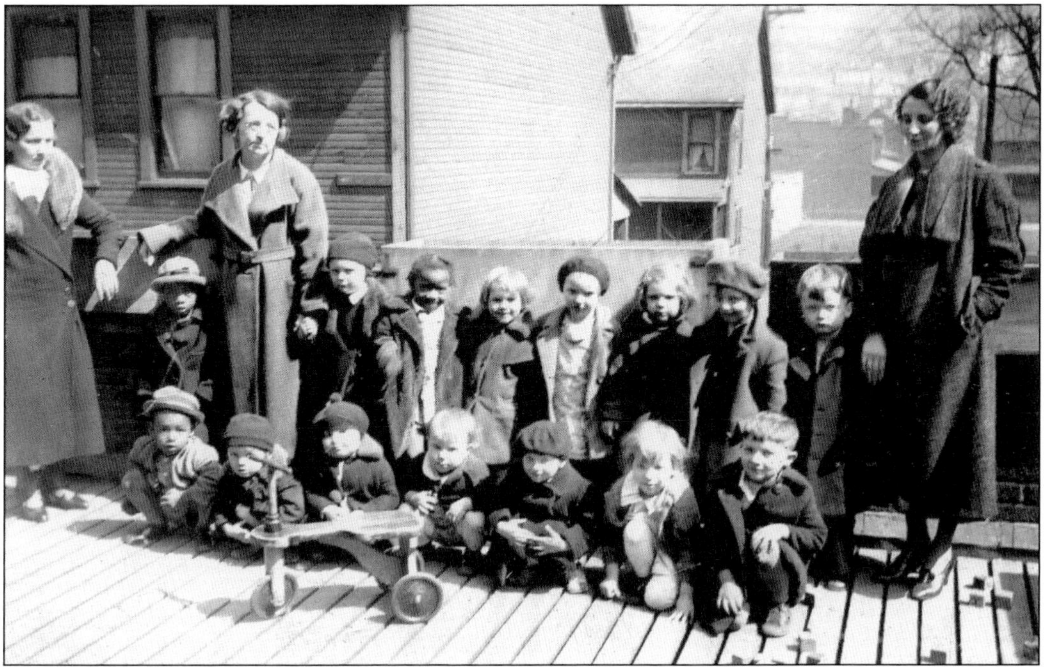

DAY NURSERY. Special ministries visited homes where industrial conditions and economic need often forced women into the workforce. The employment bureau found work for mothers and assisted them in maintaining their family by providing their children with care in the Rankin Christian Center's nursery. The Rankin Christian Center Day Nursery helped many families deal with these economic issues. Shown here is a nursery scene from 1930. (Courtesy of Rankin Christian Center.)

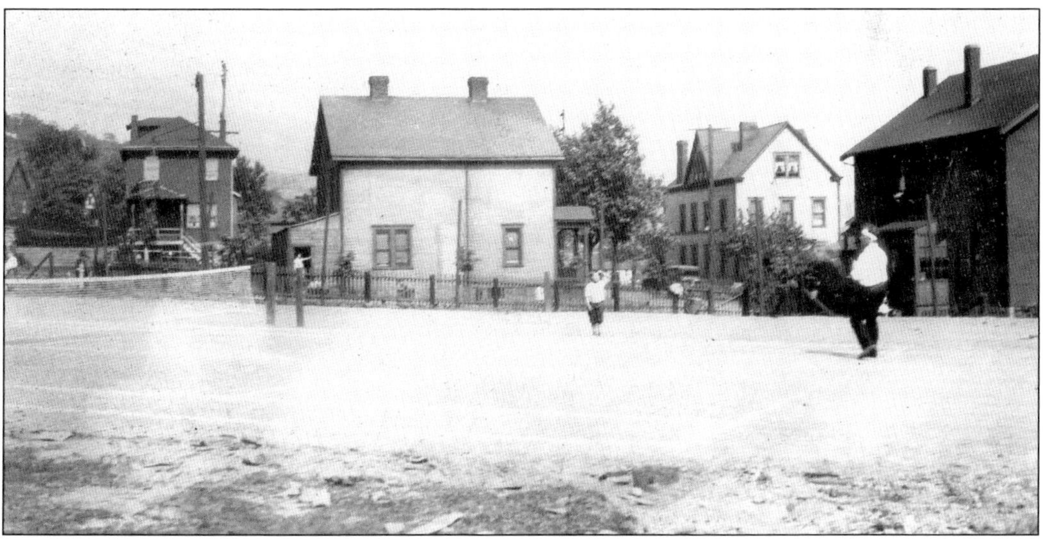

TENNIS, ANYONE? In the summer of 1925, funds were raised from members of the Rankin Christian Center board to purchase property for development of tennis courts. The property was located near the center and was among the last properties in Rankin available for sale. (Courtesy of Rankin Christian Center.)

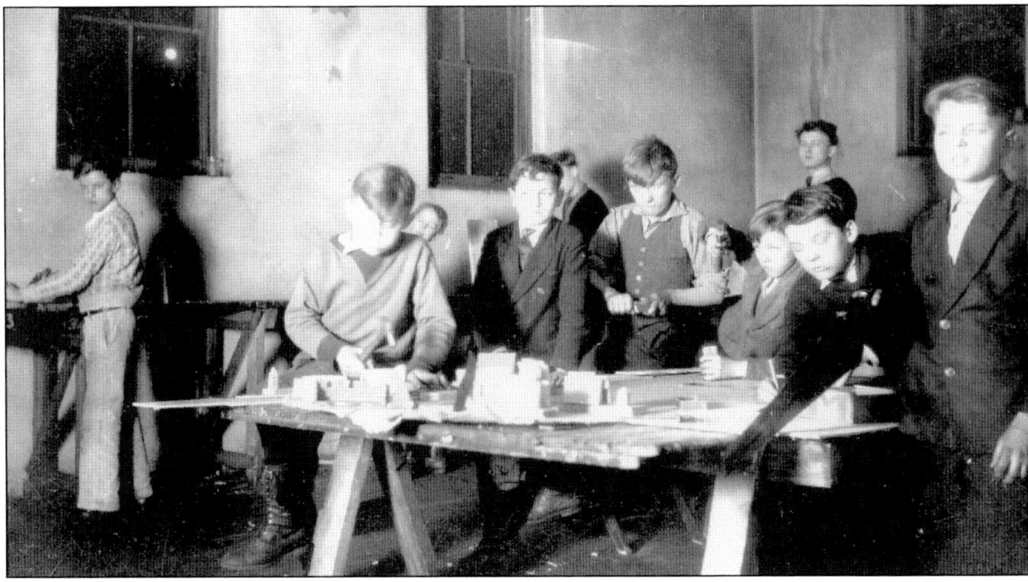

Manual Training for Boys. Working with tools or drawing with a pencil, boys at the Rankin Christian Center engaged in art, clay modeling, and woodworking in order to help them choose a vocation and assist them in gaining basic business ability. The center's manual training group for boys is shown in this 1927 image. (Courtesy of Rankin Christian Center.)

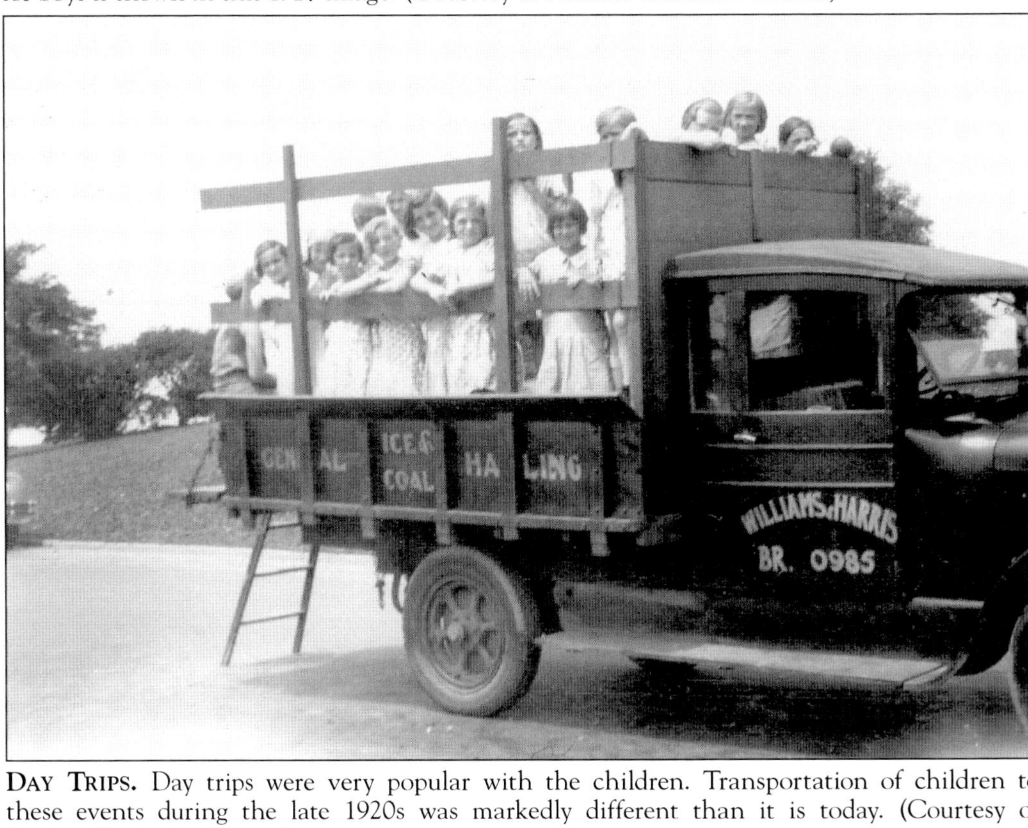

Day Trips. Day trips were very popular with the children. Transportation of children to these events during the late 1920s was markedly different than it is today. (Courtesy of Rankin Christian Center.)

BASEBALL. Baseball was a popular game among adolescent and teen boys during the late 1920s. Teams from the Rankin Christian Center readily participated in this spring and summer sport. (Courtesy of Rankin Christian Center.)

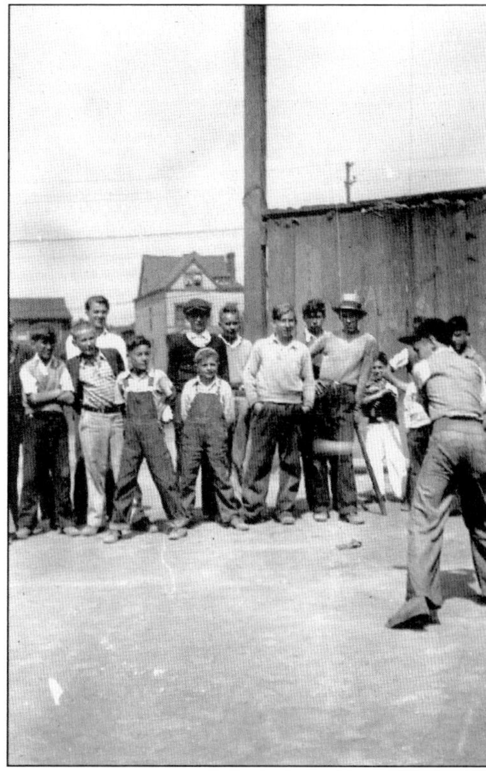

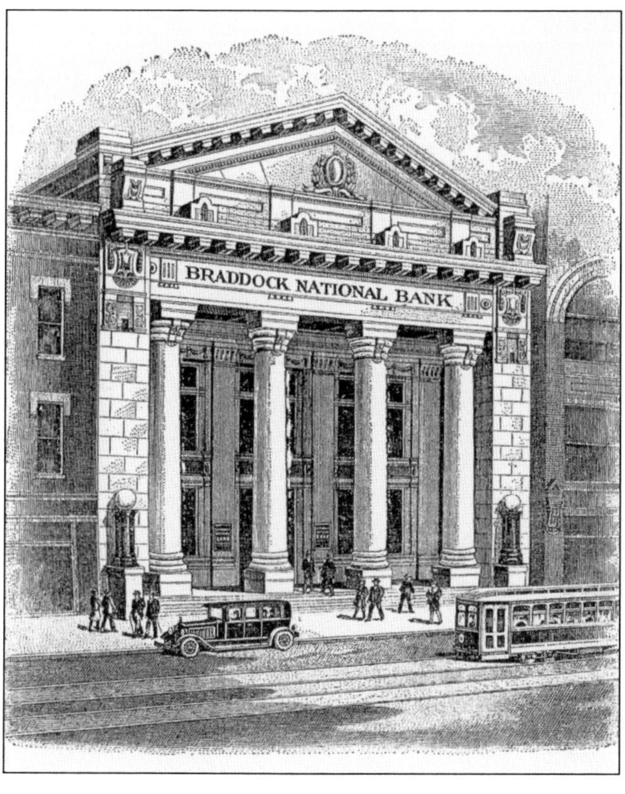

KELLY'S FOLLY. Completed in 1906, the Braddock National Bank building was considered a "palace." Constructed as a fire- and burglar-proof facility with state-of-the-art manganese vaults, the structure was built to such extreme that it was referred to as "Kelly's Folly" after its chief proponent, banker John G. Kelly. (Courtesy of Braddock Carnegie Library.)

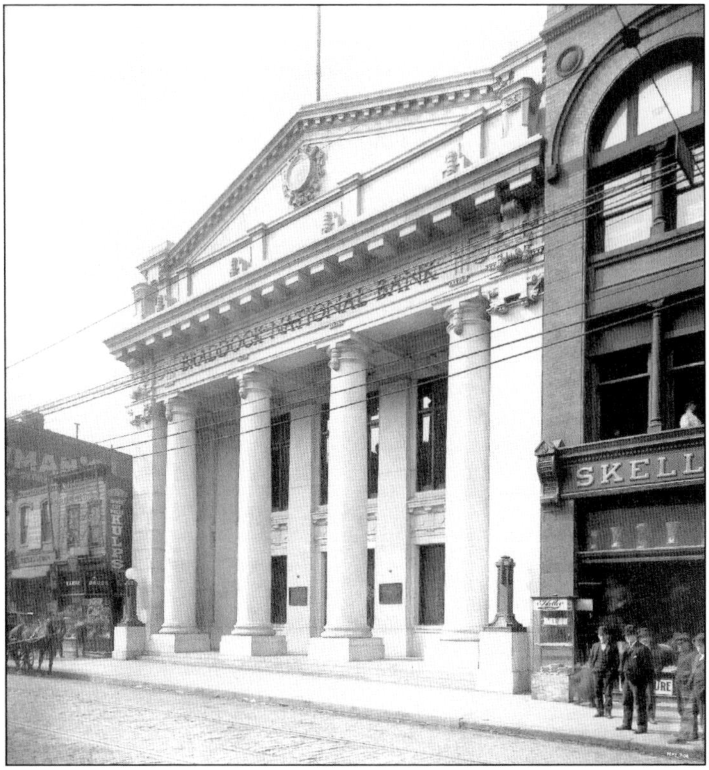

BRADDOCK NATIONAL BANK. The new bank was situated at an advantageous spot on Braddock Avenue. Its marble was imported and their sections scrupulously matched by talented artisans. In basic construction, the facility was built as a one-story bank, which was considered highly unusual at the time. Along with its extraordinary 40-foot high ceiling, the facility was a marvel of modern-day bank building design. (Courtesy of Lisa Silberman.)

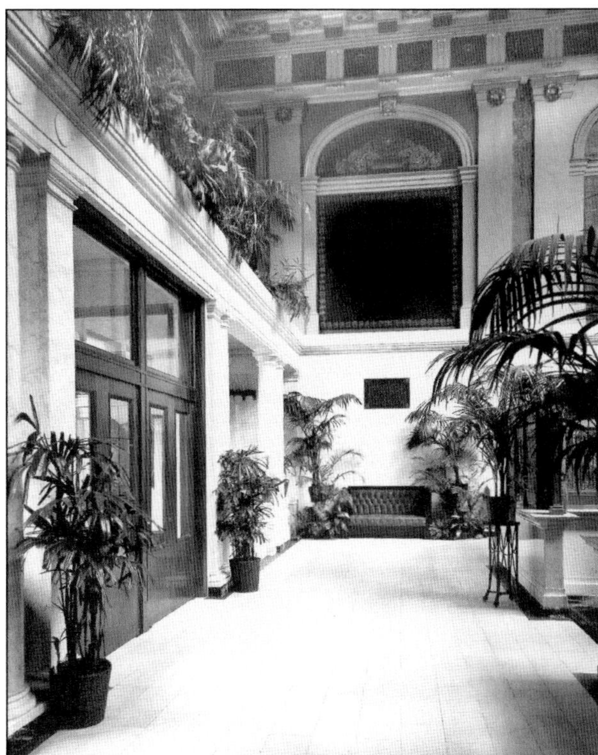

KELLY'S BANK. When the bank first opened for business, the sheer splendor of the facility made many wonder whether or not the ordinary workingman would ever feel comfortable in such opulence. It did not take long, however, for the doubters to be proven very wrong. Within 10 years, the number of depositors and deposits grew three times their original. Kelly's Folly was now endearingly referred to as "Kelly's Bank." (Courtesy of Lisa Silberman.)

BRADDOCK TRUST COMPANY. The Braddock Trust Company was organized during January 1901 as the People's Trust Company. It was affiliated with Braddock First National Bank. During the early 1920s, it boasted the third-largest amount of financial resources available in the borough. (Courtesy of *The Unwritten History of Braddock's Field.*)

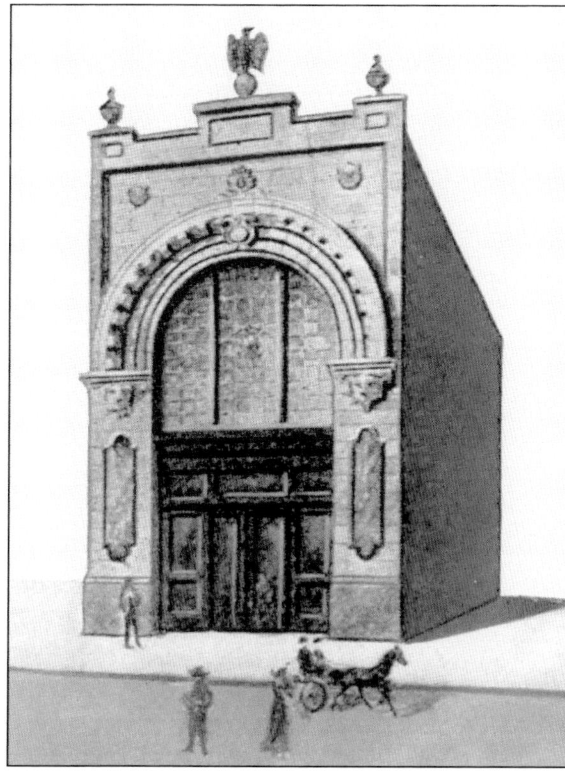

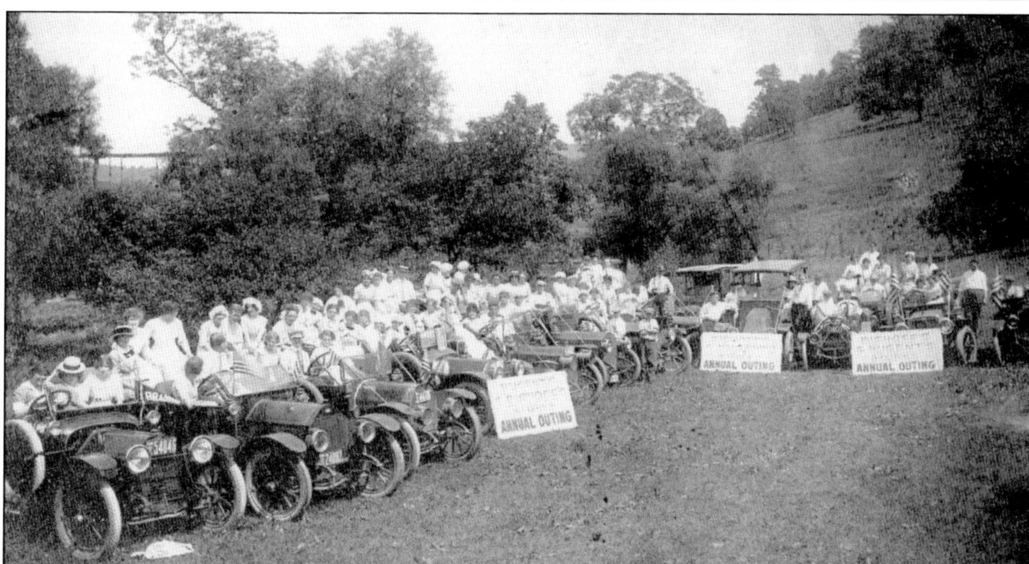

BISHOFF'S AND NUGENT'S ANNUAL OUTING. Bishoff and Company, a retail grocery business, was founded in 1886. In the store's early years, the owner served as buyer, salesman, and delivery person. By the 1920s, the store had grown tremendously; it soon occupied an entire block, employed almost 40 employees, and operated 18 vehicles for sales and delivery. Bishoff and Company and Nugent's Department Store employees often joined together for special events like the annual picnic seen here. (Courtesy of Braddock Carnegie Library.)

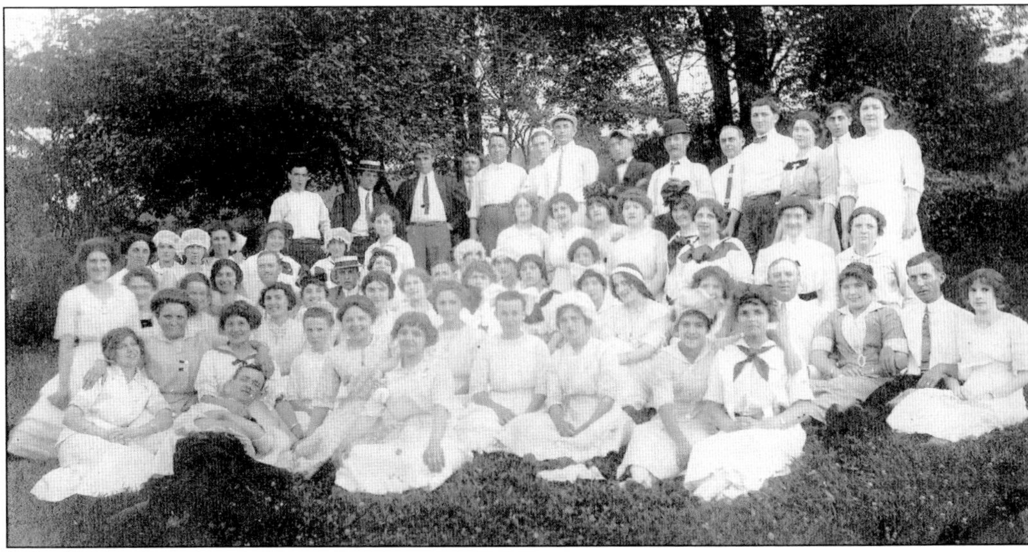

CELEBRATING SUCCESS. Business was good for most of Braddock's businesses during the first two decades of the 20th century. While competition was often fierce, it was not unusual for businesses to celebrate success together. Employees of Bishoff and Company and Nugent's Department Store are seen here relaxing at one such event. (Courtesy of Braddock Carnegie Library.)

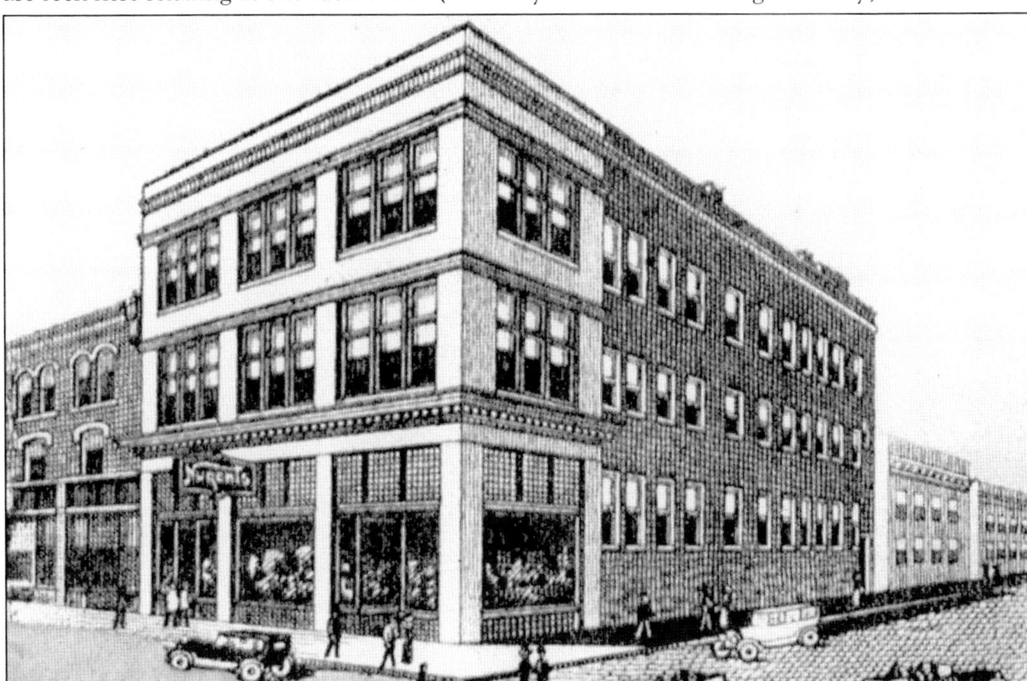

"BRADDOCK'S BEST STORE." Nugent's Department Store was one of Braddock's leading businesses. Founded in 1894 by Mary Nuggent, the store originally sold women's clothing and millinery. The first store was located at 823 Braddock Avenue; in 1898, it moved to 851 Braddock Avenue. Upon moving, the store began handling men's furnishings and a broad assortment of dry goods. It advertised itself as "Braddock's Best Store." (Courtesy of *The Unwritten History of Braddock's Field*.)

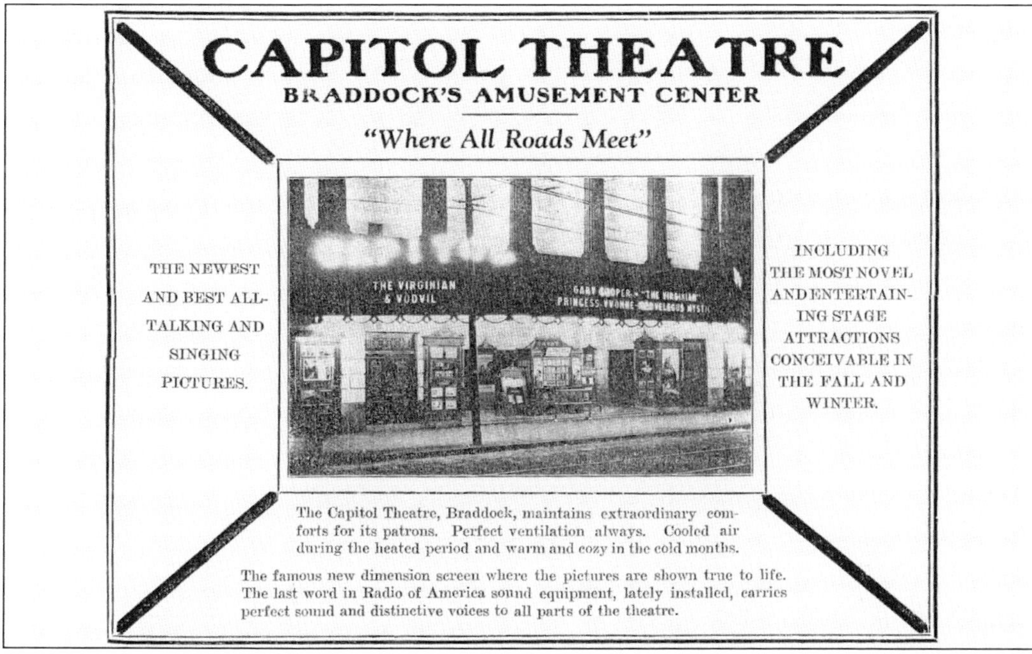

CAPITOL THEATER. Between the 1920s and 1950s, residents and visitors could find a dizzying array of shops, stores, and places of entertainment along Braddock Avenue. The Capitol Theater was one of the largest and most frequented entertainment venues, offering some of the country's most memorable first-run movies. (Courtesy of Braddock Carnegie Library.)

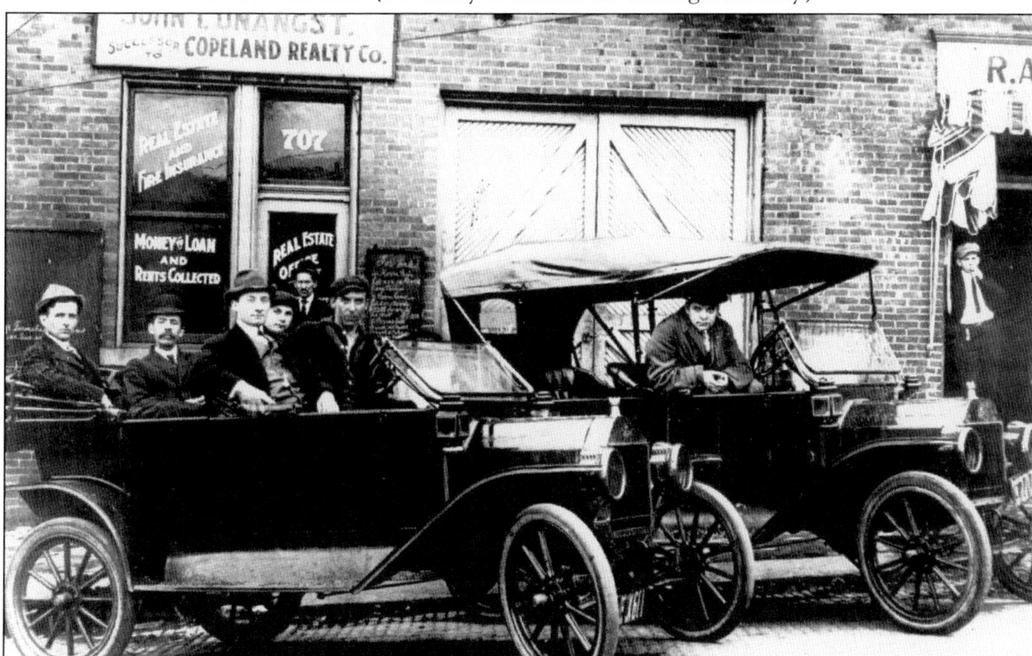

VINTAGE AUTOMOBILES IN NORTH BRADDOCK. The driver of the automobile on the left is Daniel Berthold. He and his associates sit in front of the John T. Unangst real estate company in North Braddock. (Courtesy of Braddock Carnegie Library.)

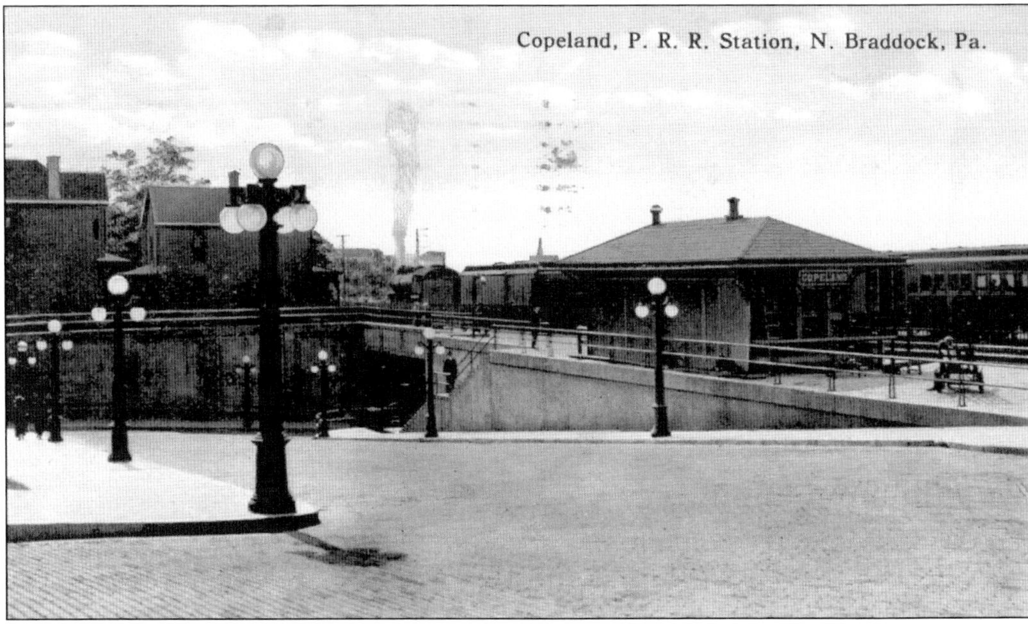

COPELAND STATION. Pennsylvania Railroad's Copeland Station was a place that connected people with the Braddock Electric Rail Company that traversed Fourth Street, Mills Avenue, and Hawkins Avenue. Around 1880, the railroad widened from one track to four. In 1913, various other improvements were made, including the elimination of an at-grade crossing and the building of an underground passageway at Fourth Street. (Author's collection.)

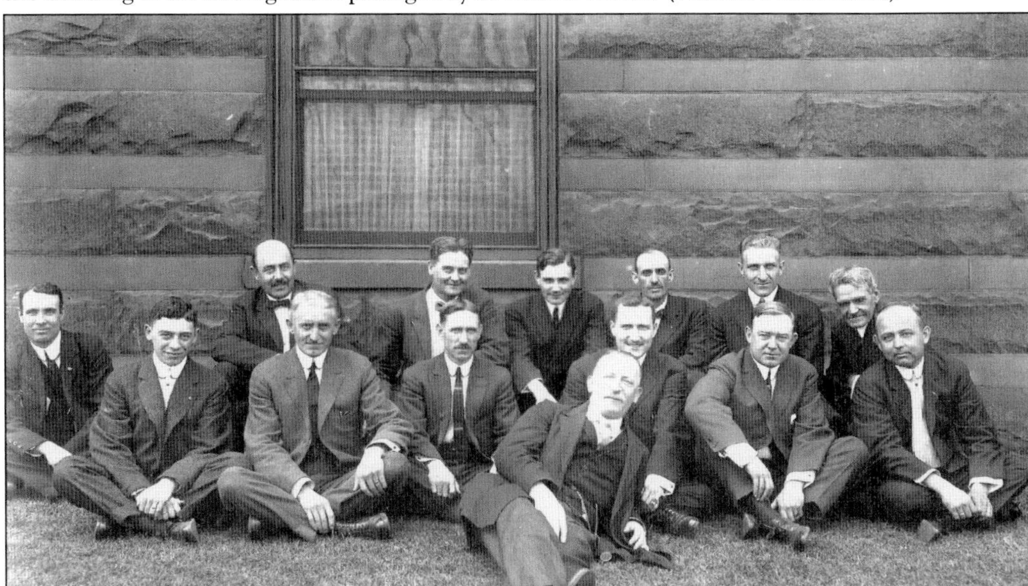

CARNEGIE STEEL SAFETY COMMITTEE. At the dawn of the 20th century, few steel mills in the country valued organized safety work. In Upton Sinclair's book *The Jungle*, Sinclair had written that at one of U.S. Steel's mills between 1906 and 1910, almost one out of every four workers would be killed or injured. Whether directly or indirectly a result of Sinclair's prodding, U.S. Steel Corporation is credited with pioneering a safety program that was later copied by many manufacturers around the country. (Courtesy of Braddock Carnegie Library.)

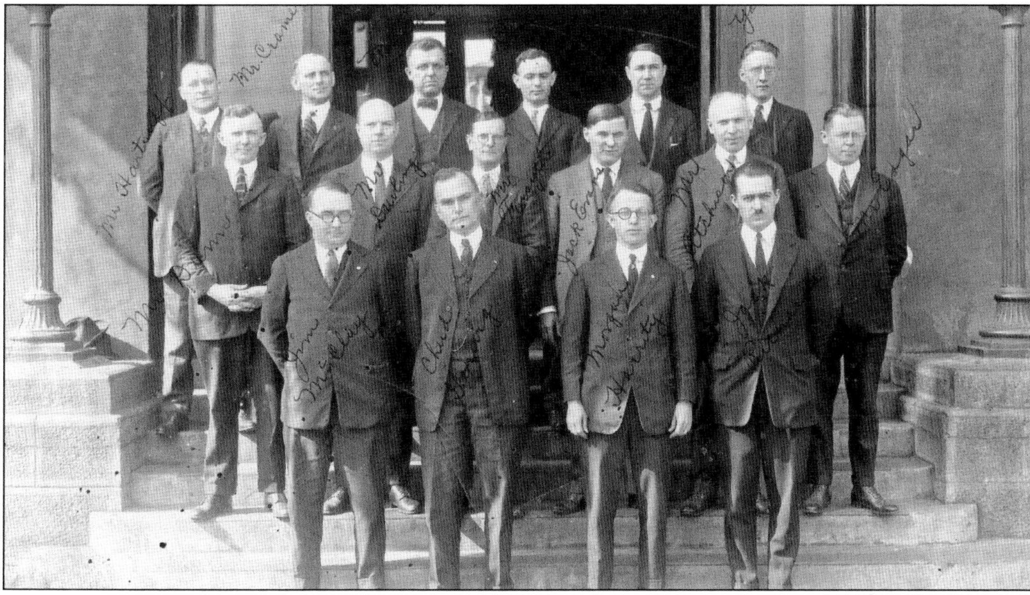

EDGAR THOMSON GENERAL SAFETY COMMITTEE. The Edgar Thomson Steel Works General Safety Committee is seen in this 1921 photograph. As U.S. Steel's safety plans evolved, they added several new layers, including the requirement that each subsidiary corporation have its own safety committee. The top layer ultimately became the Central Safety Committee, which included a representative of U.S. Steel and a representative from each subsidiary. (Courtesy of Braddock Carnegie Library.)

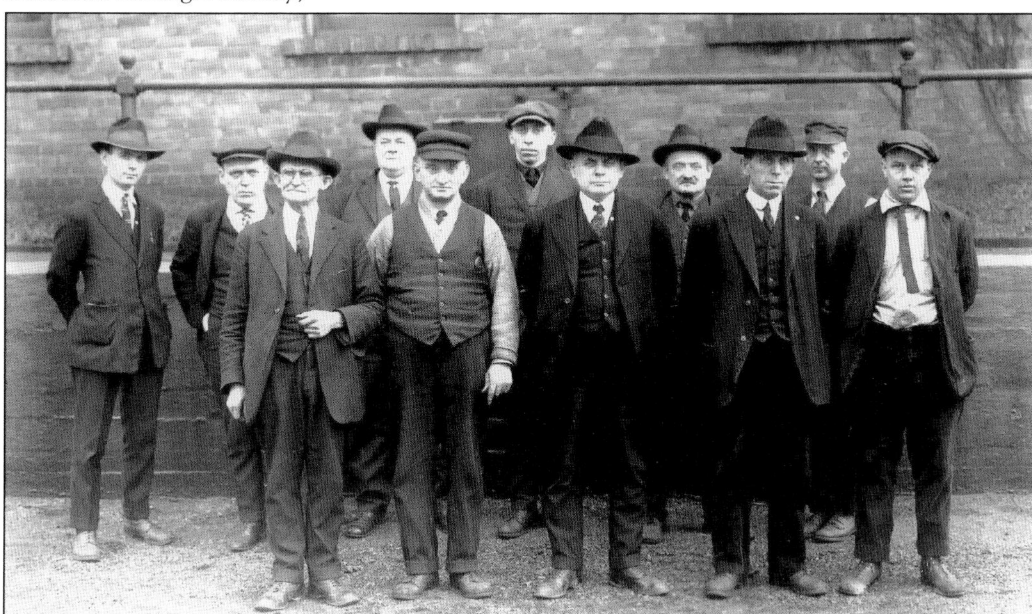

NO. 8 SAFETY COMMITTEE. The Edgar Thomson Steel Works, No. 8 Safety Committee appears in this group photograph taken on January 4, 1922. Over the first several years of operating, the safety committees could count many major improvements to plant operations. Its efforts had a positive impact on other industries as equipment manufacturers now had incentives to produce safer equipment and to create new markets. (Courtesy of Braddock Carnegie Library.)

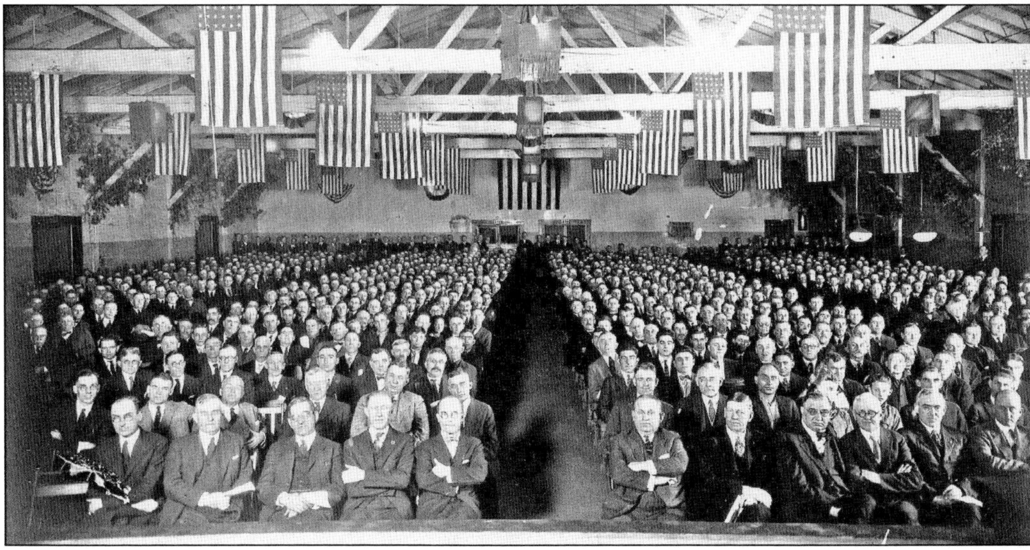

SAFETY AND QUALITY CONTROL. It was not long before safety became a major focus of operations and quality control. Groups of safety officials routinely met to learn the latest in plant safety. One such group is seen here. The setting suggests that safety was now almost a patriotic endeavor as evidenced by the large display of flags. (Courtesy of Braddock Carnegie Library.)

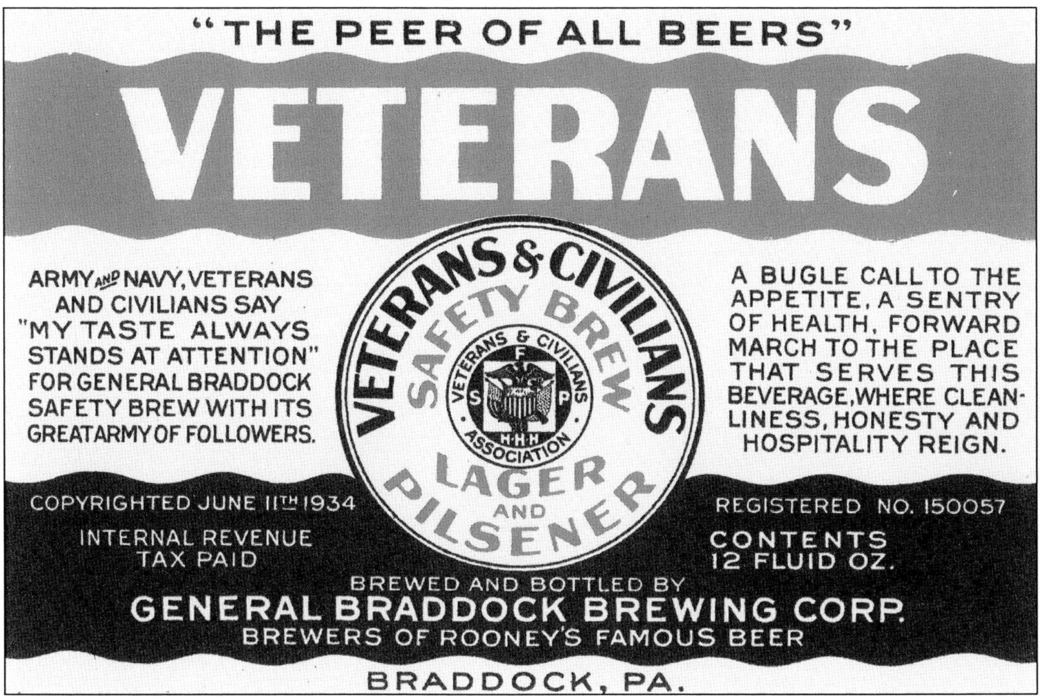

GENERAL BRADDOCK BREWING CORPORATION. Shortly after the beginning of the 20th century, Irish immigrant Dan Rooney opened the Dan Rooney Café and Saloon on Pittsburgh's North Side. Shortly afterwards, he and his son Art founded the General Braddock Brewing Company in Braddock. Rooney's Irish Red Ale and its Veterans and Civilian Lager soon became their best-known brands. In 1933, son Art became the founder of the Pittsburgh Steelers football team. (Courtesy of Joe Kirsch.)

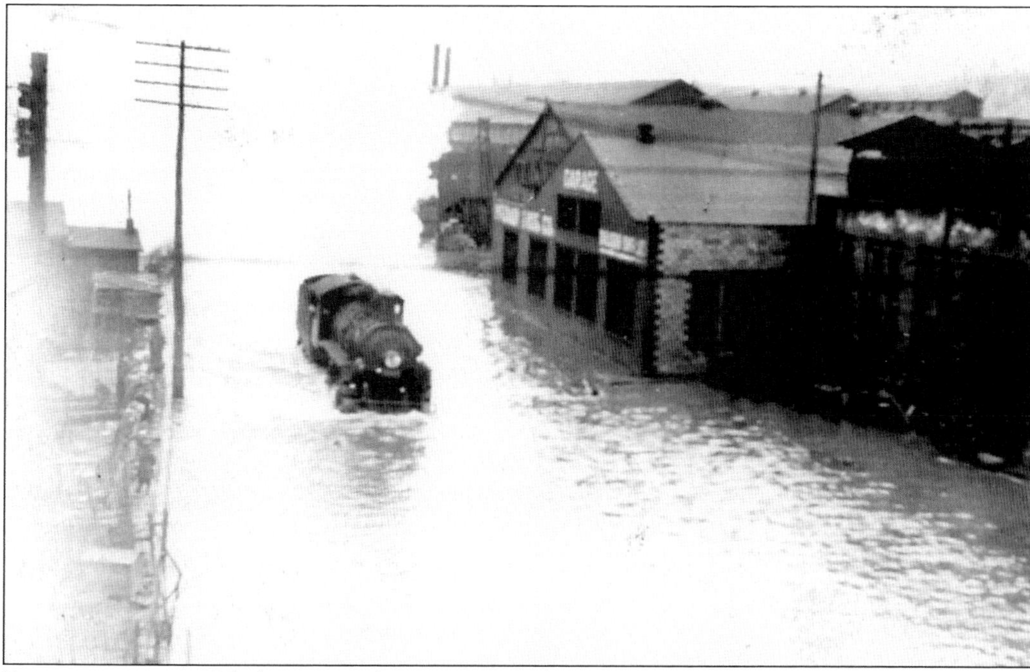

FLOOD OF 1924. While not as devastating as the St. Patrick's Day flood of 1936, the 1924 Monongahela River flood caused significant damage to the Braddock area. With the river cresting at a little over 30 feet, Braddock's Pittsburgh and lake Erie Railroad tracks were flooded. (Courtesy of Braddock Carnegie Library.)

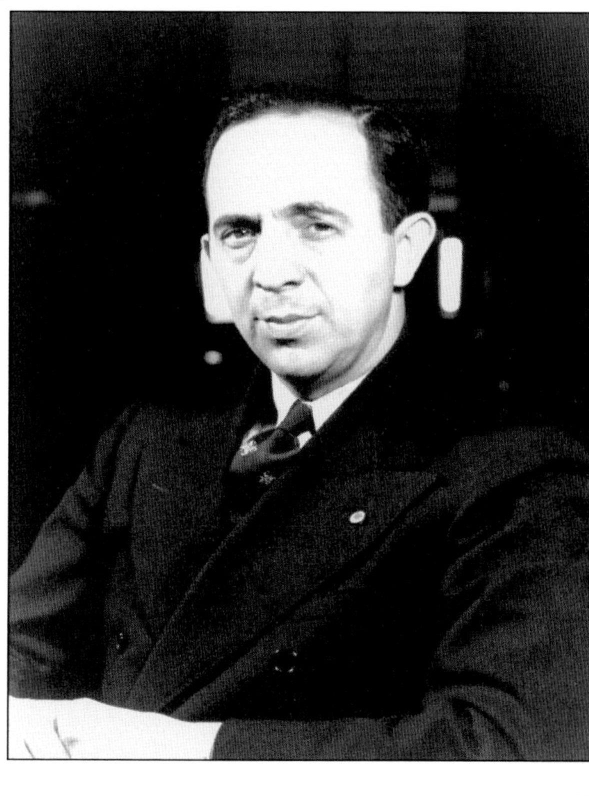

HERB MAGIDSON. Herb Magidson was the winner of the first Academy Award for Best Song in a Motion Picture. He won for the lyrics he wrote for "The Continental" from the 1934 movie *The Gay Divorcee* starring Fred Astaire, Ginger Rogers, and Betty Grable. He was born in Braddock in 1906. His parents owned a second-hand furniture store on Braddock Avenue. Magidson moved to New York in 1928 after graduating from the University of Pittsburgh. He was inducted into the Songwriters Hall of Fame in 1980. (Courtesy of the American Society of Composers, Authors and Publishers.)

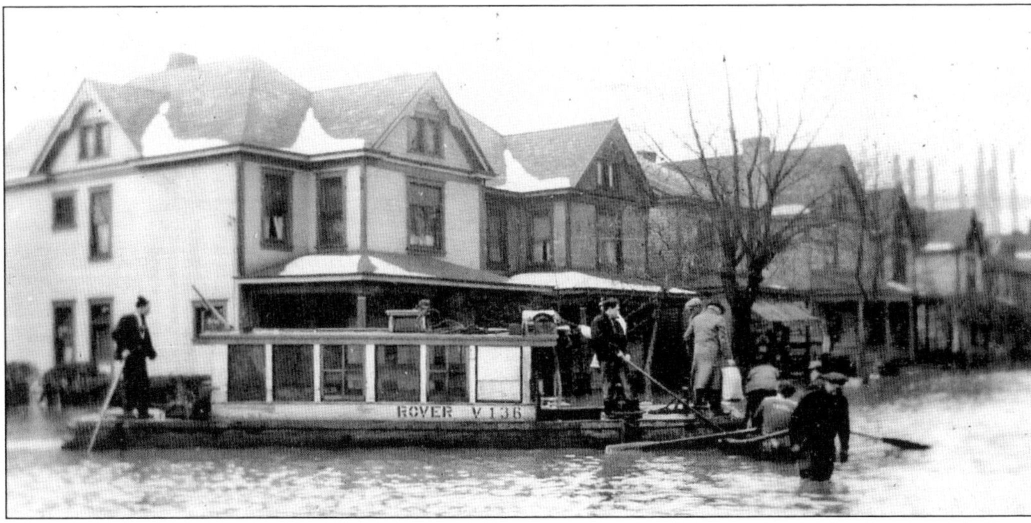

ST. PATRICK'S DAY FLOOD. Braddock streets became waterways in 1936 as the St. Patrick Day's flood took its toll on the area. This flood is remembered as one of the region's most devastating natural disasters. Business throughout the region was brought to a standstill. All along the Monongahela River, railroad and streetcar service fell hours behind schedule with tracks covered by several feet of water. Hundreds of residents were forced from their homes and many motorists were marooned. (Courtesy of Ron Zdrojkowski.)

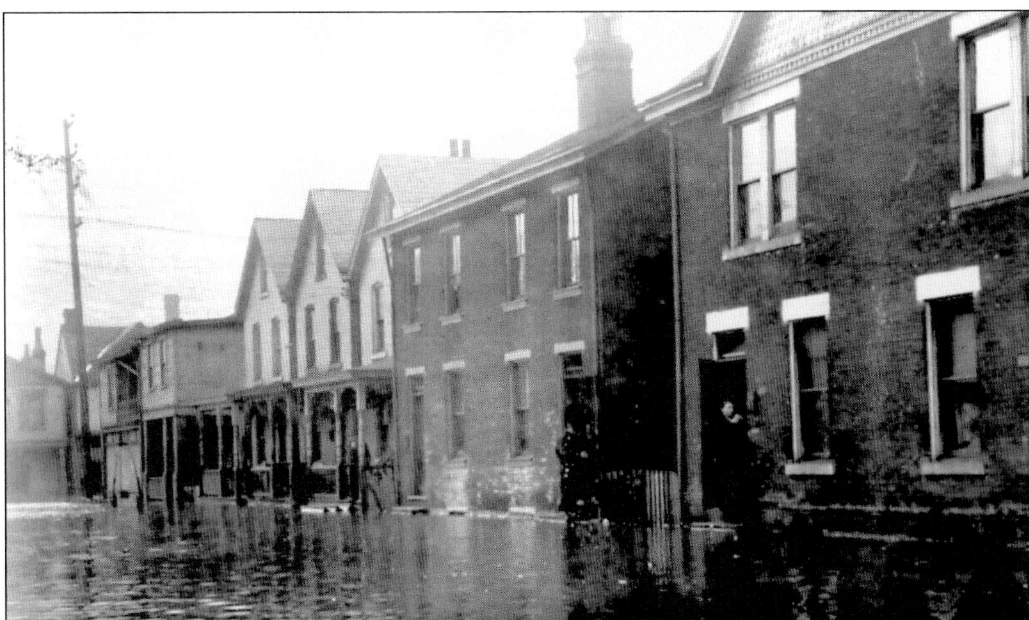

PENN STREET FLOODED. Within days, emergency hospitals were opened in the Braddock brewery and municipal building, where patients were being treated for cuts, bruises, colds, grippe, and similar illnesses by staff from Braddock General Hospital. (Courtesy of Ron Zdrojkowski.)

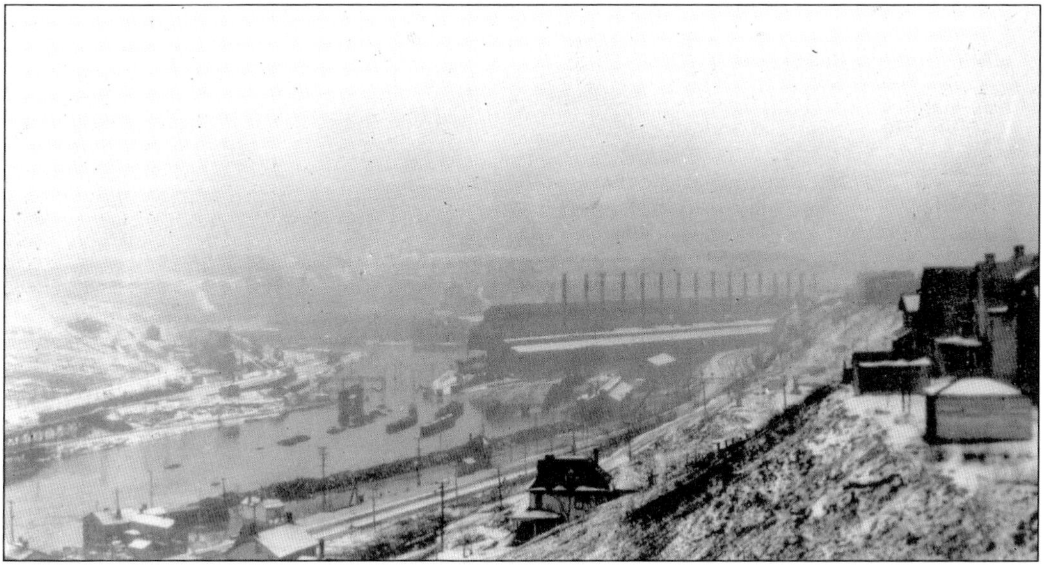

EDGAR THOMSON MILL FLOODED. This view, looking southwest from North Braddock, shows the flood's impact on the Edgar Thomson plant. Braddock Avenue toward East Pittsburgh was flooded for almost one-half mile and automobiles from East Pittsburgh had to be rerouted over Bessemer Terrace. Four thousand people were marooned in two garages in Turtle Creek, where the whole town was under water. (Courtesy of Ron Zdrojkowski.)

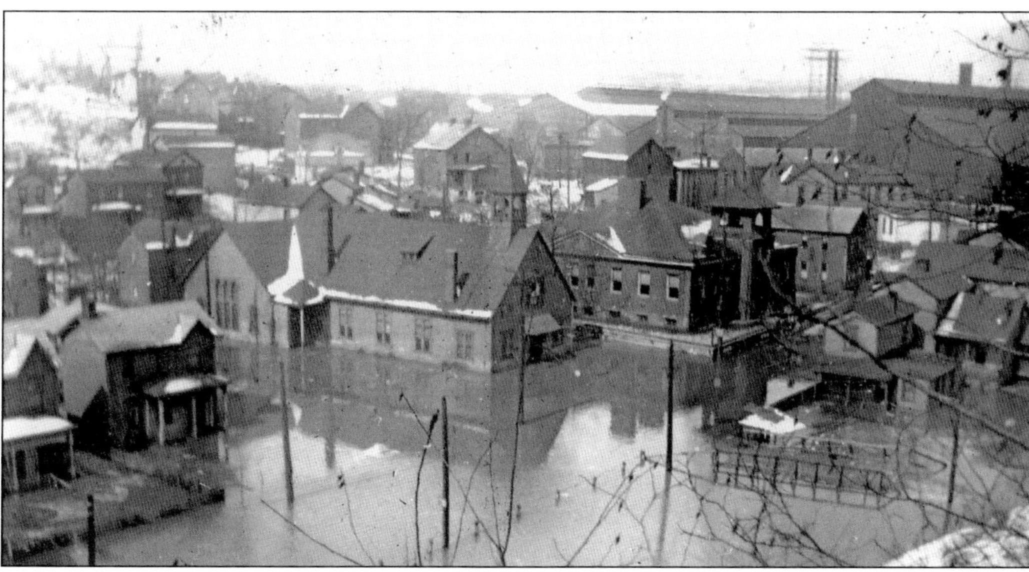

FLOOD OF 1936. The water dramatically impacted the entire community around the Edgar Thomson plant. Buildings and homes were seemingly swallowed. As reports from around the Monongahela Valley were collected, it was determined that the communities of Braddock and Homestead were two of thc hardest hit. (Courtesy of Ron Zdrojkowski.)

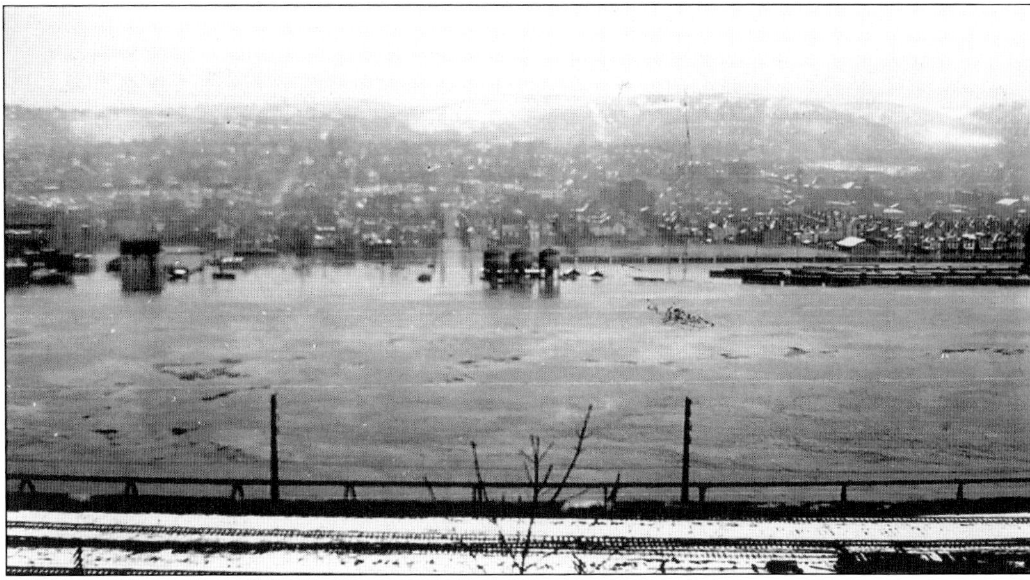

BRADDOCK FLOODED. This scene of Braddock viewed from the Duquesne side of the Monongahela River shows the flood's devastating impact. Industrial activity along the river came close to a standstill. A few days after the flood, Braddock burgess James H. Rose reported that Braddock was taking care of 1,300 homeless residents, while another 1,000 were being cared for in the homes of friends and relatives. (Courtesy of Ron Zdrojkowski.)

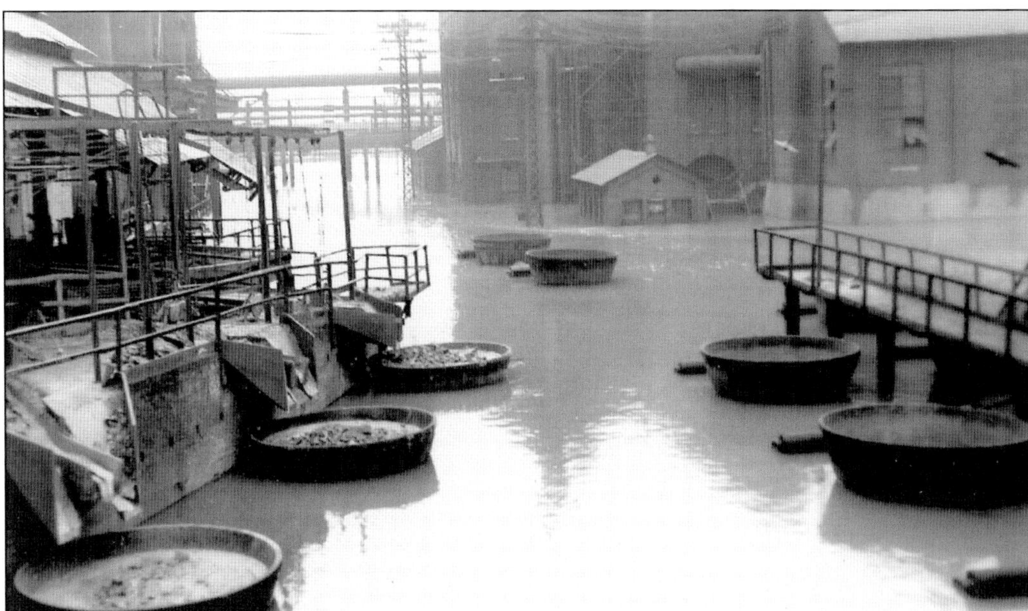

INSIDE EDGAR THOMSON. Edgar Thomson Steel Works's H Furnace cinder run is seen flooded in this image. In mills and factories along the Monongahela River, laborers were rushing to rebuild the flooded sections in order to fill the orders that were critical to the local economy. It took days for the full impact of the damage to be assessed and for work to commence in an effort to return all parts of the plant to working order. (Courtesy of Ron Zdrojkowski.)

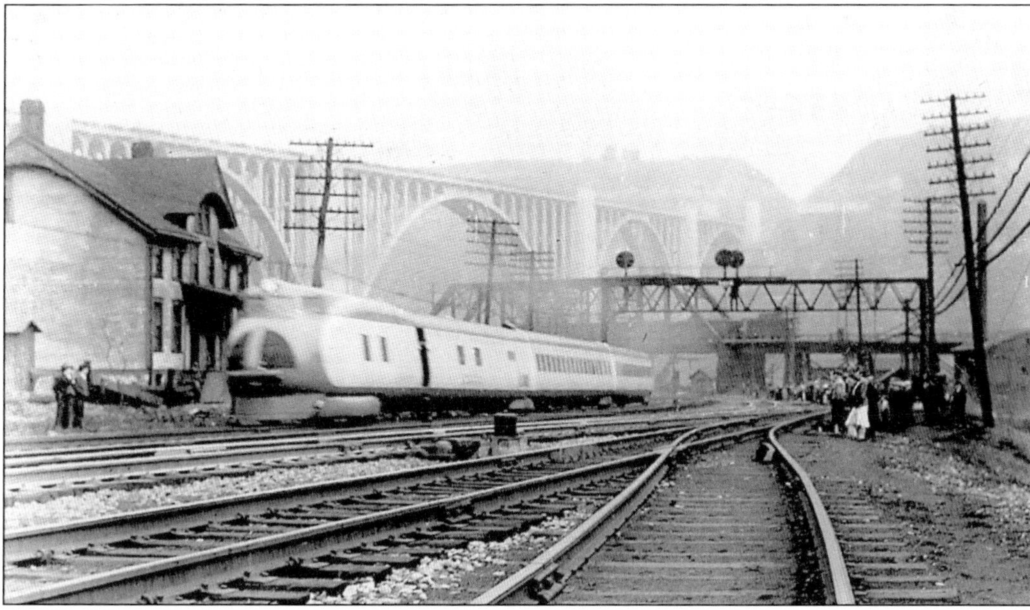

UNION PACIFIC STREAMLINE FLASH. The Union Pacific Streamline Flash was a modern, sophisticated passenger train capable of speeds of up to 100 miles per hour. It is seen here in this 1934 image as it speeds along tracks from East Pittsburgh into North Braddock heading toward the Braddock stop. The George Westinghouse Memorial Bridge can be seen in the background. (Courtesy of Braddock Carnegie Library.)

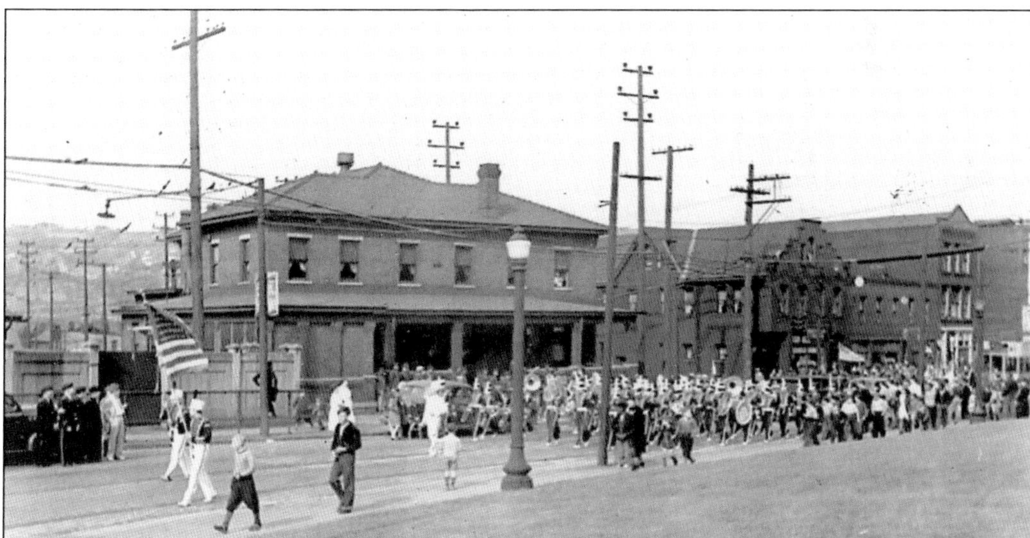

MEMORIAL DAY PARADE. Braddock's citizens have always loved a parade and, over the years, images of many of these parades suggest much about the people and the context of the community in which they resided. This picture of the 1938 Memorial Day parade captures both the people and background. (Courtesy of Braddock Carnegie Library.)

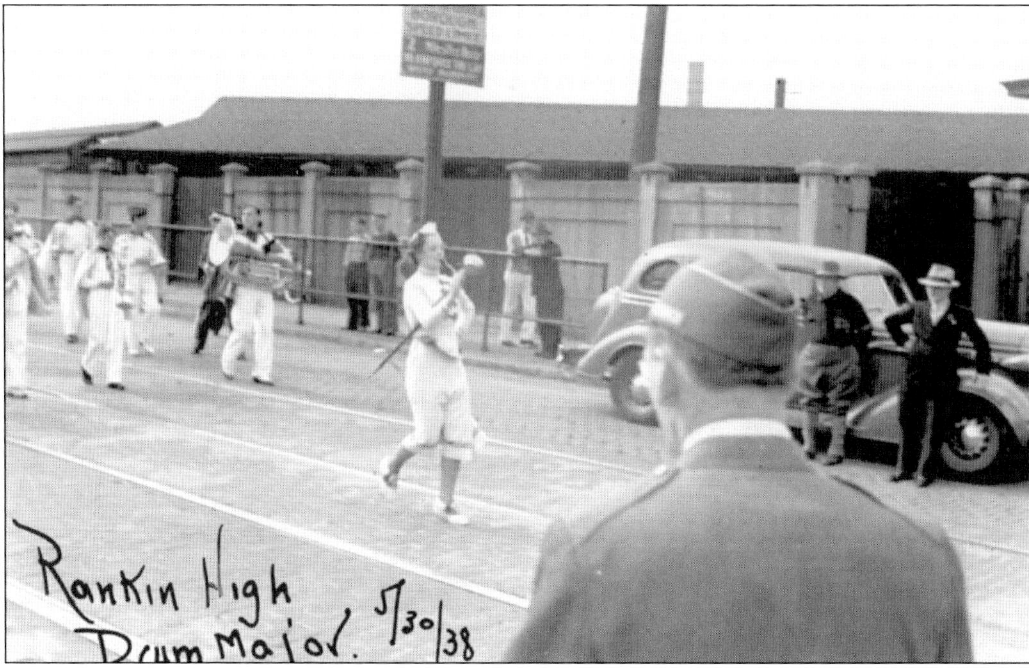

RANKIN HIGH SCHOOL BAND. Rankin High School's drum major leads the band through the streets of North Braddock during the 1938 Memorial Day parade. (Courtesy of Braddock Carnegie Library.)

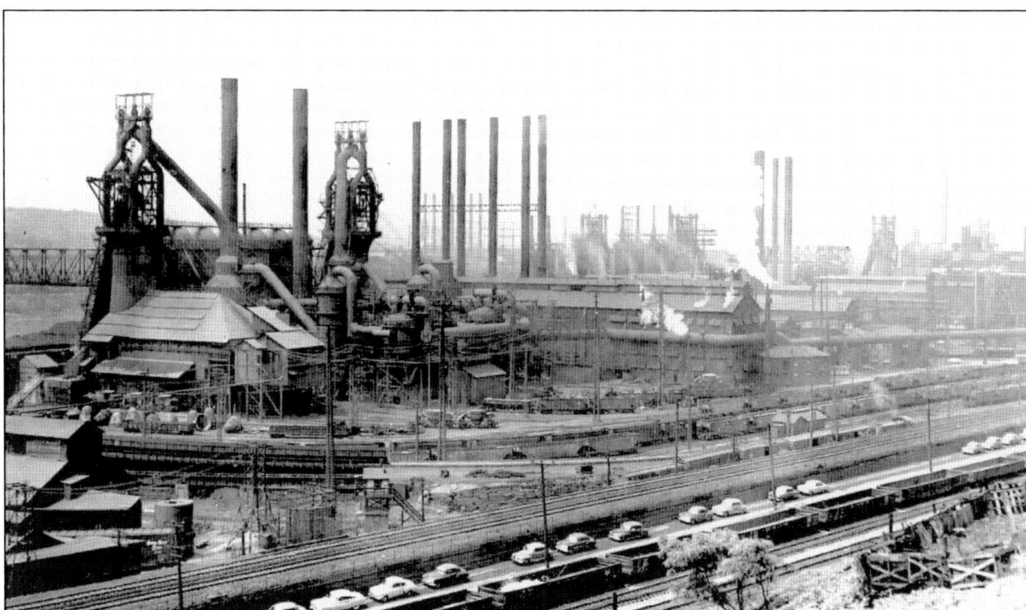

CARRIE FURNACE DURING THE 1950S. Carrie Furnace began operations in 1884 with one blast furnace. In 1900, a second furnace was brought on line, just in time for the company's merger into the Carnegie Steel Company. Once the ink was dry on the sale, two additional furnaces were installed. By 1907, additional furnaces had been added bringing the total to seven. (Courtesy of the Rivers of Steel National Heritage Area.)

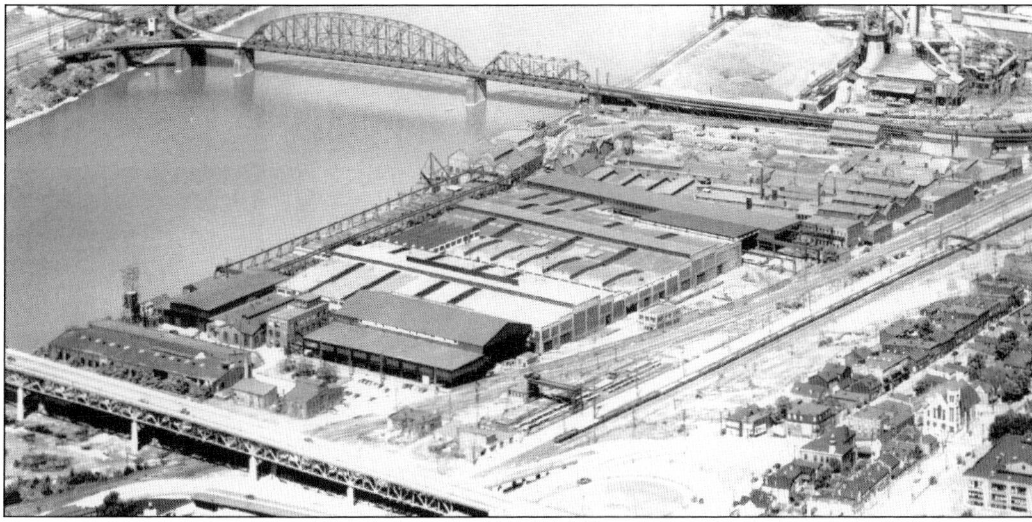

BETHLEHEM STEEL-RANKIN. Howard H. McClintic and Charles D. Marshall formed McClintic and Marshall Construction Company in 1901. Operating their main plant out of Rankin, the company became one of America's largest independent steel fabricating firms. Some of their most notable projects include the Panama Canal lock gates, the Golden Gate Bridge, and the University of Pittsburgh's Cathedral of Learning. In 1931, the company was acquired by Charles Schwab's Bethlehem Steel Company. (Courtesy of the Rivers of Steel National Heritage Area.)

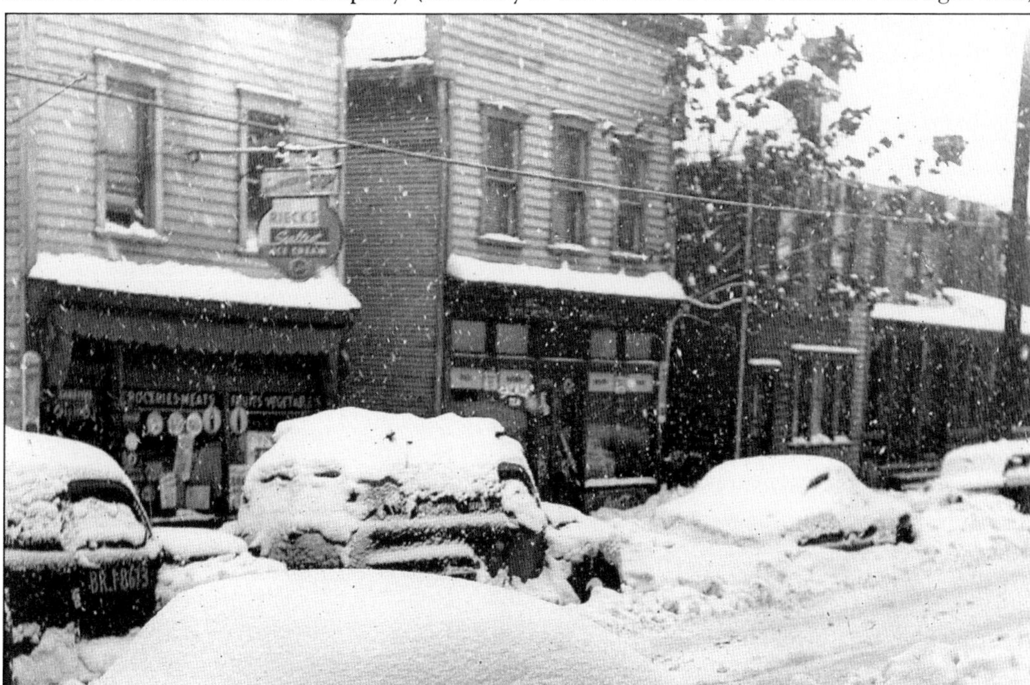

THANKSGIVING DAY RECORD SNOW. This Washington Street snow scene shows the situation shortly after the record 1950 snow. It was the snowstorm that made history when more than 30 inches of snow fell over the Thanksgiving holiday. As a result, travel came to a standstill in Braddock and most Pittsburgh neighborhoods. Businesses and schools were closed for days. (Courtesy of Ron Zdrojkowski.)

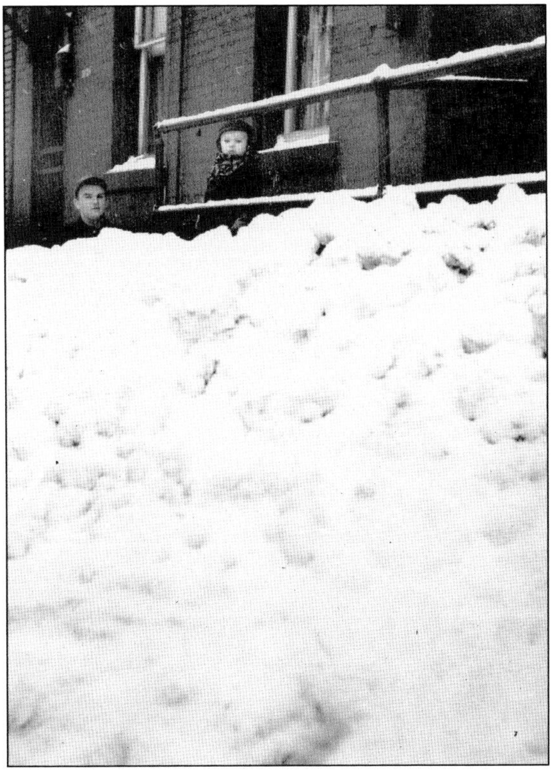

Milk Deliveries Hampered. Clean up of the snow seemed impossible on Cherry Way, as there were precious few places to put it all. Families with children panicked when milk deliveries were hampered. The army was called in to use heavy equipment to clean streets from vital areas. George Vichinsky and his son, Kenneth, are seen here behind a deep snow pile in front of their home on Cherry Way. (Courtesy of Ron Zdrojkowski.)

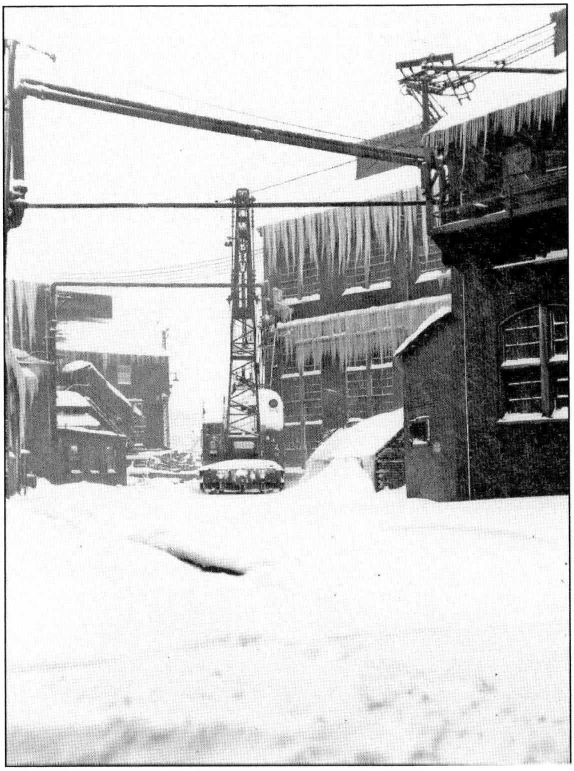

Snow Stops Mills and Factories. Operators tried desperately to remove enough snow to enable their mills to get back to normal production. The larger problem, however, was that rail transportation was so dramatically impacted that raw material could not be brought in and finished products could not be shipped out. U.S. Steel operations along the Monongahela River were virtually shut down with only minimal crews available to bank blast furnace fires. (Courtesy of Ron Zdrojkowski.)

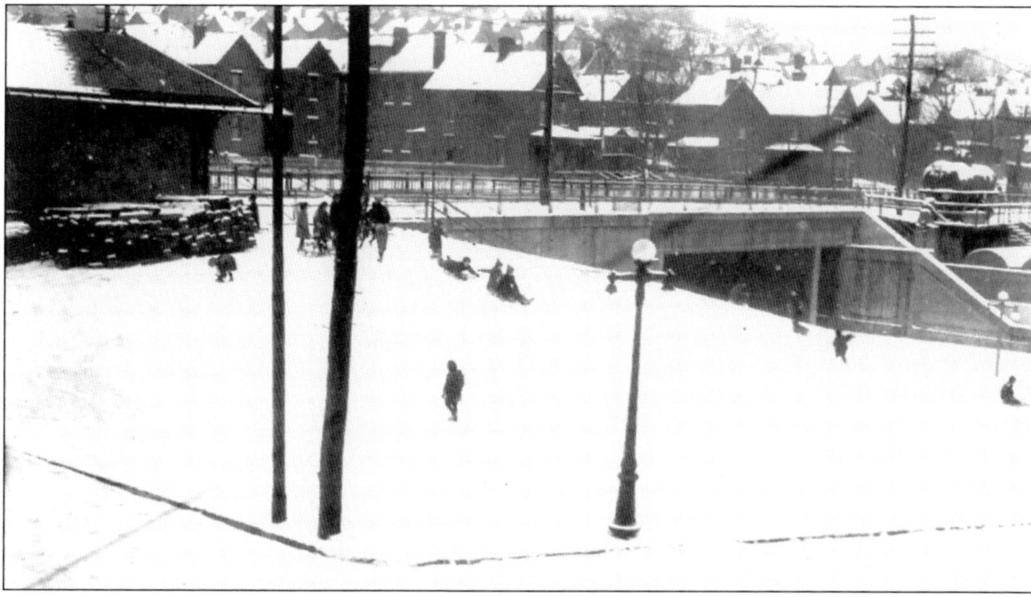

COPELAND STATION WITH SNOW AND KIDS SLEDDING. The Braddock area was well served by railroads, and a number of well-used train stations were developed in the area over time. Seen here is Copeland Station, named after the training camp that occupied the area during the Civil War. Located at the head of Fourth Street at the boundary between Braddock and North Braddock, this Pennsylvania Railroad station was an important passenger stop. (Courtesy of Braddock Carnegie Library.)

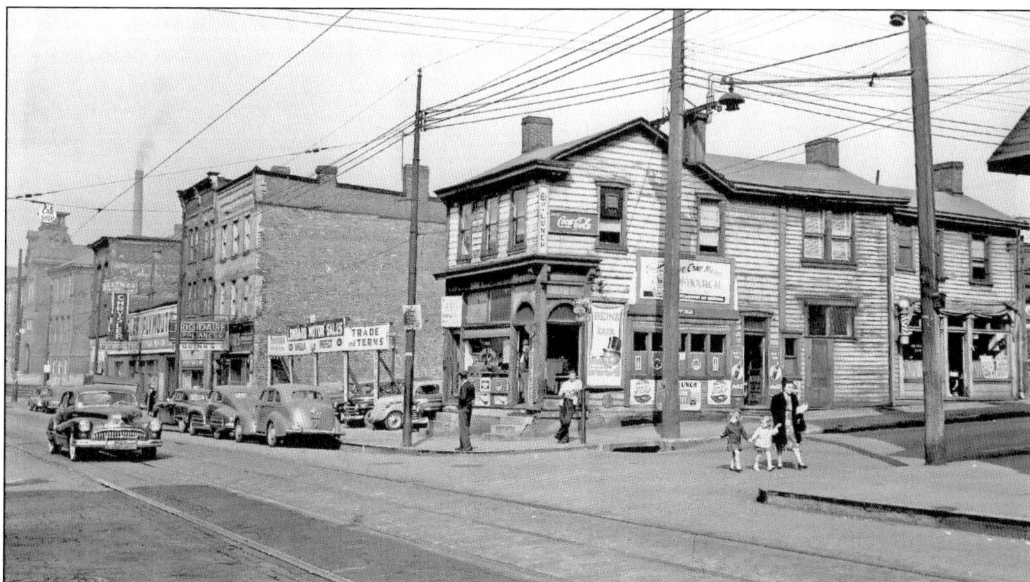

SIXTH STREET AND BRADDOCK AVENUE. The corner of Braddock Avenue and Sixth Street was a major gateway into and out of the community and a good place to shop. A few of the commercial enterprises that can be seen in this image from the late 1940s include the Sixth Street Quick Lunch, Litman Motor Company, Lombard Motors, and Quinn's Frigidaire Appliances. To the west (far left), the Hamilton Building Third Ward School can be seen. (Courtesy of Braddock Carnegie Library.)

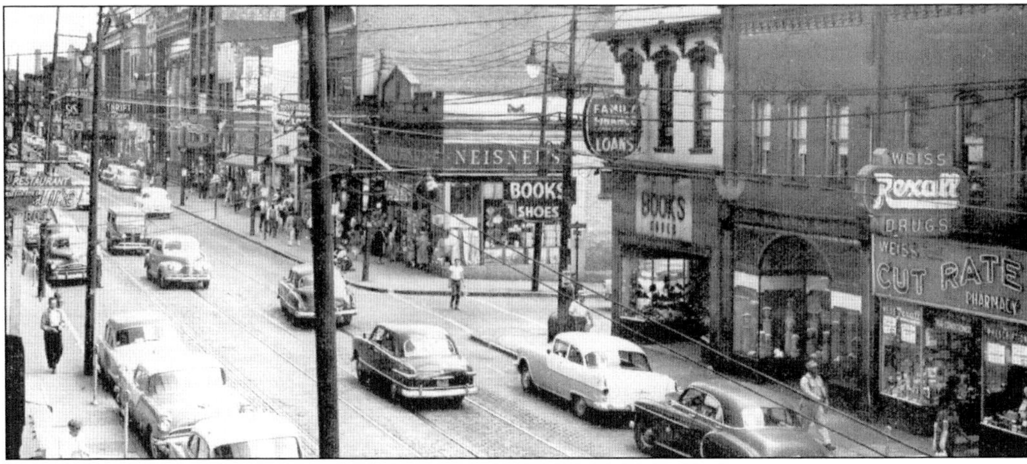

BRADDOCK AVENUE BUSINESS WAS BOOMING. Braddock Avenue business was booming in the late 1950s as can be seen in this image looking southeast near Ninth Street. Parking for shoppers was at a premium as automobile and pedestrian traffic pass stores like Ellis Hat Shop, Weiss Cut Rate Pharmacy, Neisner Brothers, Family Finance, book and shoe stores, and restaurants. (Courtesy of Braddock Carnegie Library.)

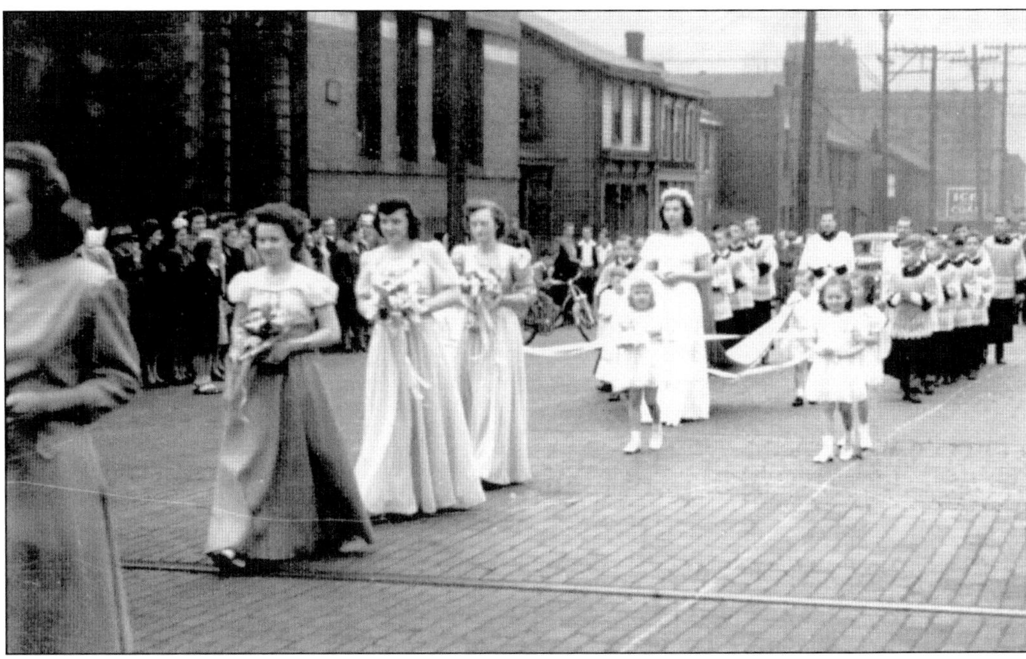

SIXTH STREET PAGEANT. Sacred Heart Church and its school kept the southern side of Sixth Street a beehive of activity. During religious holidays the street was often filled with processions like the May Crowning procession shown here during the late 1940s. Sophie Balawajder Mieldar is May Queen. (Courtesy of Mimi [Szwarc] and Joe O'Donnell.)

SACRED HEART SCHOOL. Sacred Heart Church was one of many churches in the area that served a particular nationality. In the case of Sacred Heart, its primary congregation was formed among those of Polish origin. Seen here is a procession exiting the doorway of the Sacred Heart School during the late 1940s. (Courtesy of Ron Zdrojkowski.)

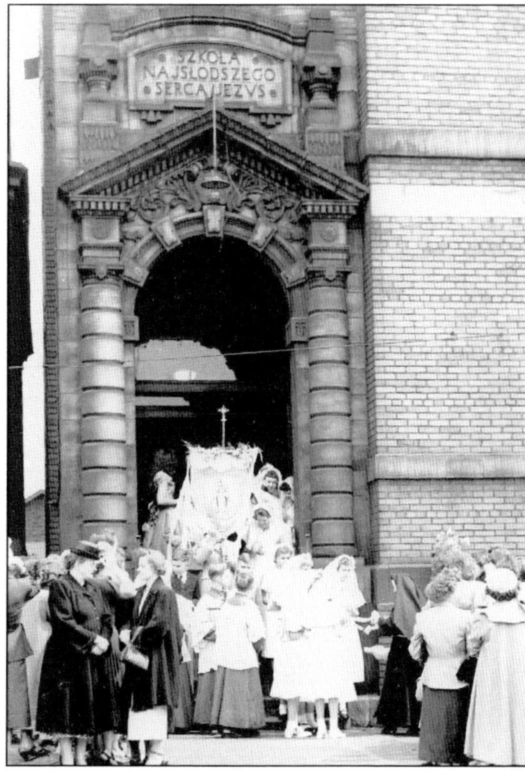

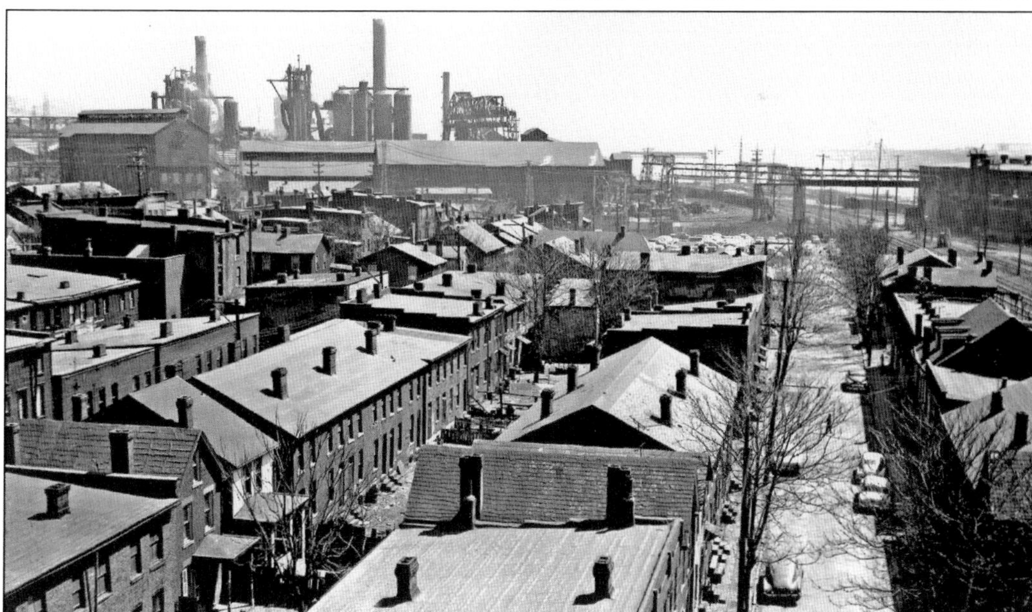

BRADDOCK BOTTOMS. Residential housing development in Braddock followed much the same pattern as had occurred in other mill towns. The earliest private and corporate-sponsored housing was built just outside of the mills. This image offers a glimpse of 1950s era housing conditions as they appeared just outside Edgar Thomson Plant in an area of Braddock known as the Bottoms. (Courtesy of Braddock Carnegie Library.)

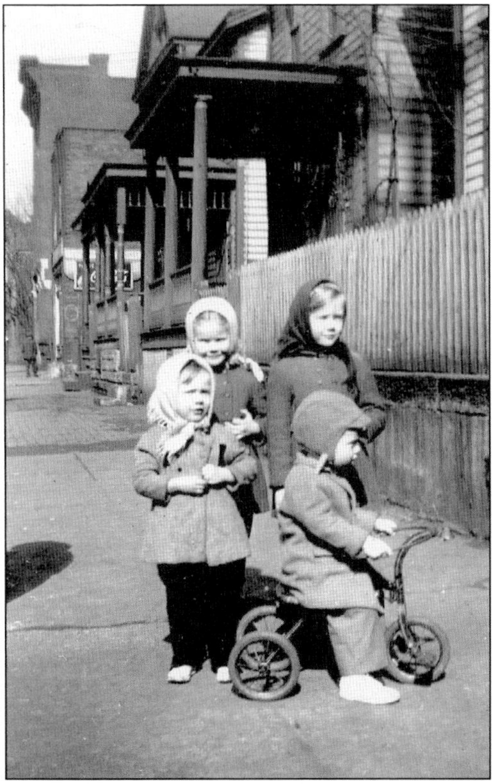

SIDEWALK PLAY. During the late 1940s and early 1950s, a period of economic transition occurred that allowed many families to begin moving out of town toward new suburban communities. Some neighborhood enclaves of extended family remained however. Sidewalks and side yards were still fun places to play, as parents visited with neighbors and everyone watched over children like, from left to right, Vivian, Gail, Jean, and Gary Krawczewicz. (Courtesy of Ron Zdrojkowski.)

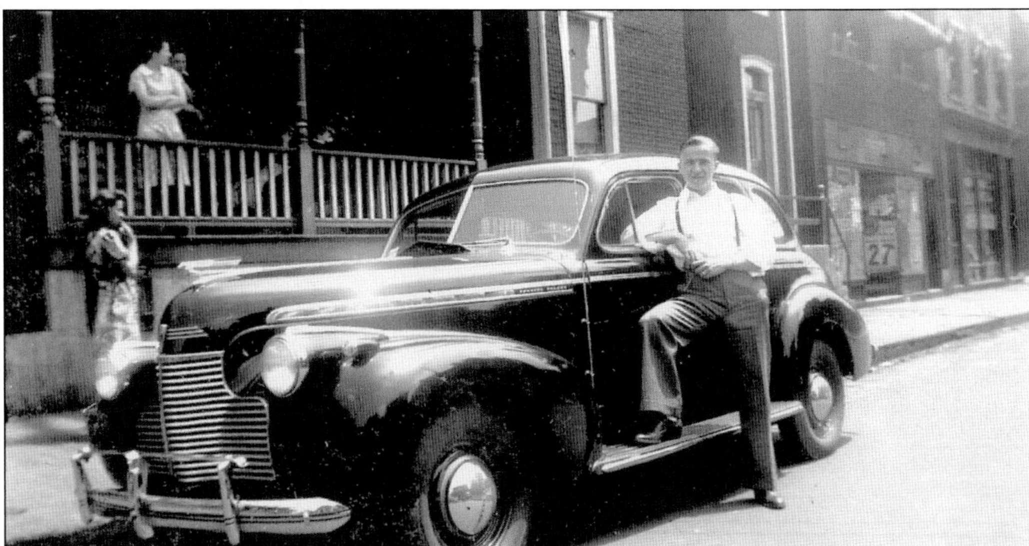

BIG CARS AND BIG DREAMS. After World War II, a period of prosperity offered consumers the chance to buy products that had previously been rationed or in short supply. Economic good fortune also allowed a whole generation of consumers to buy new automobiles, or perhaps, become owners of their very first cars. Edward Krawczewicz is seen here with his prized automobile. Helen, Julian, and Victoria Krawczewicz are seen on the porch and Jane Zdrojkowski stands on the sidewalk near their homes on Washington Street. (Courtesy of Ron Zdrojkowski.)

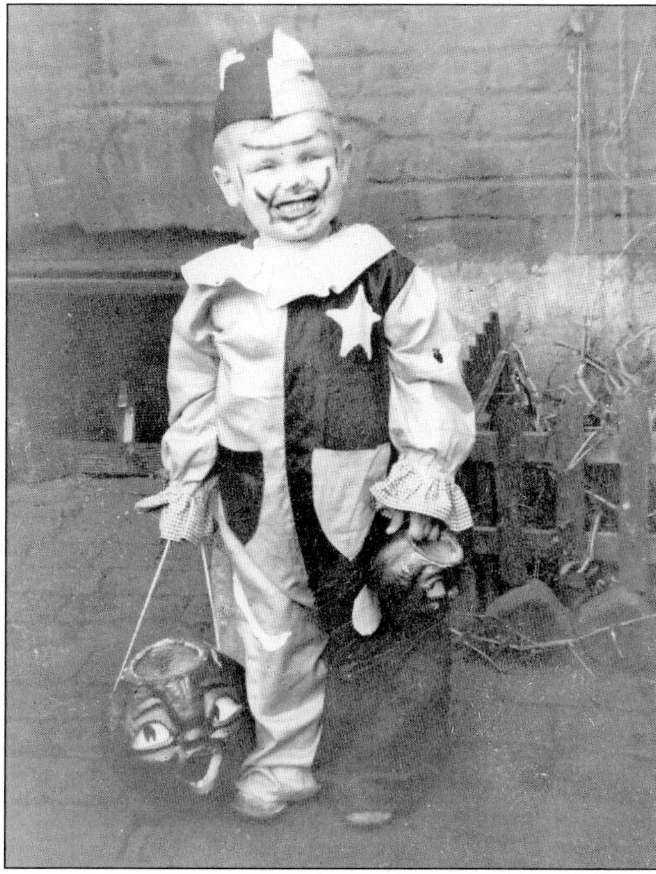

Trick or Treat. Kids were kids in the late 1940s and Halloween was an important holiday. Young Kenneth Vichinsky is seen here in his costume. (Courtesy of Ron Zdrojkowski.)

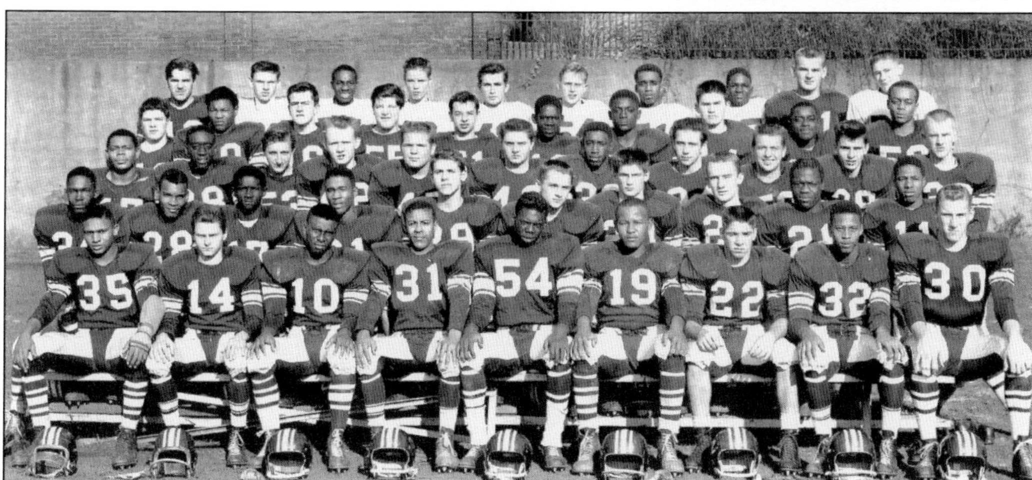

Braddock Football Team of 1957. Braddock High School had a proud football heritage. The first team began play in 1903. It was not until 1954, however, that their team and its coach would reach for almost every record in the books. That year, Chuck Klausing became the team's new coach. Klausing managed to do the impossible by creating six undefeated teams, winning six Class A championships, and creating a new record by putting together a 56 -game unbeaten streak. The 1957 team set a school record. (Courtesy of Chuck Klausing.)

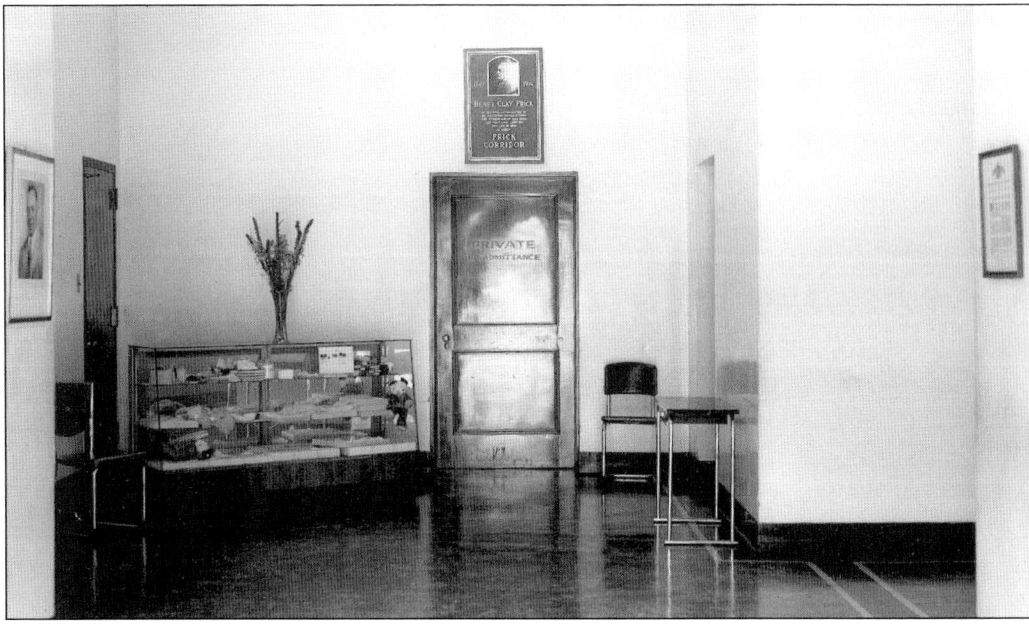

BRADDOCK GENERAL HOSPITAL, FRICK WING. The Mills mansion was demolished in 1940 to make room for the addition of a new building connecting the east and west wings. The connecting corridor, called the Frick Corridor, was completed in 1941. Upon completion of the new wing, the hospital was now able to boast 147 beds. (Courtesy of UPMC Braddock Medical Center.)

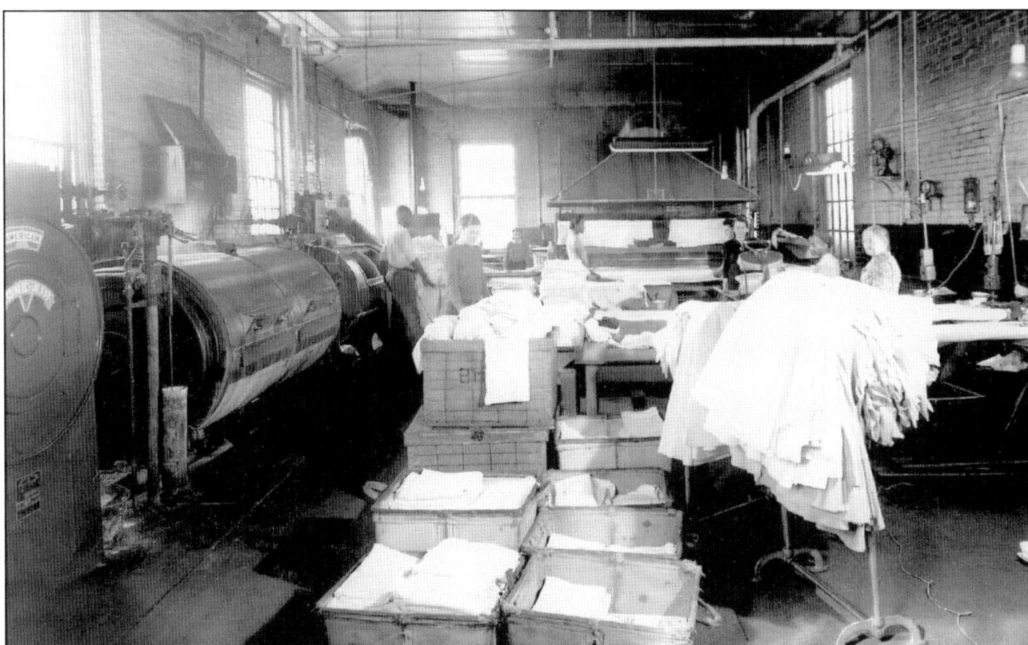

CLEAN LINEN. Braddock General Hospital, like most hospitals in the region, evolved in an effort to allow the hospital to become as self-sufficient as possible. This included construction and operation of full laundry services. (Courtesy of UPMC Braddock Medical Center.)

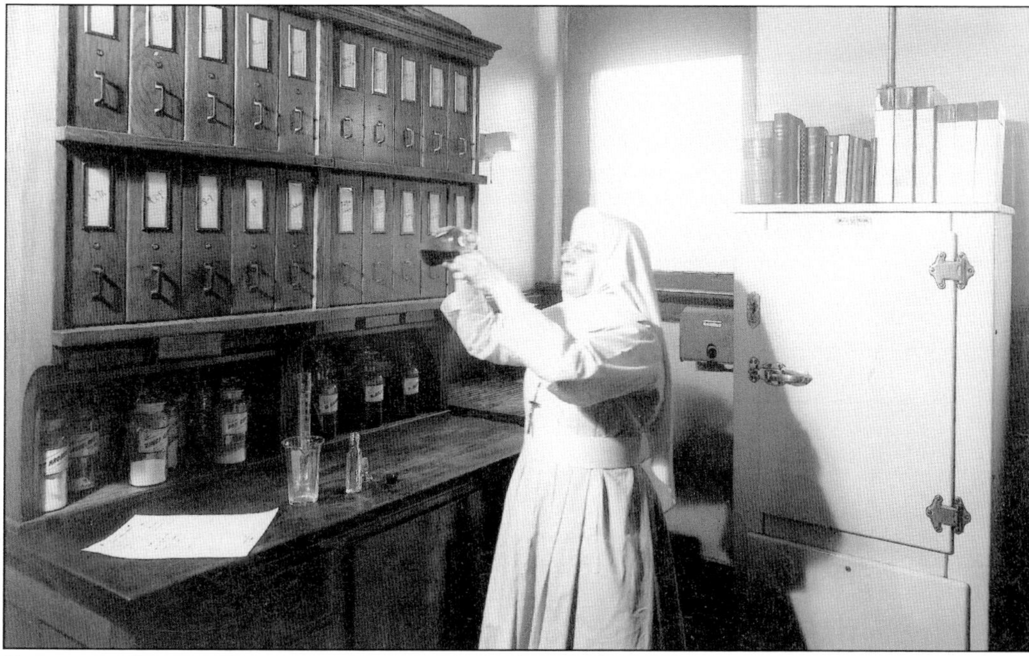

Sisters of Divine Providence. In 1935, the hospital signed an agreement with the Sisters of Divine Providence to manage the hospital. Sr. Mary Aniceta was appointed superintendent and served in that capacity until 1952. This image shows one of the nuns working in the hospital dispensary. (Courtesy of UPMC Braddock Medical Center.)

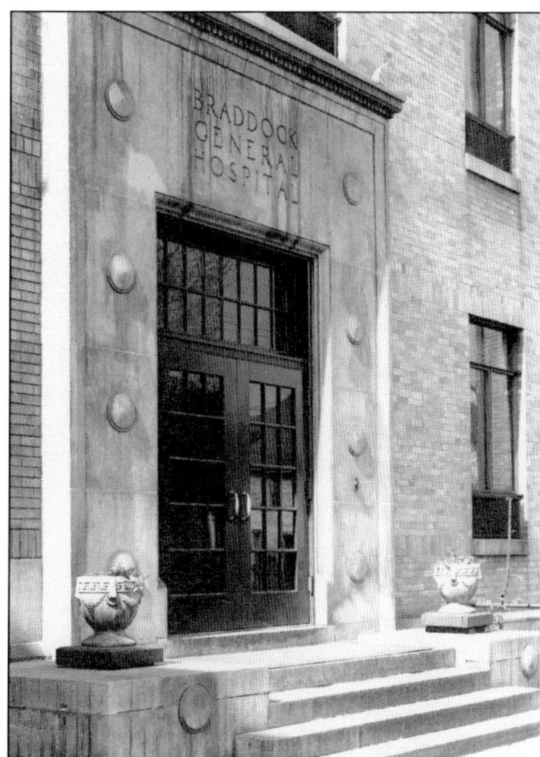

Braddock General Hospital. The hospital's entrance was both practical and functional as can be seen in this image from 1967. (Courtesy of UPMC Braddock Medical Center.)

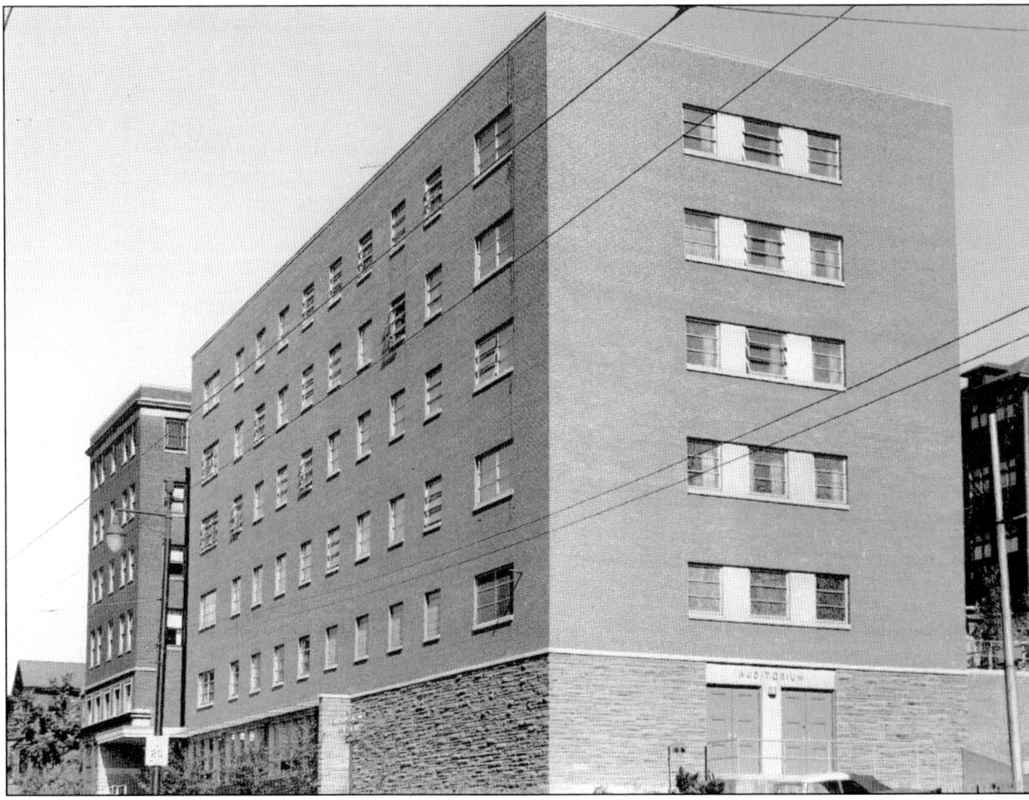

BRADDOCK GENERAL HOSPITAL SCHOOL OF NURSING. In 1955, the hospital's second nursing residence was constructed. The building was a six-story structure, capable of housing 64 student nurses, several nuns, and housemothers. An auditorium, classrooms, and a lounge were included. This view of the school of nursing on Braddock Avenue was taken around 1974. The last class of nursing students graduated in 1972. (Courtesy of UPMC Braddock Medical Center.)

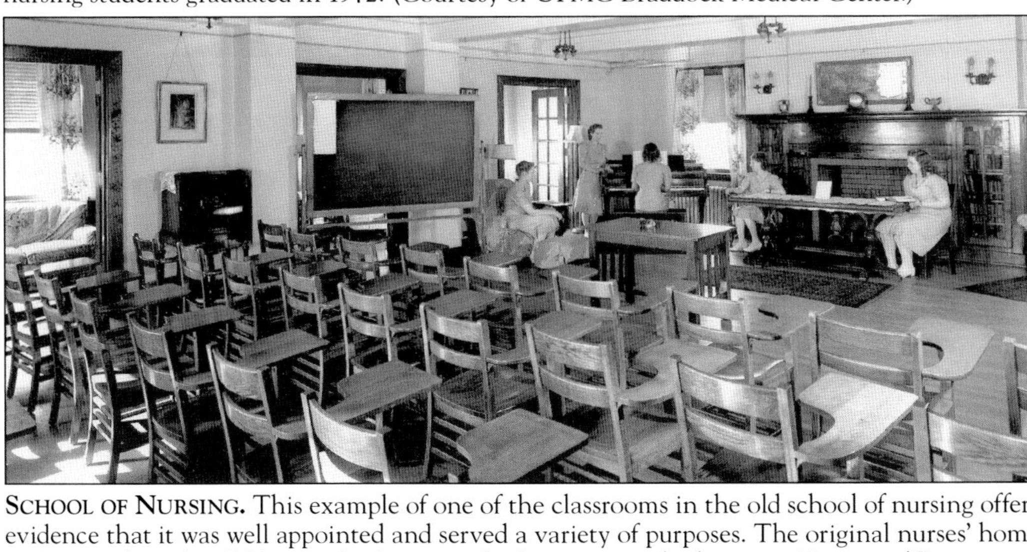

SCHOOL OF NURSING. This example of one of the classrooms in the old school of nursing offers evidence that it was well appointed and served a variety of purposes. The original nurses' home was opened in the 1920s, at which time it had a capacity for housing 48 nurses.(Courtesy of UPMC Braddock Medical Center.)

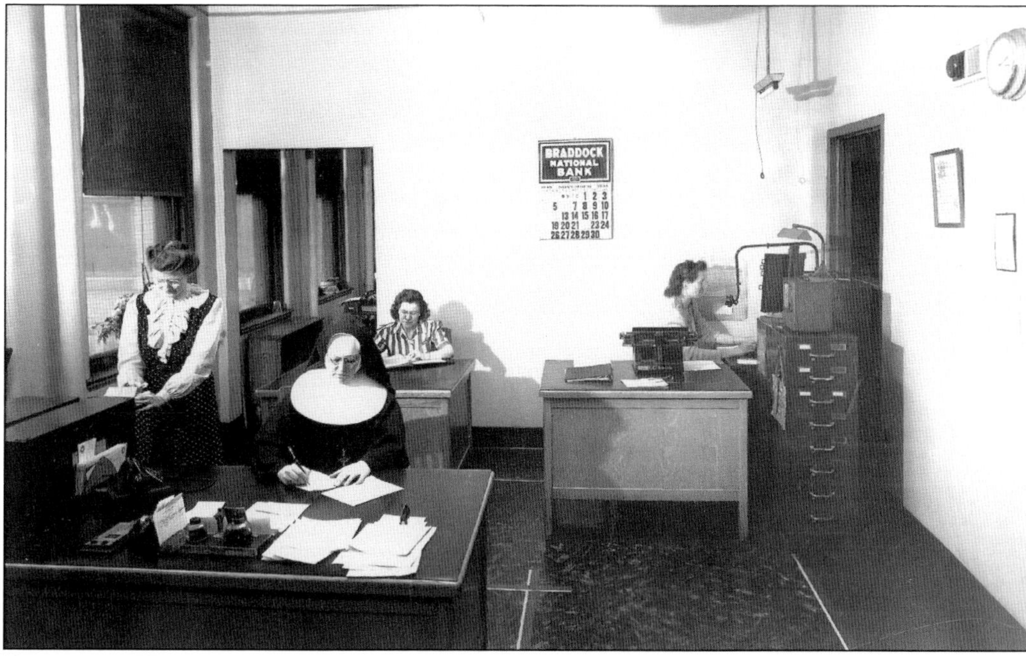

BRADDOCK HOSPITAL ADMINISTRATION. Hospital administration and routine office work were much simpler in the past. The hospital's administrative office staff and facility is seen here in this 1945 scene during the period in which the Sisters of Divine Providence managed the facility. (Courtesy of UPMC Braddock Medical Center.)

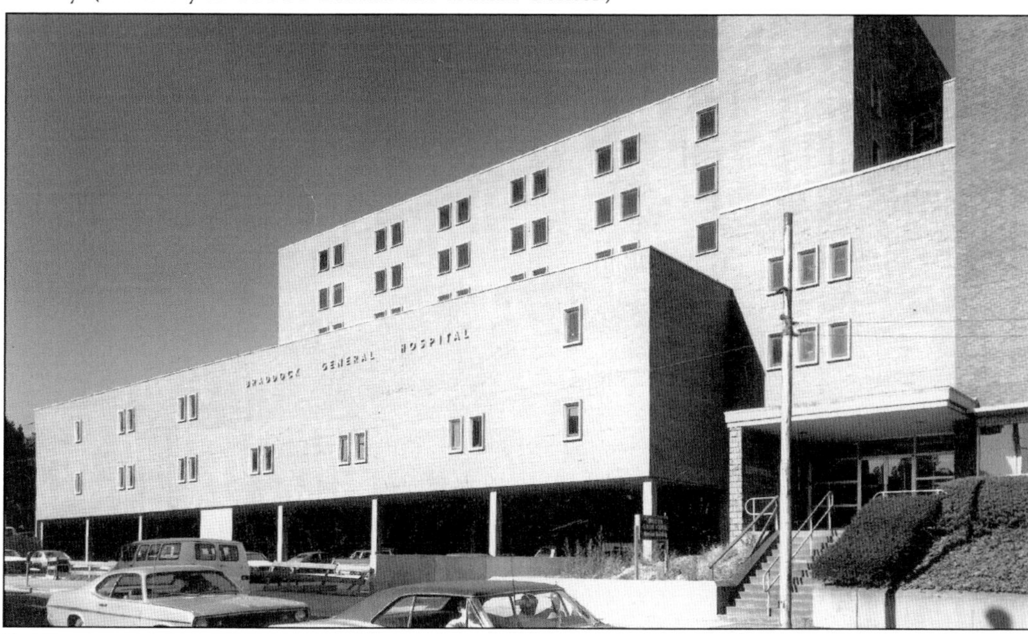

BRADDOCK MEDICAL CENTER. In October 1973, the hospital's new $10 million, 150,000-square-foot addition was opened. The facility doubled the amount of space in the hospital and included acute, critical care and pediatric care units, semi-private patient rooms, and many new staff and visitor amenities. In total, another 138 new beds were added. (Courtesy of UPMC Braddock Medical Center.)

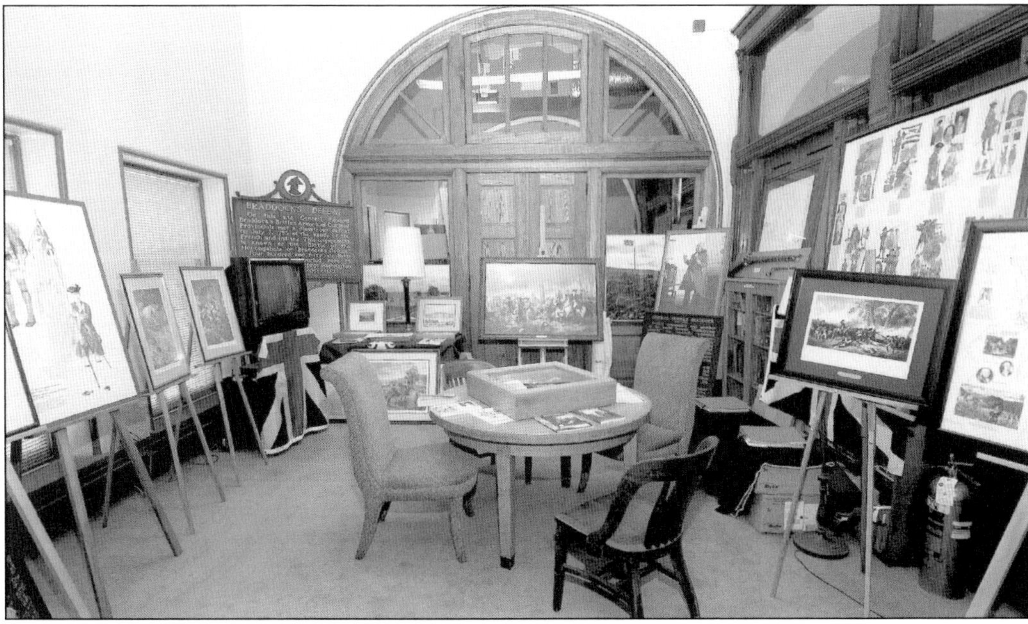

French and Indian War Museum. In 1995, a special 240th anniversary celebration of the Battle of Braddock was conceived as the Braddock's Field Historical Society began to explore interest in creating a historical destination and history tourism program. As a result of an outpouring of interest, a museum and gallery dedicated to the French and Indian War was developed within the library. It officially opened during January 1999. (Author's collection.)

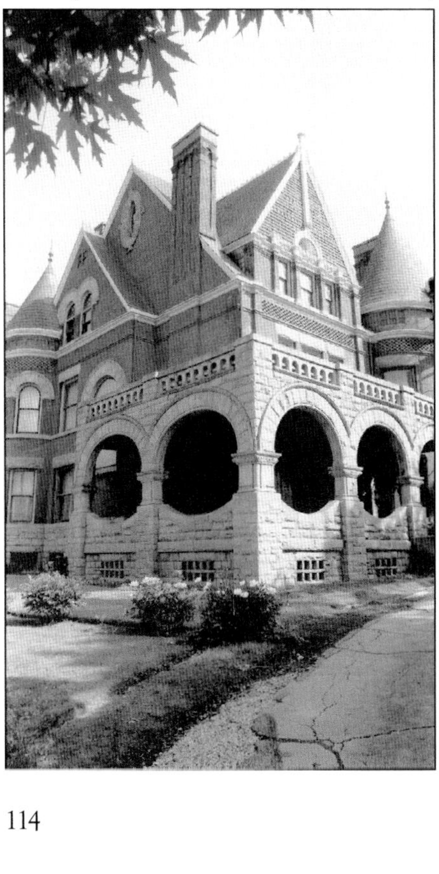

Schwab Mansion. Charles M. Schwab was known as "a dollar a day stake driver" working for Andrew Carnegie and ending up as a president of Carnegie Steel Corporation and later U.S. Steel Corporation. The Schwab Mansion was designed by Pittsburgh architect Frederick Osterling and built between 1890 and 1893, the year that Schwab married Emma Dinkey. Today the mansion sits majestically within view of Frank Vittor's statue of George Washington, both exemplars of artistic achievement. (Author's collection.)

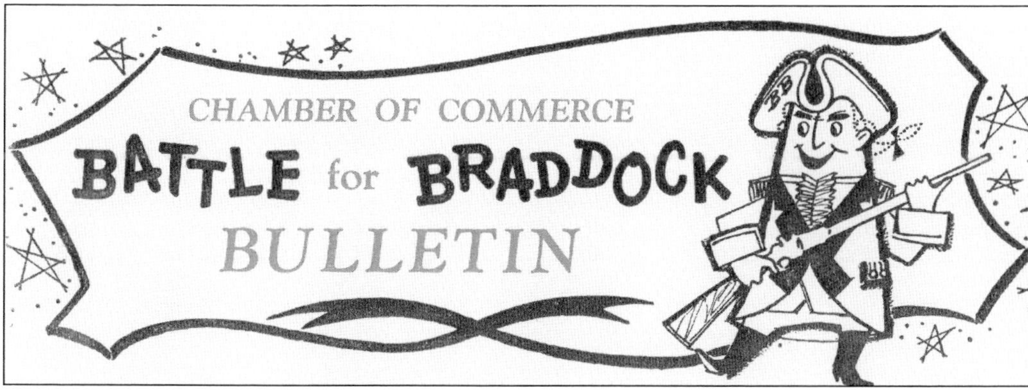

GREATER BRADDOCK CHAMBER OF COMMERCE. Organizations representing Braddock's businesses have a history extending back to before the dawn of the 19th century. The Braddock Merchants' Association had offices at the Carnegie Club. The organization later changed its name to the Braddock Board of Commerce, and still later, to the Greater Braddock Chamber of Commerce. The chamber's *Battle for Braddock* news bulletin masthead is seen here. Buster Braddock was the chamber's mascot. (Courtesy of Braddock Carnegie Library.)

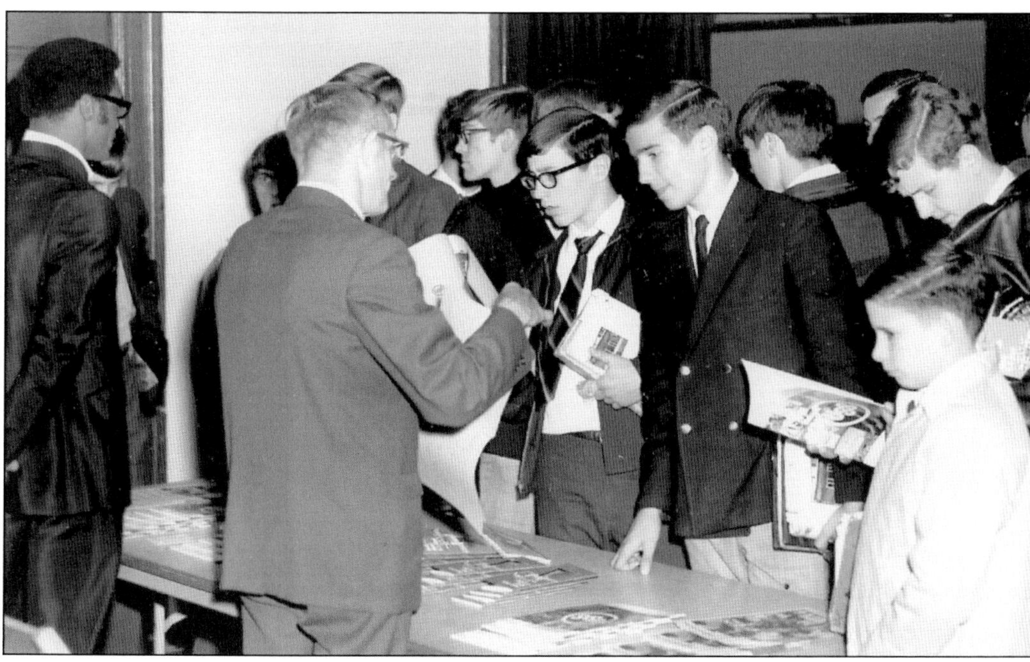

CHAMBER CAREER DAY WITH YOUNG MEN. During the 1960s and 1970s the Greater Braddock Chamber of Commerce worked to inform teenagers about careers and job opportunities with local business. Shown here are representatives of U.S. Steel Corporation interacting with interested young men. (Courtesy of Braddock Carnegie Library.)

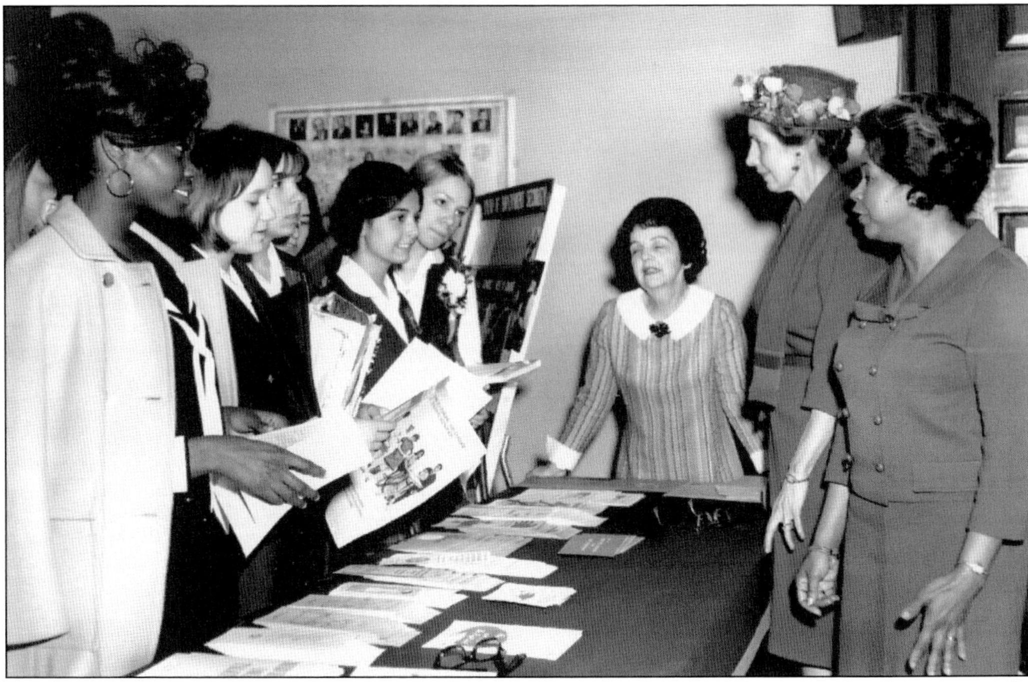

CHAMBER CAREER DAY WITH YOUNG WOMEN. Opportunities for young women were also widely promoted. Chamber representatives are seen here presenting information on a wide range of career choices. (Courtesy of Braddock Carnegie Library.)

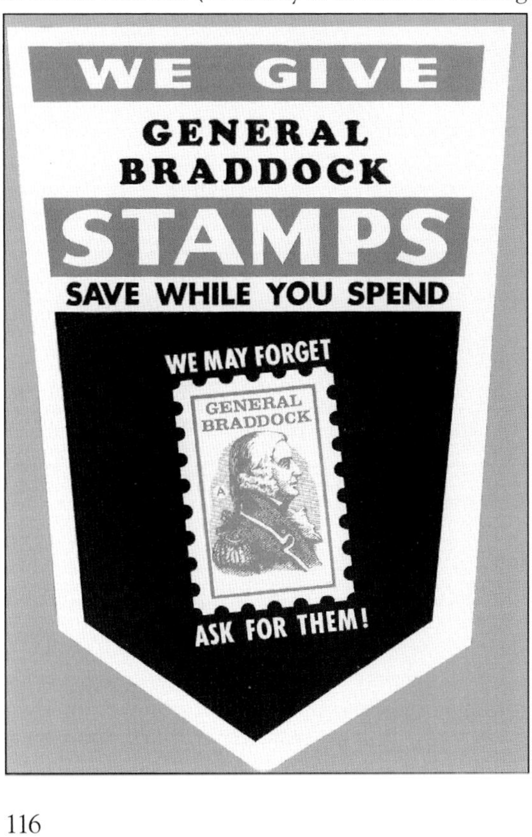

GENERAL BRADDOCK STAMP PENNANT. The trading stamp phenomena hit the United States during the 1950s and 1960s as supermarkets exploded into virtually every community. In an effort to attract and retain loyal shoppers, the concept of trading stamps was advanced. The Braddock Chamber of Commerce devised "General Braddock stamps" to attract and retain local shoppers. This advertising flag hung in local participating store windows. (Author's collection.)

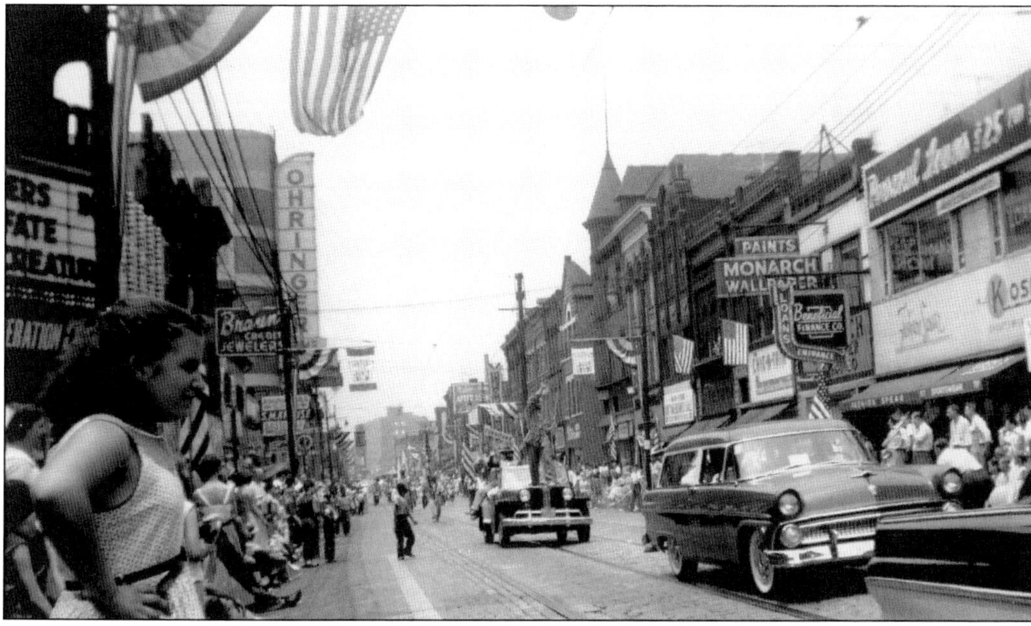

EVERYBODY LOVES A PARADE. Braddock Avenue was the perfect street for holding a parade, and it has served the community well for more than 100 years. This 1950s parade was much like many others held over the years—flags are flying, music is playing, and crowds are lining the sidewalks as veterans groups, civic organizations, and school bands participated. (Courtesy of Anna [Gilarski] Szwarc.)

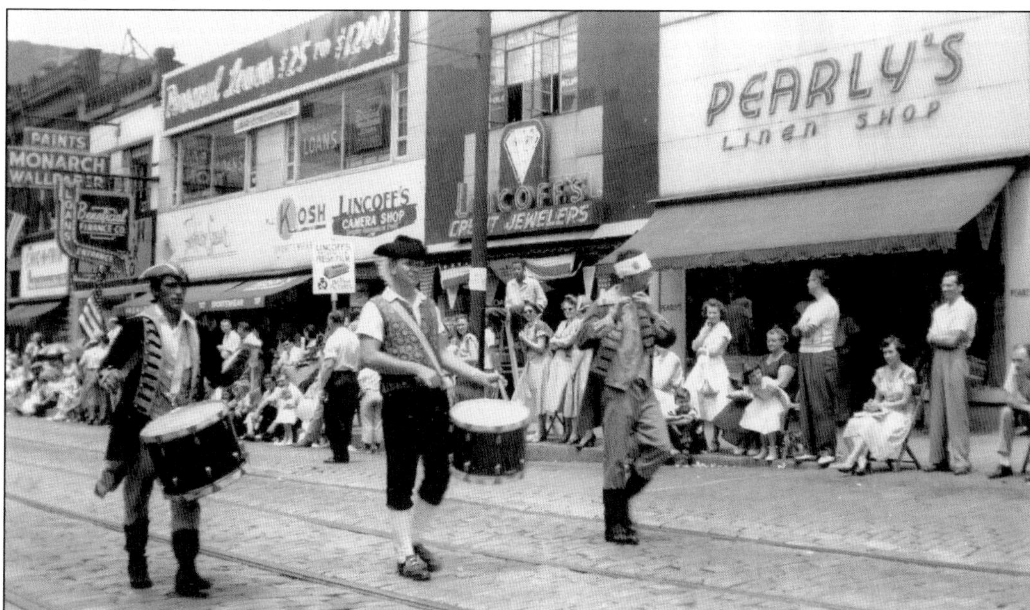

BRADDOCK'S COLONIAL ROOTS ARE SHOWING. Fife and drum actors played a prominent role in many of Braddock's parades over the years. Compared to the actors that participated in the Battle of Braddock 175th anniversary celebration, little had changed in 25 years. The only difference now was that they were viewed by a whole new generation of children. (Courtesy of Anna [Gilarski] Szwarc.)

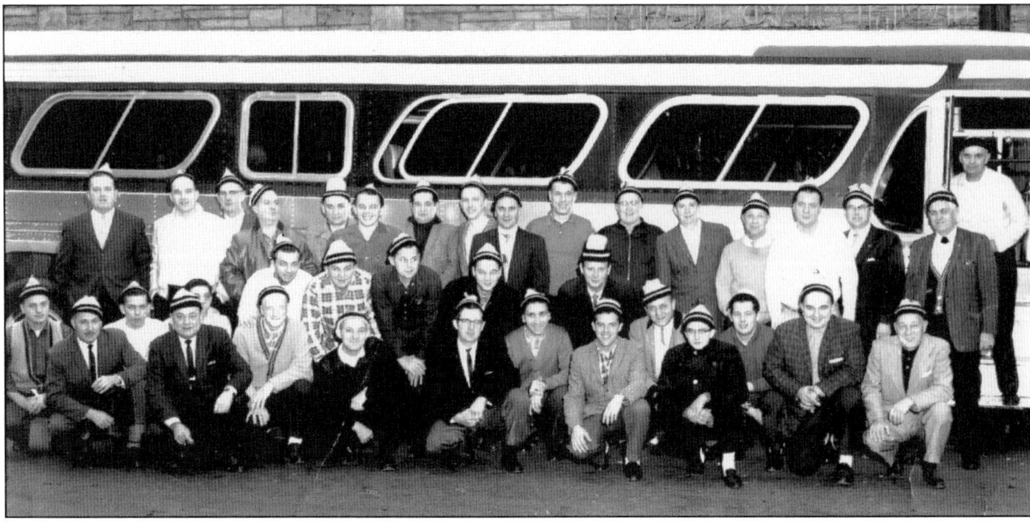

OLD FRIENDS, BIG GAME. Despite the failed local economy, many families remained. Small neighborhood enclaves remained and friends and relatives often returned for religious or social events. This group of local residents gathered for a bus ride to one of their favorite pastimes in 1961—a Pittsburgh Steelers football game. Longtime resident, World War II hero, and local barber Joseph "Red" Szwarc is the third person from the left in the first row. (Courtesy of Mimi [Szwarc] and Joe O'Donnell.)

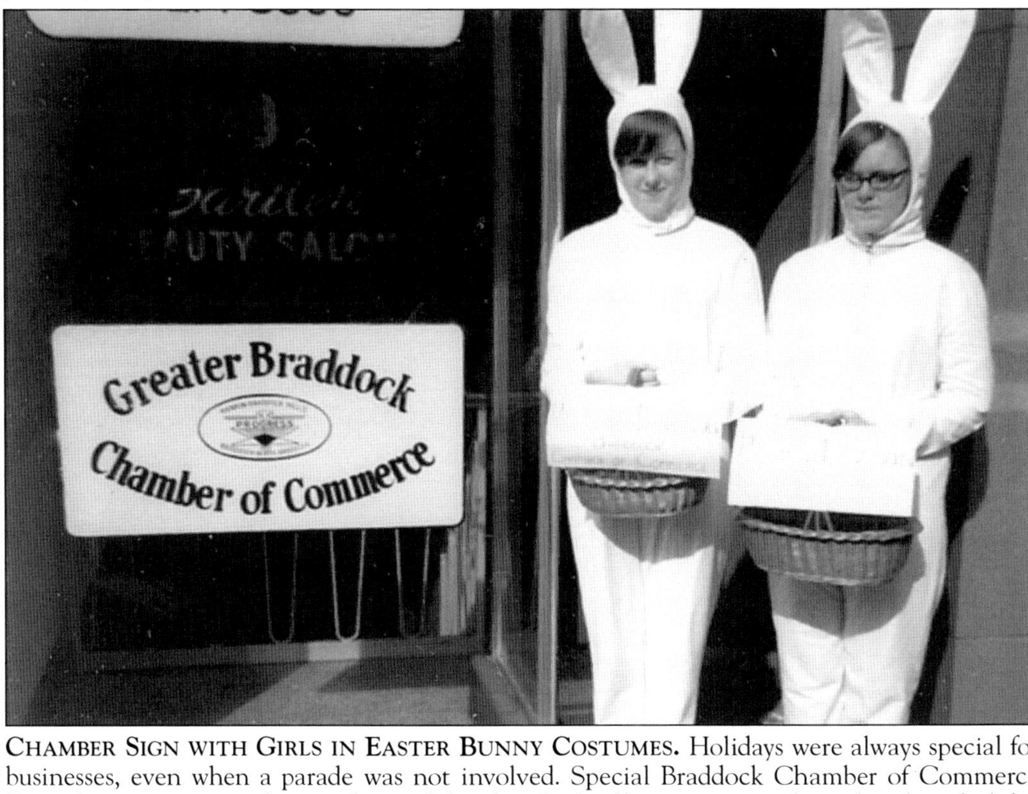

CHAMBER SIGN WITH GIRLS IN EASTER BUNNY COSTUMES. Holidays were always special for businesses, even when a parade was not involved. Special Braddock Chamber of Commerce Easter bunnies are seen here in front of the chamber's office, getting ready to distribute holiday goodies along Braddock Avenue. (Author's collection.)

Six

Deconstruction and Reinvention

Not long after the Depression, prosperity returned to the area. The post–World War II and Korean War economies seemed ripe with optimism. However, the good feelings soon waned as prosperity brought new challenges. Suburban housing development offered residents an opportunity to move away from the factories and the shabby living conditions of old housing stock. While this new housing was attractive, people were much less able—or willing—to uncouple themselves from Braddock Avenue's commercial activity. For more than two generations, the number of businesses on Braddock Avenue had grown significantly. There was little reason to shop anywhere else, since there were few retail goods or food items that could not be found within the confines of the town's main thoroughfare. Most often, Braddock's businesses had the newest fashions, fixtures, and furnishings available for sale well before most other businesses in the region. By all accounts, Braddock Avenue was a shopper's paradise.

Beginning in the late 1960s, the machines of industry began to slow and in some cases stop entirely. The retail, business, and banking activity that industry had supported for so many years, likewise began to feel the full negative impact of the changes. Seemingly running on parallel tracks, business started its decline just as new highways were being built making access to Monroeville, Penn Hills, and other new communities to the east. When people left, they took the local tax base with them. The downward spiral continued as the reduction in tax base left local governments ill equipped to deal with decaying infrastructure. As U.S. Steel, Westinghouse, Union Switch and Signal, and Wheeling Pittsburgh Steel closed major plants in the area, economic devastation of the local communities was not far away. Soon houses were abandoned, businesses vacated, and storefronts boarded up. Anyone with transferable work skills or college degrees left quickly. Retail customers that remained were now visiting the new suburban shopping malls that were being developed to serve their every "modern" need. Braddock Avenue's traffic congestion and parking shortage problems had now been solved, but in a manner that few had ever conceived possible.

A generation later, the fate of Braddock and its sister communities of North Braddock, Rankin, and Braddock Hills remains in the hands of people with strong wills, good hearts, and forward vision.

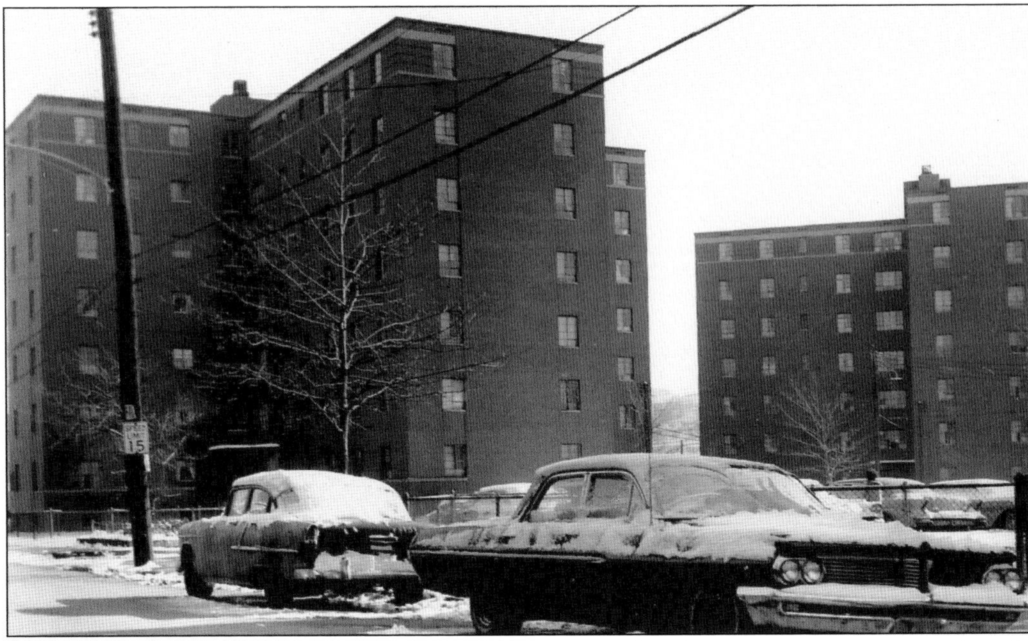

TALBOT TOWERS. Talbot Towers was one of the many public housing units constructed in the Monongahela Valley during the 1950s and 1960s. This particular high-rise and its residents became the focus of a major lawsuit in early 1988 as alleged long-term racial segregation practices by the Allegheny County Housing Authority, the Redevelopment Authority of Allegheny County, Allegheny County, and the U.S. Department of Housing and Urban Development were challenged. The federal court case was resolved through settlement in 1994 when the Sanders Consent Decree was signed. This image dates from approximately 1967. (Courtesy of Braddock Carnegie Library.)

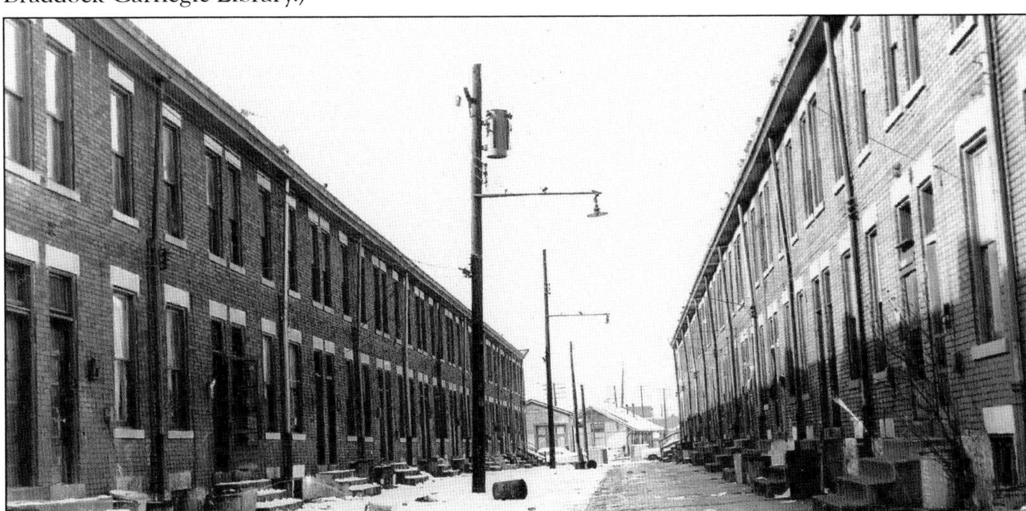

ROW HOMES. This image records the conditions of homes on Grant Street and Willow Way in the late 1960s. It dramatically attests to the severity of the harsh living conditions and stark economic realities that negatively impacted local communities during this period. Homeowners were not alone in facing this situation as municipal governments were also challenged to maintain public buildings and basic infrastructure. (Courtesy of Braddock Carnegie Library.)

SACRED HEART CHURCH. Braddock as the "City of Churches" suffered dramatically from the financial devastation of the local communities during the 1970s and 1980s. Church consolidations began to take on urgency as economic reality dictated that declining congregations could no longer afford to support as many churches. Compounding the loss of jobs, housing, and people, an unfortunate fire created even more heartache in December 1975, when it destroyed Sacred Heart Church. (Courtesy of Mimi [Szwarc] and Joe O'Donnell.)

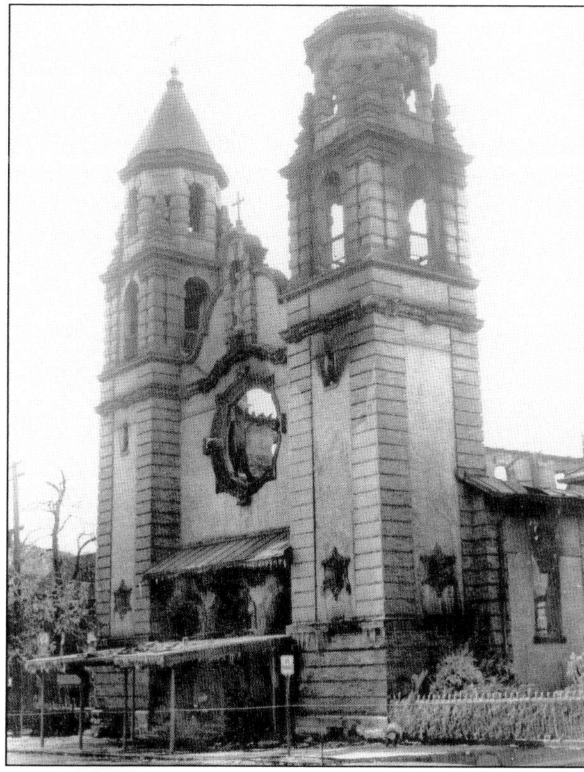

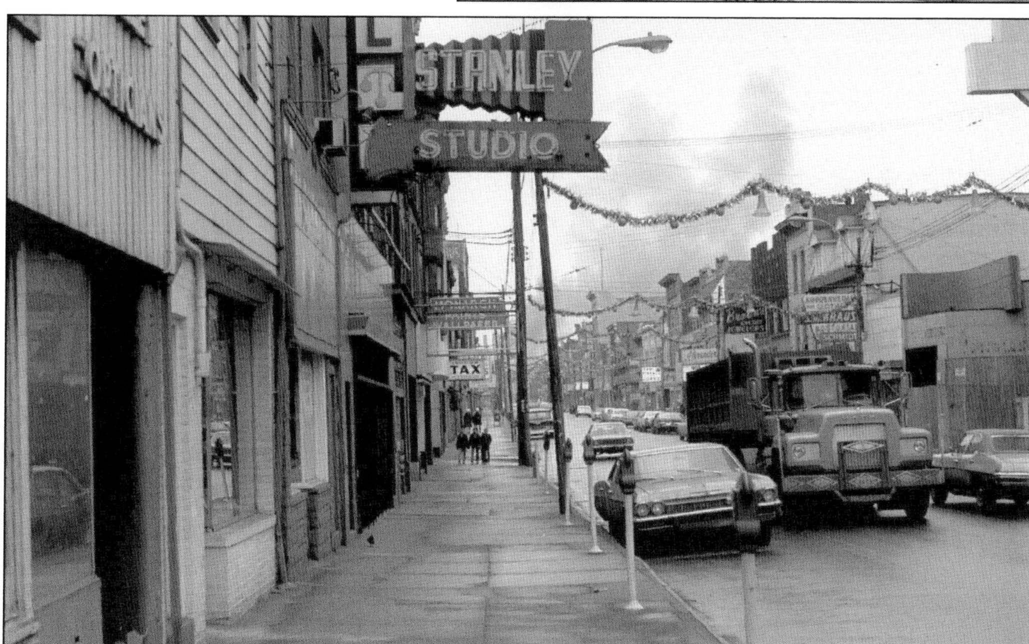

STANLEY STUDIO. Braddock Avenue has changed much over the past 20 years. During the early 1980s, stores began reducing hours or closing at an alarming rate. Automobile traffic was still heavy, but drivers were now heading out of town to jobs they had found elsewhere. (Courtesy of Tony Buba.)

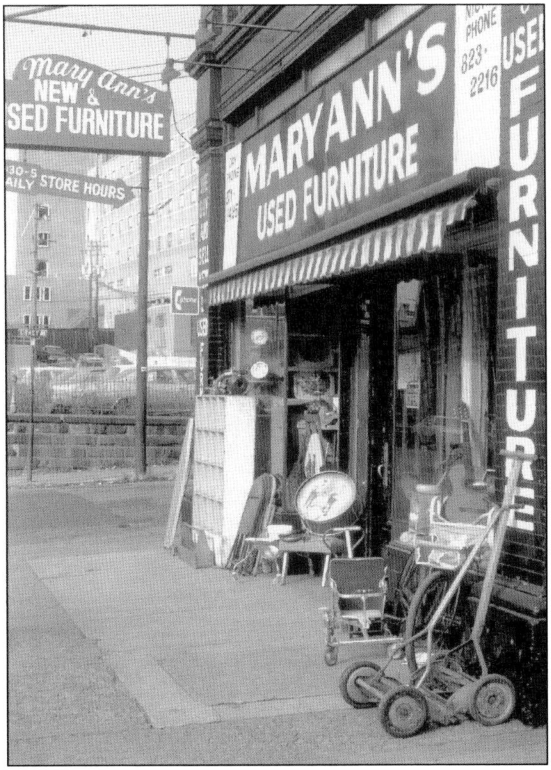

MARY ANN'S USED FURNITURE. During the 1970s and 1980s, many families found it difficult adjusting to job loss or work reductions. As the economy progressively worsened, second-hand furniture stores and used car dealers saw increased traffic. By the time 1990 rolled around, families in Braddock and surrounding communities had a median family income less than 80 percent of other Allegheny County residents. (Courtesy of Tony Buba.)

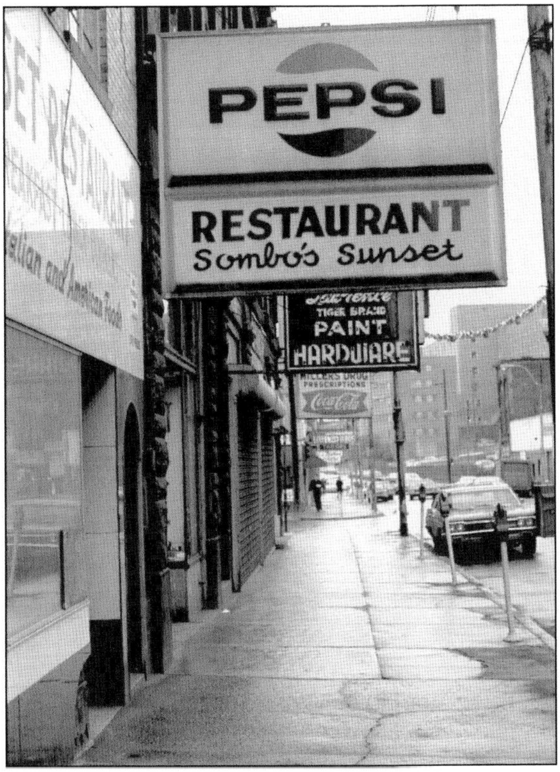

SOMBO'S RESTAURANT, LOOKING WEST. A fair number of businesses remained along Braddock Avenue in the early 1980s—or so it appeared. For those that hung on, business was not good, and every remaining business struggled to survive. With Braddock General Hospital's newest buildings in the background, one can see the increasingly harsh conditions for business along the avenue. (Courtesy of Tony Buba.)

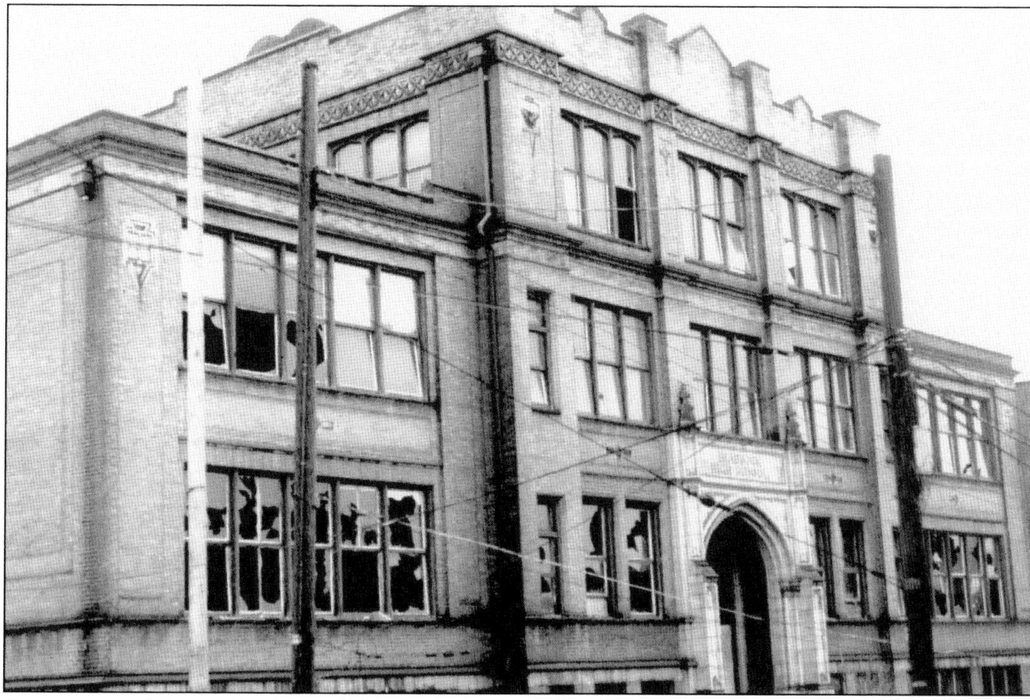

BRADDOCK HIGH SCHOOL. In 1960, average hourly wages in Braddock were $2.75 or $104.50 per week; over 70 percent of families in Braddock were homeowners. The downward spiral of industrial decline extracted both workers and homeowners from the community and left much debris and desolation in its wake. By the early 1980s, the visual impact of decay was almost too much for many to bear. Old Braddock High School was now redundant and in decay. (Courtesy of Tony Buba.)

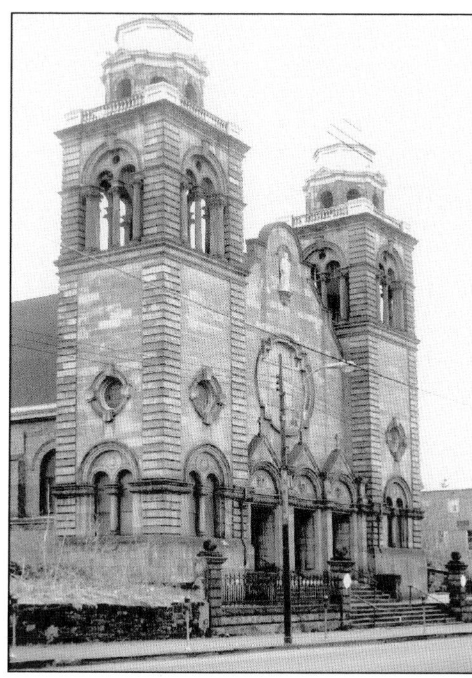

ST. THOMAS CHURCH DESTROYED BY FIRE. Organized in 1854, St. Thomas Church was one of several Catholic churches in Braddock, with its 20th-century edifice built with the help of steel titan Charles Schwab in 1902. As 1983 came to an end, so too did the church's building. A fire on Friday night, December 30, ended the aspirations of almost 300 parish families who had been working diligently to save the financially ailing church. (Courtesy of Tony Buba.)

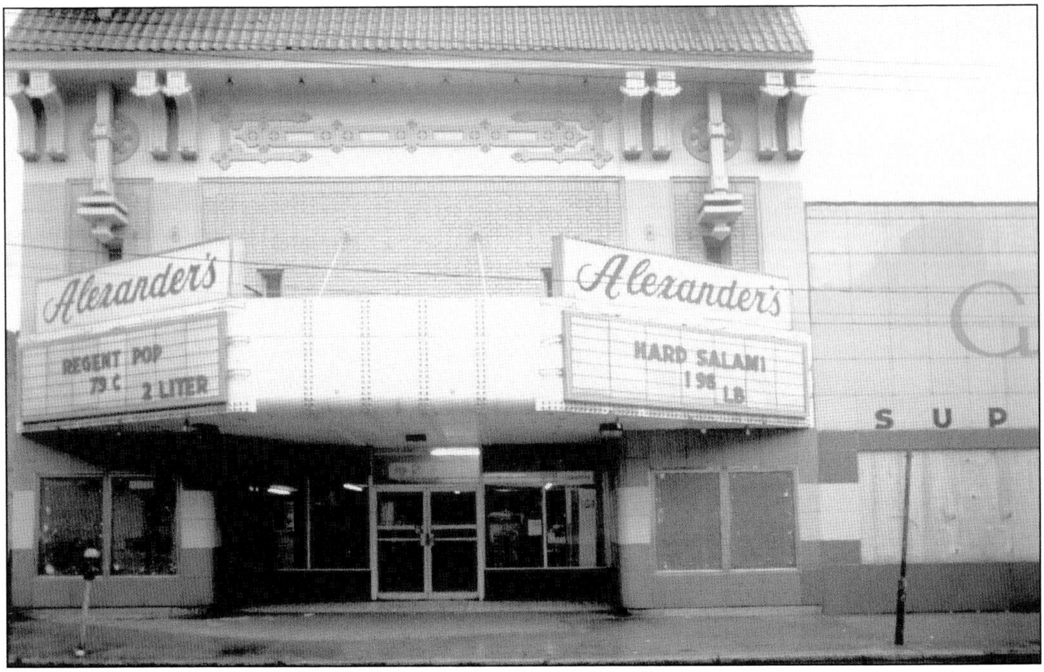

ALEXANDER'S MARKET. As the economy worsened and entertainment tastes and venues changed, some buildings were adapted to other uses. Alexander's Market was an interesting example of this conversion of the old Paramount Theater building into use as a neighborhood food market. (Courtesy of Tony Buba.)

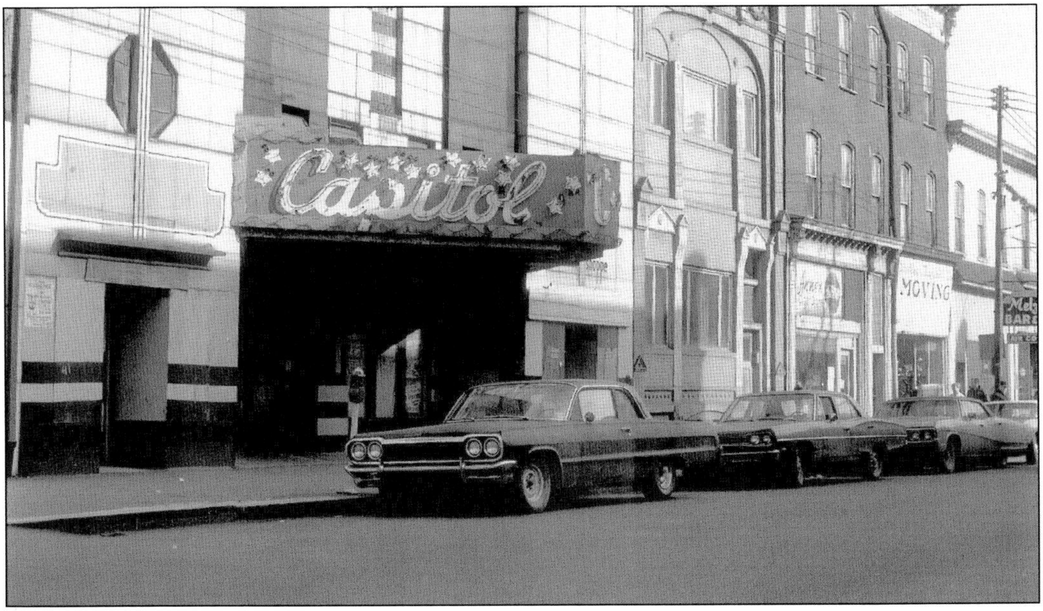

CAPITOL THEATER. Thousands of people had traveled to the Capitol Theater over the years to watch the product of some of America's best-known movie producers. After the original Capitol Theater was torn down to make way for a new Sun Drug store, another smaller theater was adapted. As a result, business was not good, and it did not take much time before the main attractions were restricted to second-run movies. (Courtesy of Tony Buba.)

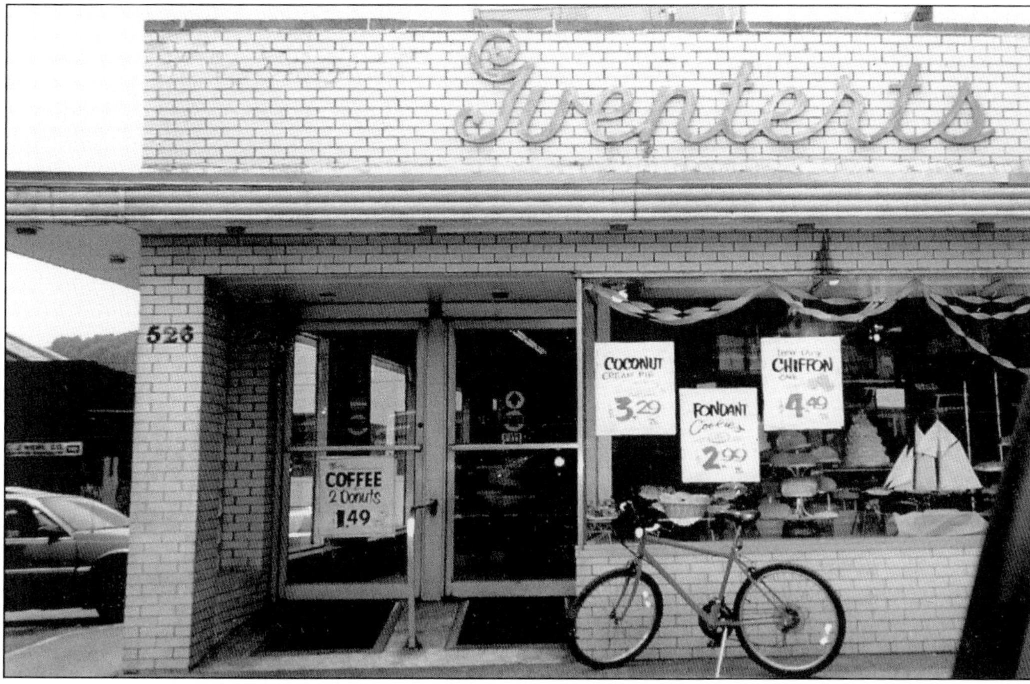

GUENTERT'S BAKERY. Braddock was home to a number of bakeries over the years, but few were able to challenge the quality of the remarkable products crafted by Ernst Guentert. He learned his trade during an apprenticeship in Germany, where his grandfather and great-grandfather had owned a bakery. During the height of operations in Braddock, Guentert employed 20 bakers and opened three additional shops, in Lawrenceville, North Side, and Swissvale. All of the bake goods, however, were crafted in Braddock. (Author's collection.)

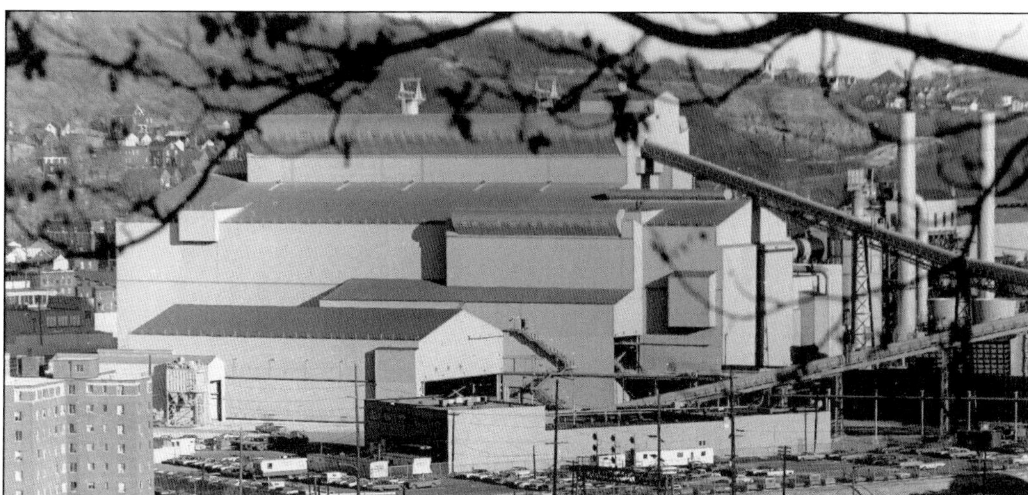

U.S. STEEL EDGAR THOMSON WORKS. During the 1970s and 1980s, the national economy was in a state of crisis. In the Monongahela Valley the crisis started earlier, but its impact was restrained until time and circumstance took their toll. In 1983, U.S. Steel Corporation began to close plants throughout the valley. Fortunately, the Edgar Thomson plant survived. Today it continues its proud heritage of making steel in Braddock. (Courtesy of UPMC Braddock Medical Center.)

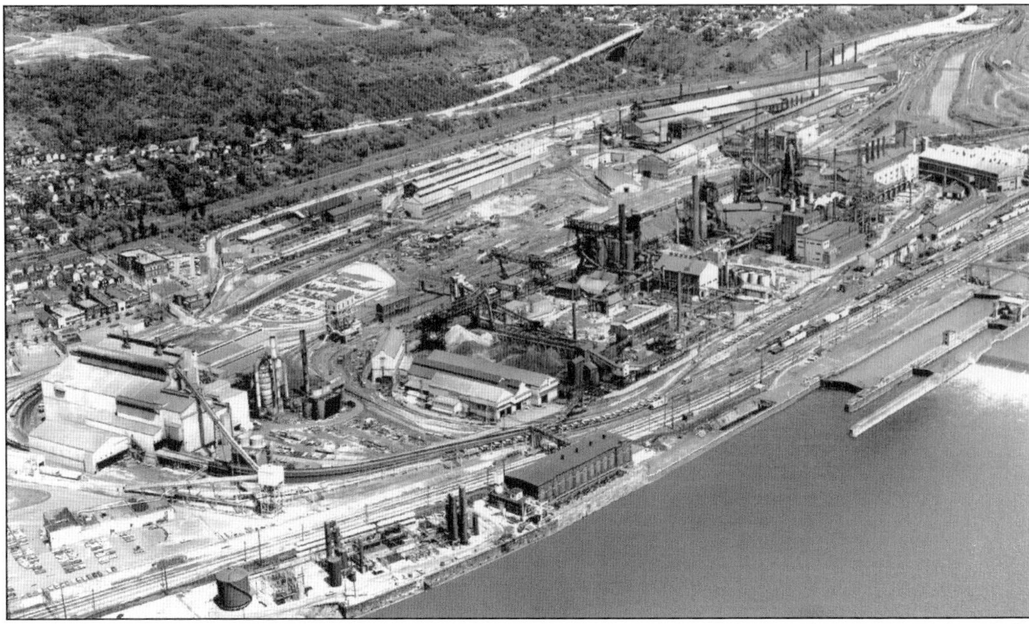

ET RULES! This modern aerial view of Edgar Thomson Works shows the magnitude of the mill that still remains on the very ground where John Frazier first built his cabin and where Gen. Edward Braddock lost his battle. After being equipped with a new continuous caster in the early 1990s, the mill once again began breaking steel-making records—just like it did for Andrew Carnegie, 100 years earlier. (Courtesy of the U.S. Steel Corporation.)

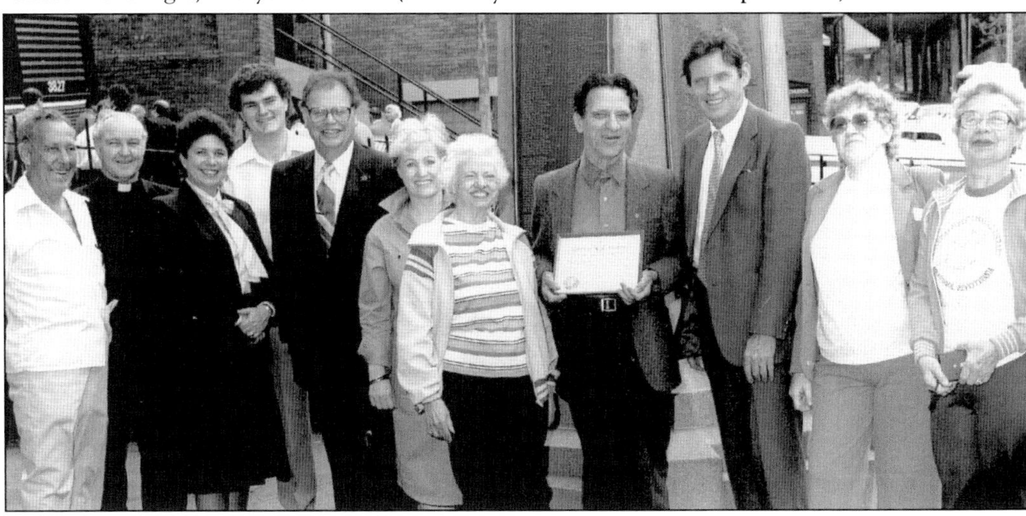

BRADDOCK CARNEGIE LIBRARY REVERSING FORTUNES. Library usage had dropped dramatically between the 1950s and 1960s as suburbanization took its toll. As patronage dropped, the library's resources and viability were severely challenged. The fight to keep the library alive and independent was aided greatly by the leadership of librarian David Solomon and a group of dedicated volunteers. Allegheny County government officials presented the library with a special proclamation in the late 1980s. It was received by, from left to right, Roy "Chook" Stell, Fr. Thomas Boyle, Allegheny County commissioner Barbara Hafer, Jeffrey McLaughin, commissioner Thomas Forester, Marilyn Collins, Peg Zinsmeister, David Solomon, commissioner Pete Flaherty, Elizabeth Haas, and Lida Stell. (Courtesy of Braddock Carnegie Library.)

DAVID SOLOMON. Principally through David Solomon's work, Braddock Carnegie Library was placed on the National Register of Historic Places in 1973. In 1974, however, it closed and David Solomon was recognized as its "last master librarian." Through his untiring efforts and those of countless volunteers, the Braddock's Field Historical Society was formed. During recent years, the society's careful stewardship has restored both the library's structural integrity and its programmatic vibrancy. (Courtesy of Tony Buba.)

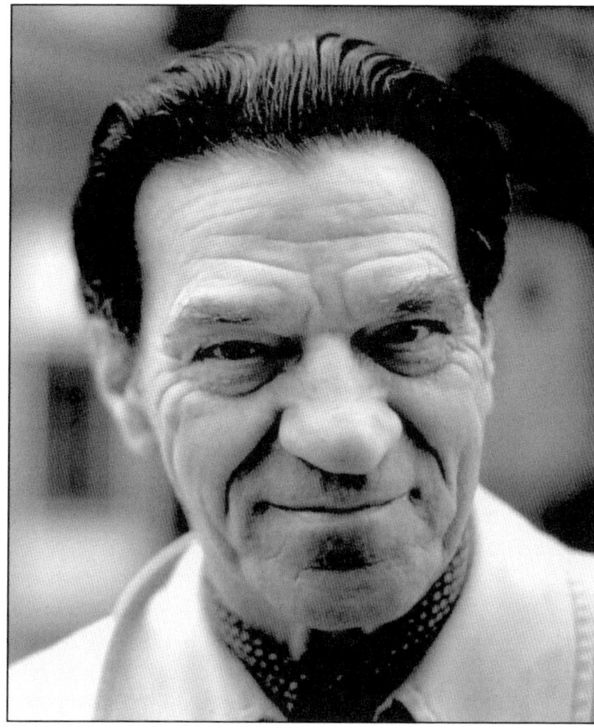

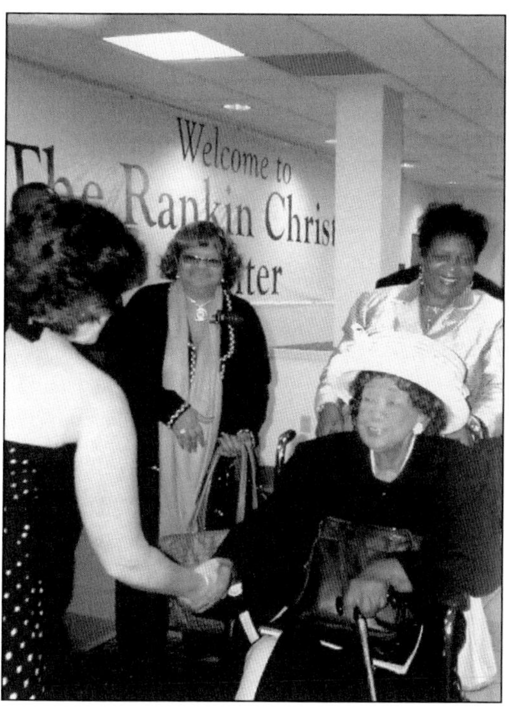

DOROTHY HEIGHT. Among the greatest gifts that any community could ever hope to receive is that of leadership reborn. Dorothy Height (seated) is a wonderful example of a recent generation's contribution. She is one of Rankin's most recognized personalities and one of America's most ardent civil rights leaders. In 1994, she was awarded the Presidential Medal of Freedom by Pres. William Clinton, and on April 11, 2003, she was awarded a Congressional Gold Medal in recognition for her work in civil rights. She is seen here during a recent visit. (Courtesy of Yvonne Spencer.)

Consistent with our mission to preserve history on a local level, this book was printed in South Carolina on American-made paper and manufactured entirely in the United States. Products carrying the accredited Forest Stewardship Council (FSC) label are printed on 100 percent FSC-certified paper.

MADE IN THE USA